PRAISE FOR *BRIDGING THE GAP: CREATING A CULTURALLY RESPONSIVE SCHOOL*

"Informative, aspirational, and inspirational. Gutierrez provides readers with rigorous, responsive, and applicable approaches and strategies to create culturally responsive schools. School leaders and practitioners will truly benefit from this much-needed book."

—Tyrone Howard, Ph.D., President, American Educational Research Association; Professor, UCLA

"Dr. Hank Gutierrez reminds us that the purpose of education is liberation. It's a reminder that should energize every educator to examine their own educational experiences as well as their current experiences and expectations as they lead classrooms, schools, and districts. Thankfully, Dr. Gutierrez provides a comprehensive blueprint to build a classroom that actively engages and reflects the culture and history of Black and brown students. As a former teacher and school leader, I'm excited that this book provides the framework necessary to elevate classroom communities. As an educator, liberator, and activist, I'm in awe of how Dr. Gutierrez's work advocates for a radical shift in how and who we educate and, hence, liberate."

—Sharif El-Mekki, CEO, Center for Black Educator Development

"Dr. Gutierrez takes us to the proverbial 'church,' in a very approachable way, reminding us that education is a tool for liberation. Instead of just another 'get folks fired up' book about equity, he provides actionable ideas for how we might give the gift of freedom to every student by allowing them to be themselves while we expand their minds and their worlds. This is definitely a worthwhile read for educators at all levels."

—Tinkhani Ushe White, Ed.D., Associate, Networked Improvement Science, Carnegie Foundation for the Advancement of Teaching

"*Bridging the Gap* is a powerful book that serves as a reminder of why educators chose to enter the profession in the first place. Through compelling realities and insightful analysis, Gutierrez underscores the critical importance of all students, especially those who are Black and living in poverty, succeeding in school. The message is clear: educators have a moral obligation to do everything in their power to close the achievement gap and ensure that every student has access to a high-quality and culturally relevant education."

—Matt Navo, Executive Director, California Collaborative for Educational Excellence

"An invaluable resource to teachers and school leaders who want to redesign and design classrooms and schools that are culturally responsive."

—Travis J. Bristol, Ph.D., Associate Professor, University of California, Berkeley

"This book necessarily contributes to the work of helping schools get better in the fight for culturally responsive education."

—H. Richard Milner IV, PhD, author of *The Race Card: Leading the Fight for Truth in America's Schools*; Chair of Education, Cornelius Vanderbilt University

"Through its insightful and thought-provoking exploration of culturally sustaining schools, this book offers a valuable roadmap for education leaders seeking to create inclusive and empowering learning environments that honor and celebrate the diversity of their students' backgrounds and experiences."

—Keilani M. Goggins, Director, Black Educators Initiative, a division of the National Center for Teacher Residencies

"Dr. Gutierrez had me at his series of 'Dear poverty' letters, in which I could see my own students. This book effectively establishes the mindset for the ideas of culturally responsive teaching, which requires building positive relationships with students from historically underserved groups that have not been a traditional focus in schools. Dr. Gutierrez does a fantastic job of clarifying why this is important and the impact of such practices on students' lives; he lays the groundwork for powerful conversations in leading and developing a plan to establish a systemwide culture of culturally responsive practices."

—Sheiveh Jones, Ed.D., Executive Director, Teacher Effectiveness and Preparation—Human Resource Services, San Diego County Office of Education

"*Bridging the Gap: Creating a Culturally Responsive School* is an interdisciplinary synthesis that draws from cognitive science, education, psychology, neuroscience, and history. Dr. Gutierrez engages the ready by weaving personal narratives and the voices of other educators with research, concrete examples of practice, and policy connections. Dr. Gutierrez's passion definitely comes through in this highly personal, fearless call to action."

—Cathy Yun, Senior Researcher, Learning Policy Institute

Bridging the Gap

Creating a Culturally Responsive School

Hank Gutierrez

ROWMAN & LITTLEFIELD
Lanham • Boulder • New York • London

Published by Rowman & Littlefield
An imprint of The Rowman & Littlefield Publishing Group, Inc.
4501 Forbes Boulevard, Suite 200, Lanham, Maryland 20706
www.rowman.com

86-90 Paul Street, London EC2A 4NE

Copyright © 2023 by Hank Gutierrez

All rights reserved. No part of this book may be reproduced in any form or by any electronic or mechanical means, including information storage and retrieval systems, without written permission from the publisher, except by a reviewer who may quote passages in a review.

British Library Cataloguing in Publication Information Available

Library of Congress Cataloging-in-Publication Data

Names: Gutierrez, Hank, author.
Title: Bridging the gap : creating a culturally responsive school / Hank Gutierrez.
Description: Lanham, Maryland : Rowman & Littlefield, 2023. | Includes bibliographical references.
Identifiers: LCCN 2023026554 (print) | LCCN 2023026555 (ebook) | ISBN 9781475872910 (cloth) | ISBN 9781475872927 (paperback) | ISBN 9781475872934 (ebook)
Subjects: LCSH: Culturally relevant pedagogy--United States. | School environment--United States. | Educational leadership--United States. | African American teachers--Training of.
Classification: LCC LC1099.3 .G87 2023 (print) | LCC LC1099.3 (ebook) | DDC 370.117--dc23/eng/20230715
LC record available at https://lccn.loc.gov/2023026554
LC ebook record available at https://lccn.loc.gov/2023026555

"Never say never, because limits, like fears, are often just an illusion."
—*Michael Jordan*

Special Appreciation
Gloria Ladson-Billings and Jessica Sabogal (Cover Art)
Debbie Neufeld, Matt Doyle, and John Kilroy

Contents

Foreword	ix
Preface	xiii
Prelude: Dear Poverty	xix
Introduction	xxiii
Chapter 1: Culturally Responsive Pedagogy: A Mindset	1
Chapter 2: A Nation at Risk—*Still*	13
Chapter 3: Culturally Relevant Pedagogy: Capacity over Contention	37
Chapter 4: The Surface-Level Examination	63
Chapter 5: Deep Instructional Undercurrents	85
Chapter 6: Culturally Responsive School Leadership	111
Chapter 7: The Prepared Leader: A Lens of Equity	125
Chapter 8: The Culturally Responsive School	149
Chapter 9: Building the Black Teacher Pipeline	165
References	183
About the Author	195

Foreword

If you have ever had the chance to ride public transportation in the bustling city of London, you might find yourself using the subway or, as Londoners call it, "the Tube." As a city girl growing up in Philadelphia and spending summers in New York, the subway was a familiar form of transport for me. Riding the Tube did not seem like a big deal. I have ridden subways in Tokyo, Stockholm, Mexico City, Montreal, and many U.S. cities. However, in London painted on the platform you will see over and over the words "Mind the Gap." This admonition alerts passengers to the fact that there is a small space between the train's edge and the platform, and if one is not careful, one can get a foot caught in between the two, with disastrous results. Thus, passengers are regularly reminded to "mind the gap."

When we talk about "gaps" regarding education, we are not talking about a small space where student achievement is separated from an agreed upon norm. No, typically academic gaps refer to large disparities between where students ought to be and where they are. For the most part, we wring our hands and bemoan the fact that the "gaps" seem insurmountable. We have taken solace in notions that these gaps are "someone else's fault." Students are not performing well because they are poor. They are not performing well because they only have one parent living in the home. They are not performing well because they come from a "culture of poverty" that does not value education. They are not performing well because they do not speak "proper" English. The list of excuses goes on and on. However, the idea that students are experiencing academic disparities because schools are not teaching them well is rarely addressed.

In the late 1980s, I began investigating teachers who *were* successful with African American students. In their classes, students' backgrounds were never used as an excuse for poor performance. The students were expected to do well, and they did under the tutelage of these teachers. After three years of intensive participant-observation in the teachers' classrooms, I was finally able to distill what they exhibited in their teaching into something I began to call "culturally relevant pedagogy" (Ladson-Billings, 2022).

There were three important commonalities among these teachers—a focus on student learning, a commitment to cultural competence, and an inspiration toward sociopolitical or critical consciousness.

Student learning is evidence that students are growing in academic and other school-related tasks. Most schools are slavishly tied to student performance on standardized assessments. Culturally relevant teachers expect students to demonstrate growth on these measures, but their sense of student learning is more expansive. They look for students' improved work habits. For example, a student who started the year chronically late begins to arrive on time. A student who never has his school supplies now brings his books and pencils. A student who often turned in no assignments or turned them in partially completed and late now brings in assignments on time and complete. These things do not show up on standardized tests but are clear evidence that the student is growing and learning. For culturally relevant teachers, moving a fifth-grade student from a second-grade reading level to a fourth-grade level is student learning, even though she will still be below grade level on the state or district exam. Student growth, not test performance, is the measure of student learning.

Cultural competence is the most misunderstood concept that is part of what it means to be a culturally relevant teacher. *Cultural competence* is one of those terms that is used throughout our society and often refers to some superficial treatment of people we see as "different." Today we have culturally competent counseling, culturally competent health care, and even culturally competent policing. Typically, what is meant by the phrase is that someone from the social mainstream is given a list of dos and don'ts to deal with people they deem as "others" (i.e., don't expect Asian immigrant students to look you in the eye, or Black parents beat their children). This approach typically exacerbates the cultural misunderstandings that exist between students and the school.

True cultural competence is helping students to be firmly grounded in their culture of origin while ensuring that they are fluent in at least one other culture. For most students of color, this other culture is what we refer to as the mainstream. However, White, middle-class students are also required to become culturally competent. They should be learning a language other than English. They should learn about histories and cultures other than their own because the world they will enter via college and the world of work is diverse and culturally complex. We do all students a disservice if we treat them as if they will remain racially, ethnically, and linguistically encapsulated. The culturally competent student should be culturally flexible.

Finally, the culturally relevant teacher develops a sociopolitical or critical consciousness among students. This aspect of culturally relevant pedagogy is the most ignored. Too many teachers see the term *sociopolitical* and believe that it means fostering a partisan agenda. Instead, it means developing in students the ability to solve problems that are important in their lives. Many times, teachers take up a cause, such as the environment, and force students to work on that cause. Suddenly, all the third graders are trying to save the rainforest. I am not saying that saving the rainforest is not a worthy endeavor; rather, it is rarely the most pressing issue in the students' lives. Students may care more deeply about school rules that are applied inequitably or disparities in suspensions and expulsions. Developing a critical consciousness allows students to use some of the skills they have learned in school—reading, writing, mathematics, history, and so on—to gather and analyze data to prove the hypotheses they may have about inequities. It may give them the language and approach they need to be heard by decision makers such as administrators or school board members. It is the kind of work that will empower students as citizens.

The culturally relevant pedagogue is a true gap bridger. She knows where to stand to help students across perilous spaces. She understands her role is to develop students in ways that make them more independent as well as safe in school environments. She is careful to ensure that each of her students "minds the gap"!

Gloria Ladson-Billings,
University of Wisconsin–Madison
April 2023

Preface

A MESSAGE TO YOU, THE EDUCATOR

What if the little girl on the cover of this book has dreams of becoming a teacher? Would you support her?

What if the little girl on the cover of this book will grow up to cure cancer? Would you believe me?

What if the little girl on the cover of this book is sitting in your classroom? Do you see her?

What if her life depended on you? Would you reach for her?

What if she loves reciting poetry? Would you let her speak?

What if she was your very own? Now do you see her?

What if she only comes to school because your class is safe? Would you continue to build her fortress?

Now, do you see your purpose? She does.

You see, for me, growing up with a single mother manifested into many life insecurities. One after another, in fact. Academic failures consumed me during childhood. I attended five different schools in five consecutive years, starting in kindergarten. By the time I entered fourth grade, my reading and mathematics skills were far from proficient. I vividly remember being pulled from class with three other classmates for reading intervention—where rote memory became an ally. It was at the age of ten, that I realized my life's circumstances had taken a toll on my ability to learn.

As fate would have it, I became an educator, just like you. My very first position in education was coaching middle school girls' basketball in 1988, my first semester of college. Since then, I've held positions as a classroom teacher, Guidance Learning Specialist, high school vice principal, high school principal (at my alma mater), and assistant, then deputy superintendent at the district and county levels. My experience with school initiatives and reform efforts run the gamut—creating a Black educator pipeline, managing positive behavioral and intervention systems, forging university partnerships for rural teacher residencies, coordinating Individualized Educational Plans (IEPs), assembling behavioral threat assessment teams, leading community of practice (COP) convenings at the county office level, implementing the Men's Alliance and Women's League for at-promise youth, and modeling instructional practices. Within my three decades of educational experience, I've taken risks at creating programs specifically designed to propel students to better academic outcomes—some have succeeded, while some did not.

During the two years leading up to completing my teaching credential, I even learned how to speak Khmer, the native language of my Cambodian students. It was my way of meeting students halfway, but it was also my first experience in culturally responsive pedagogy—bridging students' culture with a critical lens for learning. Later, my ability to speak both Spanish and Khmer would land me a teaching contract before the interview was even over. My early experiences working with culturally and linguistically diverse students would later shape my outlook on education. Looking back, I was practicing culturally responsive teaching before I truly understood the theory.

I remember one of my first experiences in being adaptive to the needs of my students. I taught at an elementary school with one of the highest rates of poverty in the district—if not the entire city. It was my first year of teaching and my first experience with *parent-teacher* conferences—remember those? As I was sitting in my classroom getting files ready for each student, one of my fellow grade-level colleagues came in and said, "You won't need all that, the parents never show up." I remember replying, "What do you mean? We don't even have school the whole week, each parent was given a specific time to show up." Mrs. Smith (pseudonym) replied, "These people don't care about their kids." To my dismay, the silent majority of my fellow teachers felt the same. No wonder we were considered an underperforming school—our kids were the recipients of low teacher expectations, their parents omitted from educational decisions, and the community at large was considered lazy and unambitious.

So, I took out my class roster and called each parent and we agreed on a day and time that was convenient for them. A simple gesture of responsiveness and a massive shift from old customs dictated by the school culture. You guessed it, every single parent showed up to their child's conference. The poorest school in the district and I learned that some of my students had older siblings studying physics at UC Berkeley, and some of their parents were teachers during the 1980s in El Salvador. Some mothers, like mine, were working two and three jobs just to make the rent payment, and some grandmothers showed up speaking little English, towing crying babies at the hip. I mean, with a few phone calls, Critical Race Theory was solved in one afternoon. So much for not caring about their kids; these parents expected academic excellence, and I quickly learned it was my job to deliver.

Later in my career, I learned that the relationships built from administrator to student are equally important as those forged in the classroom. The high school students I served had their own unique ways of navigating their surroundings, both socially and individually. I saw how unmet needs from the elementary level manifested at the teenage years—sometimes in the form of gang involvement, the inability to focus, seeking attention through acting-out, and succumbing to abusive relationships. When dealing with students sent to me on disciplinary referrals, one clear student perception came about in nearly all of them. The students invariably uttered these words each time we met: *That teacher just doesn't like me*. The rigor was there, and the relevance may have been alluring, but by and large, something was amiss.

As I took a deeper dive at disciplinary referrals (usually after playing the role of a non-trained school psychologist), I knew I had to get to the source. What observable instructional strategies *did* prove inviting or engaging to students? I surprised myself as I spent countless hours observing teachers deliver lesson after lesson—spanning every grade and subject matter. Here is what I found that directly correlated to students exhibiting *positive* behavior. Effective teachers, regardless of race, were surgical in their ability to be *adaptive*, while ensuring that students had self-agency toward the mastery of learning goals. In other words, students were engaged because the teacher shared the power of learning based on knowing students' cultural strengths. Furthermore, I saw teachers willing to be adaptive as they embraced learning progressions in the face of ambiguity—the *vulnerability* factor. These countless classroom visits (as a vice principal and principal) would ultimately bode well for the experiential knowledge shared in this book.

I've had to administer standardized tests ranging from multiple choice to response-based adaptive formats. Along the way, I've seen teachers taxed with new initiatives, new state standards, new competencies, high school exit exams, all promising student success. I've jumped all-in (with teachers) throughout the comings-and-goings of character counts, specially designed academic instruction in English (SDAIE), phonics, class-size reduction, and flipped classrooms. In today's educational landscape, promises are even greater and come in the form of high-profile grant dollars, federally funded *reimagined* programs, and the rebranding of recycled reform efforts. Every program is billed with the label that *all students* can succeed, with very little intersectionality with day-to-day classroom instruction that reflects students' diverse experiences, interests, and values in practical and proven ways (Faulkner-Bond, 2022).

These high-priced initiatives often prove minimally effective, not for sake of goodwill, but lacking the foundational elements of cultural responsiveness that translates to instructional accountability. At best, most are supplementary for the masses, yet lack the necessary intentionality that points to positive outcomes for Black students. In my career, I've come to realize that instructional practices must shift toward a more culturally and linguistically inclusive format, as well as securing a racially affirming mindset.

The point is this, the success, or lack thereof, of our Black and other historically marginalized student populations is dictated by educators' critical lens. *High-impact* practitioners do not leave Black students' racial identity out, not from the conversation, not from the planning, and not from the goals of the content standards. In *high-impact* culturally responsive schools, there is intentionality and focus on building relevant lessons and connections based on students' unique cultural perspectives.

So, I begin this book as a reminder to us, the educators, that our profession comes with the highest responsibility in the land—the power to propel students and the generations after them, toward a better life—a liberation, in fact. I was one of those students living parallel to poverty, struck by circumstances beyond my control. I depended on you, the educator, to bring to life the life my mind dreamed of. You did not disappoint.

You see, ever since I can remember, the educator, just like yourself, came to my rescue. I didn't need your charity; I needed your *belief* in me. And that is what this book is all about, illuminating the visible and invisible long-term changes that must take place within the school. I'll showcase the pivotal changes and *the work* it takes for Black and historically marginalized students to achieve success. We have dreams, we have hopes, we have hidden talents, and our intellectual genius is waiting to be validated.

But do you see us?

What a beautiful notion to own—you, the educator, can actually bring these gifts to life (or stifle them all together). Or as the hip-hop educator would say, "Are you willing to *put us on*?" To be *put on* is to be believed in, where someone in a position of power recognizes talent and projects a potential for greatness. In other words, as an educator, you must be willing to give a little of yourself—to be vulnerable so that your power can be transferred to your students. Think of it as instant street cred or in this case, instant empowerment cred.

Some of us are precocious, loud, and ultra-curious in class, some of us sit silently self-diagnosing the trauma that life has brought, some of us laugh to hide the pain. But for all of us, our potential transcends the daily dilemmas we endure. The statistical poverty you see on your roster doesn't come close to tell our true stories—yet we show up every day equipped to learn at the highest levels. But most importantly, we all show up deserving *your best* every day. You, the educator, might just be the one person we can depend on, the one person we can trust, the one person to *put us on*. For many of us, your classroom is, in fact, our safe haven.

Growing up without a father took its toll on me. Role models were hard to come by. But, at the age of twelve, I was awakened by an athlete on television, a Black man that compelled me to dream about college—that man was Michael Jordan. It was quite simple, Michael Jordan was in college, so at age twelve, I told myself, "I'm going to college." I worked hard to be somewhat successful with my high school coursework, knowing full well not many people expected me to go far. One night, while studying for an American History midterm (that never mentioned any person from my culture as a contributor to America's success), a song was playing on a local hip-hop channel. The group was called Leaders of the New School (a fitting name), and Busta Rhymes ended the song with these words that have been etched in my mind for the last thirty-two years of my life:

> *"Sometimes you gotta stand up strong for self. Do the little things on your own. Strive hard, strive for perfection."*

It jolted me for a few seconds, the words just brought clarity to where I was and where I wanted to go. At a time, when there was just *too much on my mind*—my future became believable, and the urgency became an invisible currency. Ironically, the very educators that helped me attain higher education didn't realize that my worst fear was disappointing them. So, I had no choice *but* to succeed. It's an interesting dichotomy that we in poverty face, the notion that we can't afford to fail—yet we risk our lives based on the pedagogy provided in our American educational system.

In my first year of doctoral coursework, I was convinced that I would solve the educational world's issues by learning how to motivate students. I believed *hope* was the deciding factor on what ultimately compelled students to succeed. Growing up in poverty has allowed me the understanding of the rich gifts we have as educators. You see, each day in class, the very lives of our students are at the mercy of our practice—right down to the visible and invisible moves we make. As educators, the most important gift we have is the ability to see all facets of *culture*, it can be our students' beliefs, language, values, music, sneakers (yes, there is a sneaker culture), and even the way they see the world around them.

We turn cultural anonymity into racial affinity. We know that students' cultural processes are multifaceted, running parallel to the adaptive nature in which we teach. So, my studies led me to look past hope and into the chambers of your classroom, where genuine relationships are built, culture becomes an asset, and affirming racial identity seals the opportunity for deep levels of learning to take place.

How do we seize the power of culturally relevant pedagogy and culturally responsive-transformational school leadership simultaneously? Some clues lie in the leader's ability to provide instructional leadership through a lens of equity. The goal of this book is to secure these factors as a foundation for high impact culturally responsive schools. Both qualitative research and firsthand examples from my own work with teachers and leaders are the foundation of this book.

See the prelude for "Dear Poverty"—a piece I wrote as a cleansing of my soul, to put poverty to rest, and to remind myself where I came from. I just thought it would be the perfect reminder to us, the educators, that we have the power to turn the most unimaginable dream into a crystalized reality for our Black and historically marginalized students, whose potential is limitless. We, as educators, can truly become revolutionary if we choose to do so. I guess you can say with your help, I became—*the counternarrative*.

***

My goal in writing this book is for you to find your authentic self, to find your lens of equity, and to ultimately lead in the necessary endeavors that must take place within your school context. As a school leader, you'll be compelled to ask yourself: What is my just cause?

I want you to wake up each morning (as I do) and focus on what matters most—the empowerment of Black and underserved students of color. If you are vulnerable enough, or dare I say brave enough to *Bridge the Gap* for them, then settle in and learn with me.

Prelude
Dear Poverty

Dear poverty: You have a paralyzing stranglehold on more than 45 million Americans, 13.3 million of whom are children. Your grip is even tighter on people of color in the central San Joaquin Valley. In Fresno, California, alone, nearly 150,000 students are trapped in your clutches daily—the majority being Black, Latinx, and emergent bilinguals.

I still see you every single day, whether you are a coatless child on a freezing winter morning, the false security of gangs, or the miles of rundown apartment buildings. You come disguised in so many different forms—crime, lack of job skills, drug addiction, dropout rates, and fatherless homes. You thrive in the worst conditions. The most chilling part is that you've woven your way into generations of innocent children, often offering an enticing comfort to stay.

As a four-year-old boy, I realized you had me within your clutches too. Growing up with a single mother humbled me along the way. She did everything in her power to provide a normal life for us. Sometimes working two jobs just to put food on the table and to make the next month's rent. I learned the power of perseverance by watching my mother work tirelessly to provide for us.

I met my father for the first time as he walked out of his prison cell at the California Corrections Institution in Tehachapi. In the few weeks he was with us, I witnessed domestic violence, drug abuse, and the emotional roller coaster of alcoholism and abandonment. Yet through all the obstacles, my mother remained strong—shielding me from the present trauma and never giving up on me.

Dear poverty: Because of you, my mother never found permanent housing, causing me to attend five different schools in five consecutive years. Preschool was spent at Heaton Elementary in Fresno Unified School District, kindergarten at Rowell Elementary, then first grade at Burroughs Elementary, second grade at Webster Elementary, then finally third grade at Marshall Elementary in Fowler Unified—our final destination. In Fowler, I found a permanent educational home, but we still struggled settling into a home to call our own. At one point, we even lived in my aunt's garage.

Entering third grade, I could not read, couldn't sleep, and had trouble making friends. Little did I know, adverse childhood experiences had consumed me. The statistics already categorized and entangled me in the school-to-prison pipeline. Imagine, someone so full of hope—yet destiny had already been determined.

Dear poverty: You made me feel like I was living on borrowed time—never in control of my surroundings. Early on, I saw that my skin was fair, but life was not. I remember you very well, especially the times standing in line for that long block of cheese with my grandmother or paying for our milk and bread with stamps used as money. Yet, somehow, my classroom gave me the relentless instinct to set goals and wish for more.

Dear poverty: In order to defeat you, we as educators are in the business of creating the resilient child. In third grade, Mrs. Browning and Mrs. Karle became my angels, teaching me how to read for the first time and sending me to a local museum to take private art lessons. They saw the power of my potential, not the perils of my past. For once, I felt a teacher saw me for me, and they guided me through the deepest levels of learning. My teachers were providing me with social capital, which I could use later in life.

Dear poverty: The resilient child starts with a goal, which is attainable through the learning environment and social structures educators provide—often the determining factor. Fostering concepts that speak to a child's hopes and dreams is where we start. We have the highest expectations for them because we have the highest expectations for ourselves.

Dear poverty: We know our schools and universities are ground zero in your demise—the symbol of hope for so many students. We, the educators, are the beacon of light amid the darkness and despair you've created. Any educator will tell you—recognizing and utilizing a culturally responsive learning environment builds success—and success fosters resiliency.

Dear poverty: You shrivel when lesson plans are written not as content mastery but as tickets to liberation.

In sixth grade my teacher, Mrs. Speth, referred me to a program for gifted students. Why? Because she took the time to see a brilliance in my artwork. She noticed. She understood the funds of knowledge I came equipped with and quickly leveraged that talent for my academic success. She understood that my artistic abilities reflected my world, which portrayed my desire to learn. By looking at my abilities as an asset and having a strength-based perspective, Mrs. Speth set me on a new path to success, helping me build cultural capital along the way. In less than three years, I went from being illiterate to being seen as academically gifted in the eyes of my teachers.

Dear poverty: When educators build academic resiliency through positive relationships, it allows kids to look beyond where the next meal is coming from and to see past the social pitfalls of gangs, drugs, and teen pregnancy. This intrinsic strength spawns the positive belief in their own educational journey.

Dear poverty: The future of all students affected by you hinges on what we provide in our schools and in our classrooms. Your roots run so deep with these children, especially Black, Latinx, and Southeast Asians, adversely affecting their health, access to nutrition, emotional status, and quality of life. We want their names synonymous with *power* not *pain*. We never want a child to go back to you, so we must build learning structures that develop the whole child.

Dear poverty: We know that by creating students' academic resilience, we can help them realize that when they engage confidently with a challenge, anything is possible—and failure is not something to fear. After all, it's not what students know but what they can do with what they know. That is the goal of education.

Dear poverty: I battled you through my education at Fresno State University and I gave you my all. I gave you my mind, body, and spirit. I was blessed to be accepted as an Educational Opportunity Program (EOP) student. Throughout my time in college, I felt further empowered by my professors, who recognized that I was a holder and creator of knowledge.

Dear poverty: You knew I was just one flat tire away from failure—from the sleepless nights studying for exams, the countless hours reading class notes, to walking through lecture halls as a ghost on many nights—sometimes you whispered to me. Thank you for lurking in the shadows when it was so easy to give up. When I graduated from Fresno State University, I was the first in my family to do so, gracefully stepping past the school-to-prison pipeline accepted by society.

Dear poverty: As a boy, I never accepted you. I only saw myself defeating you. You humbled me along the way, constantly pushing me to work harder and to fall forward. You blessed me with a superhuman wife, who possesses enough strength for both of us to persevere.

Dear poverty: My patience for you has grown thin. We don't share the same beliefs, and we never will. I've grown tired of looking at national report cards and dashboards that tell me what I already know. We'll conquer you by providing our students a quality education and realizing that using their cultural strengths can be the great equalizer. We'll stop making excuses and hold ourselves accountable to overthrow you.

Dear poverty: I wanted you to know I have my doctoral degree now, and I was awarded the Dean's Medal for the most outstanding research in educational leadership. You see, you've created a dreamer. I've dedicated my life to defeating you and helping students do the same.

Now it is time to say goodbye. And that's all right. I'm ready to let you go.

Sincerely,

Dr. Hank Gutierrez

Introduction

This book is intended to reach both K–16 educational leaders and classroom teachers alike. Given the academic perils facing Black and historically marginalized students of color in the United States, the need to bridge the gap between classroom-based culturally relevant practices and culturally responsive leadership has never been greater. How is this done? Answering that question is the goal of this book. Explicit tactics are shared for university- and site-level leaders in creating a transformational base—supporting teachers' enactment of culturally responsive pedagogy.

The bridge is often fragmented or misinterpreted by educators yet must remain centrally focused on Ladson-Billings's theory of culturally relevant pedagogy. With firsthand testimonies and frameworks from research, this book allows practitioners to regain an understanding of culturally relevant practices as well as the overlay of culturally responsive transformational leadership (Khalifa et al., 2016; Northouse, 2019), creating an equitable school climate where Black and historically marginalized students thrive academically.

The reader will gain valuable insight on how to become a culturally responsive educator, both philosophically and pedagogically, by engaging in critical self-reflection. In addition, current researched-based components will be shared, such as mindfulness and the relational aspect of leveraging students' *power languages* to build positive relationships. Practitioners will be immersed in examining effective classroom practices and how to provide instructional feedback centered on reaching what I call the *Apex of Student Learning* (the adaptive level). Likewise, school administrators will be able to connect to current practices while building a foundation for their own culturally responsive leadership skills. The content will provide the reader with samples of culturally responsive rubrics to analyze classroom teaching from a lens of equity. Essentially, the purpose of the book is two pronged: first, it invites the reader to understand and begin practicing culturally responsive pedagogy, and second, it sheds light on the mentorship necessary to provide instructional feedback within the real-time practice of culturally responsive pedagogy.

Practitioners will have access to usable lesson design strategies, and site principals will see a sample rubric consisting of "look fors" in content, instruction, culture, and interpersonal structures (Massachusetts Department of Elementary and Secondary Education, 2021) to measure classroom effectiveness. Educators will also gain insight into *pedagogical reasoning*, a complex yet simple approach to instructional mentorship. Untapped in the world of culturally responsive teaching, this instructional concept weaves modeling, adaptive expertise, and actionable feedback based on professional judgement in real time (Kavanagh et al., 2020). More important, and perhaps the essence of this book, is a reminder to educators that we cannot believe our students will succeed unless we believe in our own lens of equity.

Chapter 1 is an attempt to reintroduce culturally responsive pedagogy from a mindset that reconfigures rigor in relation to cultural and racial affirmation. Postpandemic, schools across the nation have seen an uptick in social-emotional stressors, and although important, these can overshadow deeper instructional undercurrents. School leaders must be reminded that social-emotional wellness should be built into culturally responsive lessons rather than appearing in offshoot curriculum unrelated to content standards, which can tax teachers' time.

The *Apex of Student Learning* (adaptation level), which capitalizes on academic success, cultural competence, and sociopolitical consciousness (Ladson-Billings, 2009) while leveraging relationships and mindfulness, is the overarching construct of this book. It is the driver in using students' cultural strengths and racial identity as assets for deep, personalized learning. Readers are reminded that students' ability to learn at the highest levels is fostered through intentional planning in which deep learning is guided in a gradual progression within a safe learning environment.

Chapter 2 quickly shifts to the origins of educational injustice and then prescribes new ideas for educational equity for Black and other historically marginalized students of color. The parallels to the past are chilling, and veteran and newly appointed leaders and teachers must be reminded of the sense of urgency in reimaging their roles. Specific to chapter 2 are pictures of continued academic paralyses based on systemic racism, academic disparities, and the nation's ill-preparedness to embrace the academic needs of culturally diverse students. In addition, common misconceptions that inhibit teachers' use of culturally responsive teaching are highlighted. Past policies and practices will be examined to help spawn the reimagining of epistemologies that embrace Black students and prospective Black teachers.

Chapter 3 discusses the theory of culturally relevant pedagogy, a multidimensional approach that addresses curricular content, learning context, classroom culture, teacher-student relationships, and individual pedagogical procedures. When practiced effectively, culturally relevant pedagogy allows teachers to tap into the multitude of cultural proficiencies, lived experiences, historical perspectives, and relationships that students possess. For novice and veteran teachers who may be exploring the shifts necessary for culturally responsive teaching, this chapter offers building blocks for common practices.

Shifting one's mindset from a deficit approach to one of continually building self-efficacy is inherently important as it pertains to three anchors of culturally relevant teaching: (1) conceptions of self and others, (2) enriching social relations, and (3) conceptions of investigative knowledge. This chapter also explores an untapped component within the research—the *vulnerability* to let go of past practices and to embrace an infinite game of teaching. As mentioned, a critical first step for teachers is to understand that their own cultural values, inhibitions, and stereotypes often shape or dictate learning expectations.

Chapter 4 offers practical examinations from teacher interviews and classroom observations from six teachers and two site administrators, using academic success, cultural competence, and sociopolitical consciousness (Ladson-Billings, 2009) as anchors. Supported by prior research, categories emerged during the research within the surface level of learning structures, as opposed to those demanding more intricate instructional tactics tied to cultural strengths. *Learning partnerships*, for example, capitalized on building mutual trust to sustain positive relationships as a way to support academic success. However, like all surface-level themes, none of the comments made by participants linked building positive relationships with developing cultural competence or sociopolitical consciousness.

Chapter 4 also highlights the overemphasis on trauma-informed practices and social-emotional learning as often practiced in our public schools. Creating a classroom environment that is intellectually and emotionally safe is a small component of culturally responsive pedagogy. However, becoming overly dependent on offshoot curriculum tied to social-emotional learning negates deep instruction tied to racial affirmation and cultural strengths in relation to the *Apex of Student Learning*. Postpandemic, this is highly critical, as site leaders and teacher preparation programs look to navigate learning accountability as it pertains to pedagogical priorities and instructional expectations.

Chapter 5 explores explicit culturally responsive instructional practices aligned to grade-level standards and core curriculum guidelines at the deeper instructional undercurrent. Distilled from educators within the study, these practices pertain to the themes *information processing*, *pedagogical tactics*, and *leveraging the attention system*. Pivotal to this chapter is the presentation of culturally responsive lesson design, often elusive to both teachers and instructional leaders. Too often lessons remain stagnant at the level of acquisition, where the gap widens and dependent learning becomes foundational (knowledge and awareness are gained in simplistic, rote fashion). Because social-emotional learning is often overused, this chapter seeks to build mindfulness techniques into lesson design.

High-impact culturally responsive teachers increase racially diverse students' motivation and interest by allowing them to create self-agency in setting mastery goals tied to academic success, cultural competence, and sociopolitical consciousness. In addition, high-impact teachers intentionally plan for and are critically conscious to include Black students' voices when making real-time judgements, considering alternative progressions, and using instructional decisions that ensure success.

Chapter 6 introduces culturally responsive leadership coupled with transformational leadership, which in tandem emerge as *macro-level* leadership traits within a culturally responsive school setting. In tandem, these traits set the tone for the overarching philosophies of instructional leadership and one's lens of equity within the *micro level* of culturally responsive leadership. Intentional efforts, such as *promoting an inclusive school climate*, begin to emerge that bode well for the ultimate configuration of the culturally responsive community school. This chapter compels the reader to consider their own leadership traits and if they lie within the midrange or full range of cultural responsiveness.

Chapter 7 focuses on both the surface level and the deep instructional undercurrents of culturally responsive leadership. Based on research with teachers and site leaders, distinct themes inform practitioners of the necessary tactics that support teachers' enactment of culturally responsive pedagogy. Explicit instructional feedback based on sound lesson "look fors," combined with effective lesson design, is featured within the chapter. Along with fostering collective capacity centered on race relations, an untapped form of instructional mentorship will be introduced—*pedagogical reasoning*. This form of instructional feedback lies at the crux of supporting teachers' self-efficacy, enactment, and ultimate expertise within culturally responsive teaching.

Chapter 8 compels the reader to imagine a unified and encapsulated educational environment in which students' culture, school, and community *overlap* with commonalities of languages, values, and experiences. The culturally responsive school must be looked at and treated as the most effective and efficient turnaround school, where strategies are intentionally centered on improving the academic outcomes of Black and historically marginalized students of color. In fact, this book is the first to introduce the culturally responsive community school (CRCS) as a secondary component to ensure student academic success. Culturally responsive pedagogy and culturally responsive leadership are the primary components.

In illuminating the anatomy of social inequities, the community school framework looks to eradicate poverty on both short-term and long-term bases. Culturally responsive leaders' tactics in concert with the four pillars of community schools provide the *impact, access, respect,* and *trust* so vital to marginalized communities of color. Current leaders can consider this, along with various examples throughout the nation, in building sound CRCSs. Further, the CRCS acts as an all-encompassing model that invites prospective Black teachers to thrive within a culturally and racially affirming educational environment.

Chapter 9 reaches back throughout the book and presents a cyclical picture based on the primary and secondary components of the culturally responsive school. From an overarching perspective, the entire system, or *bubble effect*, is the epicenter in rebuilding the Black teacher pipeline. In fact, Black teachers, as the research confirms, have a profound effect on the academic success of Black students. This chapter explores both national and grassroots efforts in shaping structures to support, recruit, and retain Black teachers—using clues from historically Black colleges and universities (HBCUs). The essence of this book is that we will not see long-term improvements in teacher diversity (especially Black teachers) unless we see sustainability in creating culturally responsive schools.

With this book, site principals and lead teachers will be able to create actionable plans and frameworks to sustain a culturally responsive school climate. Clear overviews and observable practices will also be presented. Although the two critical levels of a culturally responsive school climate include culturally responsive pedagogy and culturally responsive leadership, this book is a first in illuminating the interplay between each.

My own qualitative research will be the underpinning of the entire text, which illuminates the surface-level elements of culturally responsive practices and the necessary and often ill-sustained deep instructional undercurrents for success. *Bridging the Gap* is also the first book to illuminate the primary components of the culturally responsive school (teaching and leadership) along with the interplay of an untapped third component—community schools. As mentioned, the final bonus chapter illuminates the praxis of creating a culturally responsive school, which is the key to the recruitment, preparation, and retention of Black teachers.

Chapter 1

Culturally Responsive Pedagogy

A Mindset

"Someday, we'll be able to measure the power of words."

—Maya Angelou

Education has been viewed as the decisive vehicle out of poverty (MacGregor, 2015), the very pathway to the American dream. In fact, human capital, social capital, and long-term health are not predicted by school achievement but by the number of years in schooling (Hattie, 2012). A paradox no doubt, for educational longevity is based on meeting institutional qualifications not historically designed to ensure culturally and linguistically diverse students get there (Goodwin et al., 2022). The joy and racial affirmation we provide in our school system and in the walls of our classrooms act to fulfill those dreams. In other words, students will strive toward a destination if they believe there is a path to get there.

This sentiment rests at the core of culturally responsive schools—at its purest form, a liberation pedagogy secured by a unified effort in facilitating culturally responsive learning, while addressing barriers to achievement. Put simply, the educator infuses students' cultural richness within all facets of learning to secure academic success, embed cultural competence, and broaden students' sociopolitical consciousness (Ladson-Billings, 2009), setting achievable goals that guide deeper learning proficiency (Goodwin et al., 2022; Hattie, 2012).

Culturally responsive schools are built on a foundation of powerful, critically conscious teaching that mirrors Black and marginalized students' powerful cultural strengths and knowledge. The academic content provides equitable opportunities for students to develop personalized deep learning, while affirming their racial identities and cultural strengths

(Adelman & Taylor, 2018; Darling-Hammond & Darling-Hammond, 2022; Ladson-Billings, 2009).

Culturally responsive schools unapologetically clear the path for Black and other marginalized students of color to have access to critical thinking, in order to combat a society that thinks critically of them. Our young students must be prepared to (1) be proficient in core academic content, (2) solve problems in real-world practical and unpredictable settings, (3) communicate factually and creatively, (4) synergize collaboratively, (5) learn independently, and (6) develop a critical awareness and a sociopolitical mindset (Darling-Hammond & Darling-Hammond, 2022; Hammond, 2015).

These outcomes occur in a school with accountable measures that ensure educators shift from *race-neutral* curriculum to a more culturally, linguistically, and racially inclusive learning space (Hammond, 2015; Ladson-Billings, 2009; Villavicencio et al., 2022). Principals and school leaders must remain unwavering on these measures and, in fact, set explicit instructional expectations that illuminate students' cultural richness.

INSULATED FACTORS FOR SUCCESS

For Black and underserved minority students, the sense of urgency has never been greater to reconcile a more equitable and just educational system, one that secures pedagogical tactics that equip students to become lifelong learners with pride in who they are as individuals. We know that students' academic resiliency is fostered through a sense of belonging and positive relationships (Young & Easton-Brooks, 2022), where learning is sustained through rigor and relevance (Daggett, 2008). The fact is that the most critical component to learning is the relationship between the school system (teachers, administrators, counselors, noncertificated personnel) and the students it serves (Daggett, 2008; Hammond, 2015; Ladson-Billings, 2009).

This is not a groundbreaking discovery in the field of education; however, it often goes overlooked in today's accountability-minded school reforms and reactionary frameworks. Effective educators know that positive relationships and the trust built within are the tipping point for many of our Black and historically marginalized students—a prerequisite to their learning. Teachers and administrators practicing culturally responsive pedagogy and leadership often proclaim the following sentiment, almost verbatim:

> I pride myself on relationships with my students because in this community, if a kid doesn't trust you, or doesn't have a good relationship, they're not going to learn anything. (Julie, fifth-grade teacher)

In taking student voice into consideration, Howard (2001) found that Black students saw culturally responsive teaching in three distinct themes: (1) the importance of *caring* teachers, (2) the establishment of a *family*-type classroom environment, and (3) the teacher's ability to captivate students while making learning *fun*. From a student perspective, all three themes act as learning anchors, which facilitate access to high levels of knowledge in real-time culturally responsive instruction. More importantly, when students' voices are heard, culturally responsive teachers are signaled to intensify instruction or perhaps scaffold learning based on personal need (Ladson-Billings, 2009). In culturally responsive teaching, student voice holds power from a relational standpoint; yet based on learning progressions, the teacher is able to shift the cognitive load—a critical factor in fostering independent student learning (Rebora, 2022).

Just as relationships between partners thrive when love languages are leveraged for deeper connection (Chapman, 2015), culturally responsive teachers must be keen in utilizing each student's primary and secondary *power languages*. Although existing on the surface level from a pedagogical tactic standpoint, power languages, such as using words of praise or connections to culture, allow for positive relationships to be built in real time. For example, young James may respond well when the teacher uses his primary power language in *connections of culture* (a custom handshake filled with fun choreographed gestures); however, his secondary motivator may be *quality time* with the teacher (one-on-one conversations or reteaching).

In all, the four factors of teacher-student relationships orbit the *Apex of Student Learning* (as seen in figure 1.2). Chapman (2015) interestingly shares that "verbal compliments, or words of appreciation, are powerful communicators of love" (p. 37), and in culturally responsive teaching, the effective teacher understands that words of empowerment can cultivate students' commitment to excel despite the rigors of the content.

Essential in accentuating student learning, these four factors—*caring*, creating a *family* atmosphere, making learning *fun*, and the use of *power languages*—remain critical. As *prerequisites* in the more intricate arenas of culturally responsive teaching, they pertain to building positive interpersonal relations in the classroom. In essence, they are critical factors in securing higher levels of cognitive development. For example, students' ability to feel seen through their teacher's use of their power language enables them to learn more productively within a racially affirming and familial atmosphere.

Without teachers taking the time to learn about and tap into students' needs, trust is lost and relationships remain at the surface level. When done right, teacher investment leads students to begin to *believe* that their teachers *believe* in them—fostering an avenue to deeper instructional undercurrents within cultural responsiveness. Figure 1.1 illustrates Ladson-Billings's

Academic Success
- Students must demonstrate academic competence in literacy, numeracy, technological, social, and political skills in meaningful ways
- Teacher forges academic success in creative ways, such as having students choose ideas and issues that build leadership

Cultural Competence
- Students keep principles of their culture intact along with having academic excellence
- Parents are invited to the classroom to demonstrate cultural customs that translate to further exploration of curricular content
- Students are permitted to use their home language as they acquire English and "code-switch" to become proficient in both

Sociopolitical Consciousness
- Students must be guided to creatively develop a critical lens to see the inequities around them (cultural norms, values, or historical contexts)
- Students are allowed to engage in community issues and empowered to present solutions
- Example: Students explore and research a community issue (homelessness) and use academic skills to present to city council about building shelters

Figure 1.1. Three Propositions of Culturally Responsive Pedagogy
Source: Adapted from Ladson-Billings (1995a).

(1995a) three-pronged approach to learning criteria (or propositions), which must be explicitly tied to daily learning goals. When designing lessons toward higher levels of learning, practitioners must envision content objectives and learning goals fused to academic success, cultural competence, and sociopolitical consciousness.

For example, *high-impact* teachers help develop cultural integrity (cultural competence) by allowing students to use their home language or "nonstandard English" in class. Given the agency to use the native language and English interchangeably is known as "code switching," whereby students' culture becomes the conduit to language proficiency in both tongues. Ladson-Billings (2009) mentions that teachers fail to leverage the "nonstandard English" that Black students come equipped with, despite the rich social context it brings from community and into classroom settings.

In this case, teachers not only validate learning through the home language but affirm and celebrate student responses as a means to progress to higher learning in real time. In fact, Emdin (2021) explains, "The world requires us all to code switch in order to connect with others from different backgrounds or experiences" (p. 41). In essence, the dual language allows for cultural connections to be continually affirmed, *and* the entire class sees an appreciation for each other's genius.

The significance described above is twofold. First, trusting relationships allow learners to be authentically invested in their teacher while losing themselves in the progression of higher levels of learning. Second, students' self-efficacy works to continually build cultural frames of reference to transfer knowledge across disciplines. As described above, teachers' development of automaticity in making rapid professional judgments—in this case, validating students' language to leverage deeper learning—is paramount. Practitioners understand this clearly, for the achievement of the lowest-performing students must increase at a much higher rate if proficiency gaps are to be closed.

Moreover, effective culturally responsive teachers do not homogenize students and base assumptions on race; they leverage positive relationships, tactfully getting to know the *whole child* to facilitate learning (Darling-Hammond & Darling Hammond, 2022). As we'll discuss in more detail in chapter 4, *high-impact* culturally relevant teachers design lessons that assist students in reaching the *Apex of Student Learning* (adaptation level) by modeling strategic thinking, tapping into cultural funds of knowledge, scaffolding guiding questions explicit to content standards, and capitalizing on students' cultural strengths for personalizing learning.

When properly put into practice, academic success, cultural competence, and sociopolitical consciousness (Ladson-Billings, 2009) are embedded, students' power languages are leveraged, and the attention system is secured. The *Apex of Student Learning* will be referred to throughout this book as a guiding feature at the core of culturally responsive teaching. (See figure 1.2.) Many Black and historically marginalized students fall short of meeting proficiency levels not because of their intellectual capacity; rather, lesson designs often fail to use their cultural knowledge to personalize and deepen learning structures (Darling-Hammond & Darling-Hammond, 2022; Hattie,

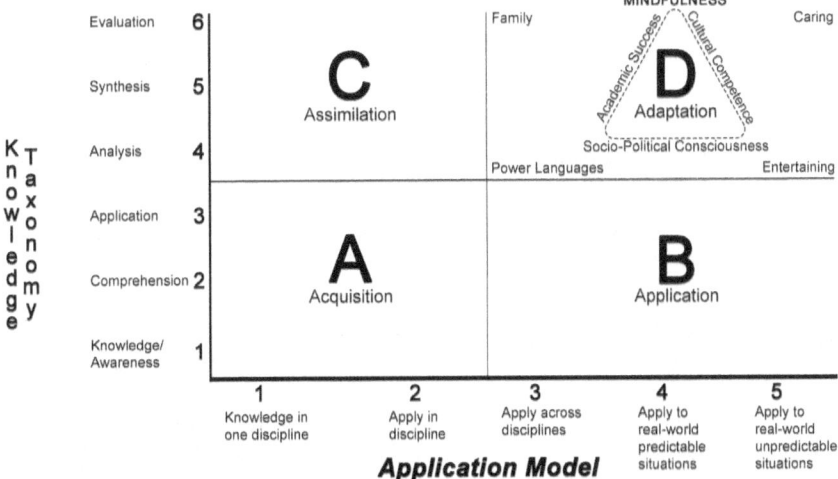

Figure 1.2. The Apex of Student Learning

Source: Adapted from Daggett (2008, p. 42). Copyright 2008 by International Center for Leadership in Education. The *Apex of Student Learning* is adapted from Gutierrez (2021, p. 151).

2012; Ladson-Billings, 2009). In the classroom, where deeper learning matters the most, the gap widens primarily when learning becomes stagnate at the acquisition level (knowledge and awareness are gained in simplistic, rote fashion).

Culturally responsive lesson plans provide a gradual progression to the adaptation level with integrated scaffolding and guiding questions beginning at the acquisition stage. In addition, instruction fosters both collective and individual learning in a racially affirming environment. If, for example, learning is geared toward and stagnated at low levels of comprehension and applied in a single discipline (acquisition), students' assessment results will continue to stagnate at lower levels—at best.

High-impact culturally responsive teaching guarantees students are engaged with the opportunity to bridge the gap, when cultural assets are interconnected with cognitive thinking, taxed at the evaluation level, where knowledge is applied in real-world unpredictable scenarios (Daggett, 2008; Gay, 2010, Ladson-Billings, 2009). Equally important, effective instructional feedback ensures teacher tactics take learning from rote to reasoning (acquisition to adaptation), affirming students' racial identity through learning goals aimed at academic success, cultural competence, and sociopolitical consciousness (Kavanagh et al., 2020; Ladson-Billings, 1995a).

Teachers and their instructional leaders must ensure that students are guided within complex chambers where unpredictable learning tasks become predictable based on cultural knowledge and lived experiences. It is at this level of instruction that culturally and linguistically diverse students stand greater chances to engage with and succeed in the skills necessary for standardized levels of proficiency, twenty-first-century learning, and college and career readiness.

Simply put, if rigor is tied to cultural *relevancy*, students' information processing abilities and performance on standardized tests will naturally mirror their everyday instruction—the *predictability effect*. Hammond (2015) explains, "Culturally responsive teaching is a pedagogical approach firmly rooted in learning theory and cognitive science" (p. 16). That said, at the heart of culturally responsive pedagogy, the high-impact teacher is keen to advance students' cognitive skills in a way that builds on their personal interests, community backgrounds, and racial identities—using them as *assets*.

This is crucial because proficiency levels on standardized tests are based on students' ability to fluidly synthesize, evaluate, and then formulate a complex response to unpredictable scenarios. As we'll see in chapter 9, Black teachers play a critical role in bolstering the necessary outcomes for Black students to succeed academically, socially, and emotionally (Bristol & Martinez-Fernandez, 2019; Carver-Thomas, 2018; Easton-Brooks, 2021; Freeman et al., 2022; Gershenson et al., 2021; Gist & Bristol, 2022; Jha,

2021; Kohli, 2009; Lindsay & Hart, 2017; Mason et al., 2021; Young & Easton-Brooks, 2022; Zenner et al., 2014).

MINDFULNESS MATTERS

In advancing through the rigors of learning and ultimately reaching levels of adaptation, it is the four themes (caring, entertaining, family, and power languages) that solidify teacher-student relationships. The critical component of mindfulness, however, also illuminates the ability to reach deeper levels of cognition (Jha, 2021). Mindfulness matters for all students, but for students affected by adverse childhood experiences (ACEs), this *attention-serving* strategy is even more crucial to learning. The Substance Abuse and Mental Health Services Administration (SAMHSA) describes ACEs as stressful or traumatic events, including abuse and neglect (SAMHSA, 2018).

The Centers for Disease Control and Prevention (CDC, 2016) explain that "childhood experiences, both negative and positive, have a tremendous impact on future violence victimization and perpetration, and lifelong health and opportunity" (para. 1). ACEs also include household dysfunction, such as witnessing domestic violence, and could include sexual abuse or an incarcerated household member (SAMHSA, 2018). Black students, particularly those who come from low-income families, are more likely than their White and Latinx peers to have had more than three ACEs during their school-aged years (Carle et al., 2013).

Many of these students experience toxic stress, which occurs when unemployment, crime, and violence are so persistent over time that they disrupt the child's neuroendocrine-immune network (Darling-Hammond & Darling-Hammond, 2022). Intentionally infusing mindfulness into culturally responsive lesson design raises the likelihood that students will be able to focus on the content and, therefore, retain knowledge to use it in transferable real-world scenarios. Many schools, in the wake of the pandemic, continue to grapple with supporting student trauma and providing behavioral interventions by using stand-alone "social-emotional" curricula, neglecting to infuse mindfulness into lesson design or real-time teaching.

Students often describe a feeling like the world is moving at hyperspeed or report episodes of mind racing. Research by Dr. Amishi Jha explains the mind's floodlight (especially in the cognitive domain) can be on overload, causing the mind to be in a toxic *racing-tension* state. In fact, in those very moments, students' minds can dissociate from the present. This is all too real for students exposed to ACEs and toxic stress, and the irony is their minds are often chasing threats yet to occur—obstacles that may or may not come to pass.

The good news is that our *attention system* can reconfigure the brain's information processing in critical ways, allowing students to focus during unpredictable and cognitively taxing learning environments (Jha, 2021).

- "Orienting System" or Flashlight: Students are able to follow and sustain a train of thought.
- "Alerting System" or Floodlight: Affords students situational awareness—students are able to notice thoughts, concepts, and perspectives that relate to learning tasks.
- "Central Executive" or Juggler: Students are able to hold goals in mind, knowing what is needed to do next to move toward accomplishing it. Students are able to overcome distractions and "autopilot" behaviors (like picking up your phone) that could derail their focus on learning.

The central executive area allows students to focus on learning, which plays a significant role in shielding students from the day-to-day distractions that may occur in school or in their home environment. In fact, mindfulness-related strategies have even proven to be effective for a wide range of stress-related problems, in particular, increasing mental well-being, strengthening immune functions, and increasing attentional capacity (Zenner et al., 2014). Routines that allow students to stop for brief moments and center thoughts also regulate impulses and feelings that enhance learning (Real, 2022). When this happens, the central executive can stabilize students' ability to plan and manage information processing that is sustained at the *Apex of Student Learning*—the adaptation level.

Major analysis suggests that incorporating mindfulness into lesson design and classroom structures for children and young adults increases cognitive capacity for learning (Zenner et al., 2014). If intentionally incorporated into lesson design, mindfulness illuminates the path for students to navigate higher levels of learning. The high-impact culturally responsive teacher capitalizes on this and builds lessons to reach the adaptation level, setting goals and setting high expectations for their students to get there. Think of mindfulness as an illuminating tool that students' brains use to guide learning toward the highest peak.

Therefore, when designing lessons, culturally responsive teachers must negotiate the curricular content in concert with principles based in academic success, cultural competence, and sociopolitical awareness (Ladson-Billings, 2009), while simultaneously navigating students' need to refocus and be present. Research suggests that with teachers and site leaders, mindfulness (often referred to as social-emotional learning) can became overused within the contextual ideology of cultural responsiveness. Although necessary, when overprioritized, it overshadows the pedagogical nature of cultural responsiveness tied to rigor. When done properly, mindfulness is embedded in the lesson, becoming an integral (albeit short) part of deeper learning progressions.

SURFACE-LEVEL VERSUS DEEP INSTRUCTION

Educators are well advised to examine programs that operate at surface-level learning versus the deeper instructional tactics of cultural responsiveness as practiced at the school site. Is funding going to programs that truly reach culturally diverse students? For example, are you leading your teachers in deep dives surrounding culturally responsive instructional expertise, or are they taxed by focusing on students' character development or social-emotional state? Time is of the essence, and leaders must critically examine school traditions that lead to academic success or hamper progress altogether.

Think of your school's practice of culturally responsive teaching like this: one set of tactics lies at the surface level, while the other carries a deeper level of instructional undercurrent (figure 1.3). The *Apex of Student Learning* (quadrant D) remains centrally focused when practicing and building lessons within a culturally responsive pedagogical framework. Below the pedagogical arrays, and equally important, lie the critical components of culturally responsive school leadership, which we'll discuss in chapter 6.

The two arrays are "real-world" tactics or critical areas that lead to deeper learning, which enhance students' cognitive progression through well-designed culturally responsive lessons (Hammond, 2015; Gutierrez, 2021). On the left wing, although surface level in regard to academic success, teachers' classroom structures secure positive relationships while looking to build academic growth (Learning Partnerships). Secondly, classroom routines revolve around building conceptions of self and students while celebrating cultural differences (Awareness). Often this critical sociopolitical *awareness*, in reimagining the implications of a teacher's work for empowering Black and marginalized students (Doucet, 2017), lies at the surface level. True culturally responsive teaching brings that domain into the deeper instructional framework. Lastly, trauma-informed instructional practices (Social-Emotional Learning) are often overemphasized in day-to-day lessons, which diverts time from the true tactical nature of content mastery tied to cultural and linguistic inclusivity (Gutierrez, 2021).

On the right, through the utilization of deeper and more critical instructional undercurrents, the teacher builds personal connections to learning (Information Processing). What is often missing are lessons centered on developing students' sociopolitical consciousness (Pedagogical Tactics),

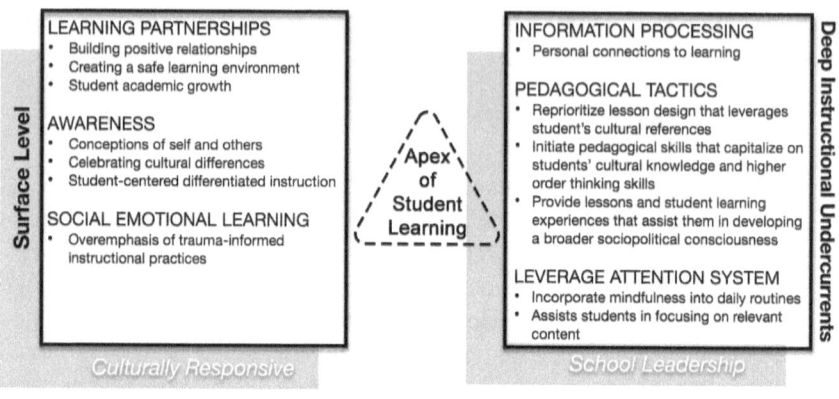

Figure 1.3. Two Arrays of Culturally Responsive Pedagogy
Source: Adapted from Hammond (2015, p. 17). Copyright 2015 by Corwin. Two Arrays of Culturally Responsive Pedagogy adapted from Gutierrez (2021, p. 151).

which capitalize on students' *cultural* knowledge tied to *depths* of knowledge. Lastly, deeper learning is achieved when teachers assist students in focusing on relevant content and being *present* (Leverage Attention System) through mindfulness.

Now, imagine yourself practicing culturally responsive teaching. As you gain expertise, you will go back and forth from each array shown above, and eventually, most of your time should be spent within the deep instructional undercurrents.

In chapter 4, we'll gain insight into teachers' attempts to employ these arrays of learning, and you'll be able to reflect on your own practice as it pertains to the *surface-level* elements versus the *deeper instructional undercurrents* of culturally relevant teaching. Pedagogical tactics from the field that have proven effective for diverse learners will be shared. It is essential to discuss theory in a manner that allows the reader to find commonalities that are tangible to their current practice. More importantly, it's critical to highlight pedagogical tactics or "look fors," which often go dismissed and, therefore, fail to become part of schoolwide instructional expectations.

We'll explore the nexus of culturally responsive leadership and the vital ways district and site leaders support teachers. This real-time support is often the missing link in cultivating academic success for Black and marginalized students of color. As you'll see, the true transformation comes with *pedagogical reasoning* (Kavanagh et al., 2020), which has untapped implications for teacher preparation programs, on-site instructional leadership, and Black teacher residency programs.

Like the two arrays of teaching, culturally responsive leadership contains actions that support teachers at the surface and deeper levels, simultaneously centered on the *Apex of Student Learning*. In essence, high-impact culturally responsive "teachers' beliefs and commitments are the greatest influence on student achievement *over which we have some control*" (Hattie, 2012, p. 25), highlighting the importance of instructional guidance and mentorship.

Further, the expectations teachers have of their students' intellectual capacity create environments conducive to reaching goals of learning at the *adaptation level*. However, without instructional leadership and actionable rubrics, most teachers remain stagnant within the surface level when practicing culturally responsive pedagogy. In the most effective culturally responsive schools, the gap is closed when the deep instructional undercurrents are fostered and sustained.

In our ever-changing world, where student diversity is our greatest asset, evidence shows that when teachers focus on cultural strengths tied to student interests, they have positive effects on learning outcomes, overall educational attainment, and future socioeconomic mobility (Darling-Hammond & Darling-Hammond, 2022; Gershenson et al., 2021; Goodwin et al., 2022). As we'll see in later chapters, Black educators play a pivotal role in bridging the proverbial gap for overall student success *and* to enlighten the tactics necessary for non-Black teachers to reach students of color.

Chapter 2

A Nation at Risk—*Still*

> "A high level of shared education is essential to a free, democratic society and to the fostering of a common culture, especially in a country that prides itself on pluralism and individual freedom."
>
> —*A Nation at Risk*, 1983

Our nation is at risk—*still*. Over forty years have passed since the National Commission on Excellence in Education released a sobering report, titled *A Nation at Risk: The Imperative for Education Reform*, detailing the failures of schooling in America. American schools, the report pronounced, were once a superpower of educational attainment, but at the time of the report, schools were unconsciously disarming themselves in the name of mediocracy.

Reform efforts prescribed to gain ground on the battlefront looked to reset the definition of quality schools based on high expectations for *all* students. Yet, ironically, the commission failed to mention that systemic racism within American schools continued to stifle the academic achievement of Black and other racially diverse students. The metaphoric "risk" was that students who were nonproficient in literary skills and mathematics would be unable to achieve social and human capital in their futures (National Commission on Excellence in Education [NCEE], 1983).

The *Brown v. Board of Education* decision, which determined that racially segregated schools were unconstitutional, made it easy for society to believe the fallacy that Black students were accepted and given equal opportunities within public schools (Wright, 2022). Desegregation closed Black schools, not White schools, leaving White teachers ill-equipped to culturally connect with their Black students. Black students, who by and large were not welcomed in the first place, were forced to assimilate to an educational system that was not built for them. Throughout the decade following the *Brown* decision, Black educators, who had a direct positive effect on Black student achievement, were essentially erased from the teaching profession (Wright, 2022).

Fenwick (2022) highlights that prior to the *Brown* ruling, Black principals and teachers comprised 35 to 50 percent of the public school workforce, depending on the state. In today's public school systems, only 9 percent of leaders are Black—a microscopic number compared to the highly qualified leaders in all Black segregated schools prior to *Brown* (National Center for Education Statistics, 2019a).

At the time of the commission's report, President Ronald Reagan noted, "Certainly there are few areas in American life as important to our society, to our people, and to our families as our schools and colleges" (NCEE, 1983, p. 114). No doubt, a concise reaction to the dismal realities of the educational disparities at the time. However, it's unclear what Reagan meant by *our people* or *our families*. Throughout his presidency, Reagan seemed blind to the causal factors of educational attainment tied to poverty and the consequent lack of social mobility.

Policies that reduced child poverty by half in the 1980s, such as housing subsidies, food stamps, student loans, and employment compensations, were heavily reduced during the Reagan administration (Darling-Hammond & Darling-Hammond, 2022). Along with cutting children from food benefits, which equated to three million students losing school lunch and another million stripped of food stamps, Reagan remained vigilant in the "War on Drugs" (Darling-Hammond & Darling-Hammond, 2022; Lopez, 2014). The race-related criminalization of street crime led to nearly eleven million dollars in slashed funds to educational antidrug efforts, shifting those dollars to bolster the nation's police forces (Lopez, 2014). Cemented stereotypes live on today about Black and historically marginalized students' families being "Chicago welfare queens" and buying a "T-bone steak" on the government's dollar (Lopez, 2014; Real, 2022).

In the mid-1990s, nearly a decade after the original call for education reform (NCEE, 1983), Hillary Clinton and others referred to inner-city youth as "super predators, with no conscience, no empathy" (DuVernay et al., 2016, 28:50), politically capitalizing on America's War on Drugs. Seemingly overnight, this rhetorical war became a war against Black youth, who became subject to the dehumanizing effects of racial profiling as school discipline policies looked to mirror America's 1994 crime bill (DuVernay et al., 2016).

As described in later sections, America's current juvenile justice system statistics continue to reflect adult incarceration rates for Black inmates. For most of the American psyche, criminality equated to color, while law and order became synonymous with whiteness (Real, 2022). Unfortunately, this is a sentiment (whether conscious or unconscious) that remains today—in many cases, within the walls of our public schools.

Aside from the underlying racial disparities, the commission, among other pieces of evidence, found two substantial factors that demanded immediate improvements: teaching and leadership.

Teaching findings:

- The United States was experiencing a teacher shortage, coupled with the need to revamp teacher preparation programs.
- Over half of newly hired teachers in core subjects were not highly qualified.

Teaching recommendations:

- School districts should seek plans to develop mentorship and teacher capacity-building networks.
- Incentives should be provided to attract outstanding students to the teaching profession, particularly those in critical need.

Although the report failed to list findings that questioned specific principal actions, there were recommendations within the realm of leadership.

Leadership recommendations:

- Leadership at both the district and school levels should stress coherence in setting academic goals and synergizing community.
- Meeting the needs of culturally and linguistically diverse students, along with socioeconomically disadvantaged students, is paramount.

Ultimately, the solutions pointed toward creating an academic culture, where, prophetically, learning extended into students' homes and into every place where the individual can thrive, perhaps encapsulating students in a system that affirmed their racial identity and mirrored their cultural identities and strengths. In essence, the reform efforts called for a *prepared leader*, one who swiftly recognizes and adapts to crisis, while building a culturally inclusive environment (James & Wooten, 2022).

OUR PRESENT EDUCATIONAL STATE

What would the National Commission's report on educational reform efforts entail today?

Ironically, educational analysts and reformists would be hard-pressed to distinguish the old from the new. Although the original document's premise was based on America's educational system losing ground to foreign advancements, today's report would surely highlight the barriers stemming from domestic affairs. Certainly, the pandemic would take center stage, particularly its effects on students' social-emotional wellness and the paralyzed educational progress of all students.

What is not readily talked about is that the pandemic exposed the ever-present individualistic self-protection mindset. What does this have to do with schools? Real (2022) posits, "The culture of individualism minimizes social inequality and places one's central concern with oneself, thereby both justifying and serving the status quo" (p. 99). The massaging of the individualistic mindset invariably places race at the center of contention, while essentially disintegrating the creativity that propels collective efficacy. Schools were not isolated from these happenings, and, sadly they are the ones that serve our most impoverished and underserved students of color.

Like yesteryear, America's school systems remain fraught by political polarization surrounding civil liberties and controversial topics related to race, racism, and cultural diversity (Rogers et al., 2022). A broad-scale poll showed that 79 percent of principals (and 92 percent of Black principals) reported that systemic racism existed in public schools (Woo et al., 2022). White teachers, for example, "tended to emphasize concerns about possible threats to their instructional autonomy, which in many cases stemmed from parents' or school board members' objections to teaching about race, racism, or bias" (Woo et al., 2022, p. 6). Not surprisingly, these factors often manifest as job-related stressors, resulting in educators, particularly educators of color, leaving the profession altogether.

Similarly, in a recent poll, 72 percent of newly hired teachers in Philadelphia felt unprepared to work in an urban classroom, while 62 percent felt ill equipped to teach culturally diverse students (El-Mekki, 2019). Many of these educators leave the profession, and, chillingly, their decisions are based on principal leadership and school culture. A significant factor in shaping a school's response to sociopolitical issues and contentious topics is the leader's ability to guide critical professional development (Kohli, 2009), in which teachers are given a degree of collective control and a platform to safely discuss race-relations.

As mentioned, teacher and leader preparation programs must use epistemologies that center students' cultural strengths and lived experiences while looking to dismantle existing racial hierarchies (Darling-Hammond & Darling-Hammond, 2022; Goodwin et al., 2022; Kohli, 2009). The NCEE today would surely report the racial diversity gaps between teachers and the students they serve (Gist & Bristol, 2022). In fact, as the number of ethnically diverse students continues to grow across America, so does the racial gap between them and their teachers (Ahmad & Boser, 2014; Gershenson et al., 2021; Gist & Bristol, 2022).

Nationally, students of culturally and linguistically diverse backgrounds comprise nearly 35 percent of the student population, while teachers of color represent 10 percent, and a shocking mere 7 percent are Black (National Center for Education Statistics, 2019b; Wright, 2022). In California, arguably the nation's most diverse state, students of various ethnicities make up 72.8 percent of the 6.2 million public school students (National Center for Education Statistics, n.d.-b). Black students make up 5.4 percent of that population, while White teachers comprise 60.1 percent of the workforce (California Department of Education, 2023), a nearly 55 percent racial gap.

HIGH-IMPACT PRACTICES

Today, based on national disparities in academic achievement, *A Nation at Risk*'s findings for educational excellence would keenly center on culturally responsive practices in three critical levels: highly qualified teaching, leadership expertise, and community partnerships. For all educators, a primary focus of learning would include *high-impact* culturally responsive teaching and leadership, while a secondary focus would address barriers through the implementation of transformative community schools (detailed in chapter 8):

High-Quality Culturally Responsive Teaching

- Teachers and the principals that lead them must design deeper learning, "where meaningful academic content is paired with engaging, experiential, and innovative learning experiences" (Darling-Hammond & Darling-Hammond, 2022; Howard, 2001).
- Teachers must design lessons that assist students in reaching deeper learning (adaptation) by modeling strategic thinking, tapping into cultural funds of knowledge, and capitalizing on students' racial identity, with academic success, cultural competence, and sociopolitical consciousness (Daggett, 2008; Gay, 2010; Kohli, 2009; Ladson-Billings, 2009) embedded within the curricular goals.

- Culturally responsive teaching must be observable through sound lesson design with measurable rubrics in the following areas: (1) content, (2) instruction, (3) culture, and (4) interpersonal relationships (Massachusetts Department of Elementary and Secondary Education, 2021; Young & Easton-Brooks, 2022).

Culturally Responsive Leadership

- Creates policies, sets and monitors expectations, and guides faculty to facilitate successful implementation of culturally responsive instruction (Intercultural Development Research Association [IRDA], 2022; Kavanagh et al., 2020; Ladson-Billings, 1995a).
- Builds teacher pipelines and residencies through university partnerships that support the recruitment, retention, and resurgence of Black educators (Freeman et al., 2022; Gist & Bristol, 2022; Ingersoll et al., 2022; IRDA, 2022).
- Secures a school climate free from implicit biases toward culturally and linguistically diverse students (IRDA, 2022; Kohli, 2009).
- Centers leadership approaches toward (1) leading critical professional development, (2) promoting an inclusive school climate, (3) developing positive community relations, and (4) establishing critical self-awareness (Kezar & Eckel, 2008; Khalifa et al., 2016; Kohli et al., 2015; Sinek, 2019).
- Raises awareness for racial justice built on asset-based approaches for students and staff based on transformational, culturally responsive, and instructional leadership, while fostering collaborative inquiry through the development of all members' lens of equity (Kohli et al., 2015; Matschiner, 2022; Paris & Alim, 2014).

Culturally Responsive Educators

- Advocate for continuous critical reflection in three distinct tenets: (1) community centered on care, (2) content mastery and an understanding of the sociopolitical contexts that undermined academic success, and (3) a courageous mindset to apply humanizing care for students while promising a rich and accurate curriculum in an inviting system (El-Mekki, 2023).
- Understand and build awareness around the progression from surface-level to deeper instructional undercurrents of culturally relevant pedagogy (Gutierrez, 2021).

- Ensure all forms of micro inequalities are interrupted to create a safe, inclusive learning environment, along with ensuring Black students are placed in college preparatory classes (IDRA, 2022; Kohli, 2009).

Culturally Responsive Schools

- Build the primary learning focus around high-impact culturally responsive instructional practices and inclusive leadership (Ladson-Billings, 2009; Kavanagh et al., 2020; Khalifa et al., 2016; Northouse, 2019).
- Define success by all Black students being qualified for college and career readiness (A–G eligible) in an environment that is supportive, is asset-conscious, and fosters positive cultural identity.
- Set a foundation (as mentioned above) for Black students to embrace the school system that embraces them, securing a K–16 pipeline for millions of Black teachers to return to the education profession.
- Encapsulate students of color in a three-component educational system that ensures the highest levels of learning through (1) *culturally responsive teaching* and (2) *culturally responsive leadership*, along with the implementation of (3) *community school partnerships* to address barriers to learning (Adelman & Taylor, 2018; Gutierrez, 2021; Partnership for the Future of Learning, 2019).

In addition to the above, university chancellors, educational policy makers, state superintendents, and governors must allocate funds for, and invest in, teacher residency programs that redesign teacher preparation practices (National Center for Teacher Residencies, n.d.) that allow school districts and university partnerships to

- invest in "home grown" recruitment pipelines that reflect the communities of color predominantly served in Title I schools;
- reduce barriers for aspiring Black educators to enter and remain in the profession through scholarships, stipends, emergency funds, and licensure testing support;
- increase teacher effectiveness through rigorous clinical preparation and coaching from an expert mentor teacher;
- adopt culturally and linguistically sustaining practices as well as trauma-informed practices that affirm, engage, and challenge students of color attending high-need schools; and
- improve the retention of effective Black educators through affinity groups that reduce isolation, build community, and empower them to collectively lead transformation in their schools and districts.

These reform efforts, which address structural inequities, will allow students of color, and in particular Black children, their entitled promise: the tools to excel in school and a fair chance at higher education, the development of their full academic and social-emotional wellness, along with shaping their individual powers of mind and spirit to the fullest (Emdin, 2021).

Building and sustaining more culturally responsive schools can bridge these opportunity gaps for educational attainment. A gracious opportunity has been placed on educators (as it should be) to right the wrongs of the past, yet our educational system today remains paralyzed by the failures it produces for Black and underserved students of color. Surely today, the commission's report would highlight educational goals tied to a growing diverse democracy, where educators advance a just cause, seize the power of diversity, and facilitate upward socioeconomic mobility for students of color.

In this chapter, we will look at the ever-present disparities in educational and disciplinary outcomes for Black students and historically underserved students of color. In doing so, the reader must imagine their very own classroom or school and ask themselves the following:

- "For the school I lead, am I willing to look beyond the current time and space and take ownership of a new world of opportunity for marginalized students?"
- "Am I willing to do the 'inner-work' (as a teacher or as an administrator) and self-examine my own teaching and leadership tactics—the deep dive necessary to build academic success for my culturally and linguistically diverse students?"
- "Am I willing to be *vulnerable* and engage in the pedagogical practices and the examination of teaching (pedagogical reasoning) that can empower my Black and underserved students?"
- "Am I willing to foster a detoxification—'clearing of the space'—so my Black and historically marginalized students experience an equitable education in my classroom and in my school?"

If your answers are yes, then this book is for you.

To fully embrace and then enact culturally relevant pedagogy and the instructional leadership necessary to enhance it, readers must also ask themselves, *Does my individual pedagogy ensure students of color "acquire academic knowledge, knowledge of self, knowledge of how to navigate one's immediate surroundings, knowledge of the systems in which one is embedded (particularly those that are structured to disempower), and knowledge of the world"* (Emdin, 2021, p. 1)? As already mentioned in chapter 1, the answers lie in daily relational academic settings, in systems of higher-order learning, and in leveraging the racial identity and genius our culturally diverse students come equipped with each day.

THE BALANCE OF HYPE AND HOPE

Mirroring the country as a whole, our public school system is afflicted by a wide range of inequities often defined along the lines of race and social class (Wald & Losen, 2003). This is particularly problematic for Black and underserved minority students when examining pedagogical practices in relation to academic outcomes. The inequities our students of color face stretch far beyond statistics and data—the bigger picture involves the tension between hope and frustration.

In the recent past, the two major components of the No Child Left Behind (NCLB) legislation—testing and more accountability imposed by the federal government—were intended to radically transform our public education system for the better. Instead of improving proficiency levels and graduation rates for Black students and categorical subgroups, such as English language learners (ELLs) and socioeconomically disadvantaged (SED) students, the policy only illuminated academic failures based on standardized test scores (Franquiz & Ortiz, 2016).

As history has unveiled, the NCLB Act neither produced higher academic success rates for these students nor reduced poverty through educational attainment. What NCLB did accomplish, which is alive and thriving today, is reinforcing societal (and educator) stereotypes in judging students based on race, rather than considering cultural strengths tied to learning needs (David & Cuban, 2010; Kohli, 2009).

The Every Student Succeeds Act (ESSA), the 2015 reauthorization of the 1965 Elementary and Secondary Education Act (ESEA), allows states greater local control for designing and building accountability systems and for determining supports and interventions for schools and districts (Darling-Hammond et al., 2016). As schools experience changing student demographics and varying instructional needs, "knowledge about student experiences has the potential to inform teaching practices, professional development for educators, and decision-making around curriculum policies for multicultural school contexts" (Chan, 2007, p. 179).

In fact, highlights of ESSA include an expectation that heightened accountability and action would be taken by local educational agencies (LEAs) to effect positive change in our public school system's lowest-performing schools, where students are not making progress and where graduation rates are low over extended periods of time (U.S. Department of Education, n.d.-a). Indicators of student achievement and social well-being paint a stark contrast to the foundational goals of ESSA when analyzing grade-level proficiency, suspension rates, and high school completion rates for Black students and underserved students of color. Heavy on the hype, easy on the hope!

DISPARITIES IN ACADEMIC ACHIEVEMENT

Nationally, the disparities in standardized test scores and high school graduation rates for students of color continue to plague our public school system. Black students' mean SAT score was 177 points lower than their White counterparts, while Hispanic students' mean SAT score was 133 points lower (National Center for Education Statistics, 2018). On average, Black and Latinx students are 9.5 percent less likely to graduate high school compared to their White peers (National Center for Education Statistics, n.d.-a).

The numbers for "limited English proficient" students are even more alarming, as the graduation rate drops to 68 percent, compared to White students graduating at 89 percent (National Center for Education Statistics, n.d.-a). In California, Black students are 13 percent less likely to graduate from high school compared to their White peers (California Department of Education, n.d.-c). For foster youth and homeless children in California, graduation rates are chilling at nearly 56 percent annually (California Department of Education, 2021).

Over the past few years, school dropout rates have also remained disproportionately consistent. According to the California Department of Education, in 2016–2017, Latinx students dropped out at a rate of 2.8 percent compared to their White counterparts at 1.5 percent, whereas Black students were four times more likely to drop out at a rate of 4.5 percent (California Department of Education, n.d.-e). Harsh disciplinary approaches equating to disproportionate suspension rates, which lead to school dropouts, have also perpetuated the school-to-prison pipeline for students of color (Wald & Losen, 2003). In fact, within the California Juvenile Justice System, Black youth make up nearly 20 percent of the inmate count (Becerra, 2019), despite being only 5.4 percent of the total student population in grades six through twelve (California Department of Education, n.d.-b).

In California's K–12 public school system, 2019–2020 demographic data indicate students of various ethnicities make up 72.8 percent of the 6.2 million student population, with Black and Latinx students comprising 60.1 percent of the total (National Center for Education Statistics, n.d.-b). Despite being the overwhelming majority population, the disparities remain bleak for Black, Latinx, and other subgroups such as emergent bilingual students.

Black students (lowest performing) scored 47.6 points *below* standard for English language arts (ELA) on the 2019 Smarter Balanced Assessment, as compared to White students, who scored 30.7 points *above* standard—a nearly *eighty-point proficiency gap* (California Department of Education, n.d.-d). Hispanic students scored 26.6 points *below* standard on the 2019 ELA Smarter Balanced Assessment, while socioeconomically disadvantaged students scored 30.1 points *below* standard (California Department of Education, n.d.-d), further depicting the proficiency gaps when compared to their White peers.

Along with standardized test scores, student discipline continues to spotlight the racial disparities within our school systems. In 2014, the U.S. Department of Education's Office for Civil Rights released data that showed Black students were suspended and expelled at three times the rate of White students in districts large and small (Loveless, 2017). In California, Black students were suspended at a rate of 9.1 percent, compared with White students being suspended at 3.0 percent, in the 2018–2019 school year (California Department of Education, n.d.-a).

POLICIES ADDRESSING STRUCTURAL INEQUITIES

As NCLB touted more testing and accountability, the task for ESSA was to re-create the central frame of education, more equitable within the infrastructure of curriculum and pedagogical design, testing and accountability, and teacher education (Cohen et al., 2018). Early critiques of ESSA stated that the policy does not require addressing the wide range of structural inequalities based on school funding, mobility, and segregation by race and social class that contribute to learning and achievement gaps (Franquiz & Ortiz, 2016). Although ESSA does require that LEAs ensure low-income and minority students are not disproportionately taught by "ineffective, out-of-field, or inexperienced teachers," this self-evaluation process lacks the thorough analysis and federal accountability that leads to structural changes.

Furthermore, there are no mandates within ESSA to ensure that teaching methods in high-poverty schools are culturally relevant so that they provide meaningful learning structures for all students, specifically those who struggle socially and academically (Franquiz & Ortiz, 2016; Gay, 2010; Hammond, 2015; Ladson-Billings, 2009). Without such provisions, accompanied by accountable measures, the dismal proficiency rates and subpar academic outcomes for minoritized students will continue across all dashboard measures within our public schools.

Usher in California AB 2774, the 2022 bill that illuminated the proficiency gaps mentioned earlier in this chapter, finding that Black students who are unfunded (meaning they are not already included in subgroups such as low-income, English learners, or foster youth) are the only student population performing below the California state average on ELA and math. This bill would have expanded the definition of "unduplicated pupil" (low-income, English learner, or foster youth) for Local Control Funding Formula (LCFF) purposes by adding a pupil who is classified as a member of the lowest performing subgroup or subgroups, commencing with the 2023–2024 fiscal year.

For California, this essentially means Black students, according to nearly two decades of data. And the irony (or wake-up call) is that low-income White students, pre- and postpandemic, still outperform *non-low-income* Black students in math (California Assessment of Student Performance and Progress, 2022). Critics of the bill knew that in California, at least 72.2 percent of Black students *already* qualified for funding as an unduplicated pupil, varying among county and individual district.

For example, in the 2021–2022 school year, 81.9 percent or 32,000 of the Los Angeles Unified School District's Black students were unduplicated and received funds, as they fell into the socioeconomically disadvantaged or foster youth categories, while 87 percent or 4,800 of Fresno Unified School District's Black students were unduplicated. Essentially, AB 2774 would have only secured dollars for the 13 to 19 percent of Black students not already funded through LCFF for districts throughout California (personal communication).

If the bill had come to fruition, the new grant category would not have provided any additional funding for Prop 98, the minimum state funding guarantee, funded by a mix of the California state general fund and local property tax revenue. However, it would have increased the allocation of existing funds, through the LCFF supplemental grant to schools that have a larger share of students within the lowest-performing student group. AB 2774 was eventually looked at by legislative analysts as a violation of Proposition 209, which bars preferential treatment based on sex, race, and ethnicity within a public education entity.

The potential impact of AB 2774 never came to light, but the academic achievement gap remains a looming reminder for a more just educational system—for the current one is failing to prepare the majority of Black students for academic proficiency, higher education attainment, and social mobility in general. Even the most elaborate funding propositions will fail if actionable items and accountable measures are not clearly outlined for creating a culturally responsive school. In fact, neither verbiage in AB 2774 nor California's 300-hundred-million-dollar "equity multiplier" required districts to mandate culturally responsive measures within single plans for student achievement (SPSAs) that align with a local control and accountability plan (LCAP). Although the "equity multiplier" does require that districts publicly identify

Black students' underachievement, plans to address those barriers are left to local control.

Explicit language was not mentioned in either reform for teacher or leader preparation programs centered on Black student success. The reality is that assembly bills, and other funding proposals that will come in the future, must demand that districts prove partnerships with universities and show strategic shifts toward an educational model that forces current and future educators to become proficient in racial affirmation and culturally responsive epistemologies. The true work comes in the willingness to interrogate and restructure a school system so that it results in equitable educational outcomes for students of color. No matter the dollar amount, Black students (like other subgroups in the accountability system) deserve more funding for the support of their learning. This book spells out the work needed with existing and future funding—and it will come.

CUTTING THROUGH THE HYPE

In 2022, much of the dollars funneled into the American public school system were coming off the heels of the pandemic, centered on staffing shortages, disciplinary reform, and early childhood education. Let's not forget my personal favorite—"learning loss recovery." In California, two investments—universal prekindergarten (UPK) and universal meals—are billed to be *transformative* for more positive academic outcomes.

In addition, millions of dollars were allocated for programs such as universal design for learning (UDL), the robust implementation of the Expanded Learning Opportunities Program (ELO-P), and policy changes with a focus on stronger supports and inclusion for children with disabilities and multilingual learners. Most significant, however, are the realizations of mental health concerns among youth and young adults alike. Although the issues are real, this is troublesome in that practitioners often see socioemotional learning as synonymous with cultural deficits, further stereotyping trauma or the inability to learn altogether.

Much like earlier reform efforts, the hundreds of millions of dollars being invested from federal, state, or local grants are left to be managed locally, with little oversight in accountability or restrictions in usage. For example, teacher preparation programs concerned with *filling spots* continue at the mercy of mass retirements and resignations from the profession, doubled down with accelerated recruitment efforts that bring into the profession teachers with shallow expertise in pedagogy tied to cultural responsiveness.

If dollars are not spent with a supreme effort surrounding instructional expectations (as discussed in chapter 4), they merely become a moral effort at reparation, not a driver for academic proficiency (Pinar, 2013). Instead of narrowing the focus toward race-conscious classroom pedagogy and site leadership, aspirations based on reform policy merely paint broad strokes of *hope* (or hype) for educational change.

Throughout the nation, a resurgent school improvement strategy anchored in community partnerships is looking to change the trajectory of childhood poverty and academic achievement. States like Michigan and West Virginia are leveraging funds to tackle poor school attendance and develop a more robust system of social support (Partnership for the Future of Learning, 2019). Taking California by storm is an unprecedented 4.1 billion dollars invested into community schools, a reform playbook that promises to address the *whole child* while aligning community resources to improve student outcomes.

It is said that effective community schools are comprehensive, research based, and designed in reflection to local needs and assets. A shared commitment for collaborative efforts surrounding leadership, proven support practices, and impactful partnerships are the hallmark of great community schools (Partnership for the Future of Learning, 2019). Districts and schools can apply for two possible sources of funding: (1) the Planning Grant (districts), totaling two hundred thousand dollars for up to two years, and (2) the Implementation Grant (schools) in the amount of five hundred thousand dollars annually for five years.

Although there are varying conceptions of what constitutes a model program (Campo, 2023; Maier, 2022), community schools are formatted conceptually to attain (1) *equity and access*, where all students and families will have connections to resources, opportunities, and supports to academic, social, and emotional development and well-being, and (2) *improved outcomes*, centered on student achievement and improved attendance, leading to positive social and economic outcomes that permeate the surrounding community. Within the framework of community schools, four key pillars are prevalent (Partnership for the Future of Learning, 2019).

Integrated Student Supports

- Meeting academic, physical, social-emotional, and mental health needs.
- Coordination of trauma-informed health, mental health, and social services.

Active Family and Community Engagement

- Actively tapping the expertise and knowledge of family and community members to serve as true partners.

- Home visits, home-school collaboration, culturally responsive community partnerships.
- Developing trusting, inclusive, and collaborative relationships with families and community members.

Collaborative Leadership Practices for Educators and Administrators

- Culture of professional learning, collective trust, and shared responsibility for outcomes.
- Professional development to support mental and behavioral health, trauma-informed care, social-emotional learning, restorative justice, and other key areas.
- Dedicated staff to support and facilitate partnerships and discover professional development opportunities to build capacity for collaborative education and community leadership structures and practices.

Extended and Enriched Learning Time and Opportunities

- Academic support, enrichment, and real-world learning opportunities.
- Before- and after-school care and summer programs.
- "Extended" learning and "expanded" learning.
- Tutoring and other learning supports during the traditional school day.

Fundamentally, culturally responsive schools are highly effective when focused on two components: (1) high-impact culturally responsive instruction that drives equitable outcomes, and (2) sound culturally responsive leadership that secures deep instructional undercurrents (as seen in figure 1.3). Community schools must serve as a third component in addressing both the *internal* and *external* factors that interfere with learning (Adelman & Taylor, 2018). With this three-component framework in mind, each community school is expected to mirror the specific needs, cultural assets, and priorities of the student population and community it serves. In chapter 8, the complete three-component model will be revealed in more comprehensive detail, with emphasis on combating childhood poverty.

It is important to note that the four attributes of culturally responsive leadership align seamlessly with the four pillars of community schools. For example, *promoting an inclusive school and organizational environment* (Khalifa et al., 2016) serves as a critical factor in building *trust*, complimentary to pillar four, *Collaborative Leadership and Supports*, which leverages partnerships with outside organizations for job shadowing, mentoring, and additional learning opportunities. Like the trust built between teacher and student, schools that promote an inclusive culture form trust with community members.

School district blueprints for community school implementation would be well served if written to align the four pillars with culturally responsive leadership. In addition, requirements for implementation must call for sites currently practicing highly effective culturally responsive teaching and leadership. Community school frameworks must go beyond a culture of sympathy based on free resources, such as health screenings, tutoring, and mental health services—they must have a significant impact on combating childhood poverty both in the short term (food assistance and job development) and along the continuum of sustainable social services.

Along these lines, "concerns about the whole student development, equity, and school climate all must be understood and pursued as qualities that *emerge* from the effective implementation, over time, of all three components at a school" (Adelman & Taylor, 2018). The high-impact culturally responsive school contains all three components (inclusive teaching, responsive leadership, and rich community schools) that serve to promote equitable opportunities for social mobility both in the short term and long term.

Effective reform efforts (should you deem creating a culturally responsive climate a reform) require critical conversations in which teachers feel safe and empowered to voice opinions. Good teaching does not have a grant shelf life; it can always be sustained. As we'll discover in later chapters, culturally responsive leadership is also accentuated by one's transformational leadership. Both traits emphasize that the current structural dynamics of inequity can be altered by inspiring a new belief in followers, innovating new possibilities, and nurturing individual concerns (Northouse 2019), while securing an inclusive school environment (Khalifa et al., 2016).

In diving into the work, one cannot lose sight of the deciding factor that ultimately drives student achievement—day-to-day culturally responsive instruction, coupled with instructional leadership. Many and Sparks-Many (2015) reported, "When the goal is improved student achievement, principals should focus on the attributes associated with an instructional leader" (p. 11), while cultivating a college-going culture. This is one of the main purposes of this book, illuminating the necessary instructional leadership actions that authentically complement and interconnect with culturally responsive and transformational leadership. Put another way, Black and other marginalized students' college-going aspirations must also be a driver in the work we do daily—this mentality must start the moment students walk into prekindergarten settings.

We'll revisit the wealth of opportunities surrounding community schools in chapter 8, and as mentioned, it becomes the third component for securing a highly effective culturally responsive school. For example, teacher preparation programs with local university instruction departments could serve as an exceptional use of funds. As part of a community school initiative for extended learning, preservice teachers and high school students could develop self-efficacy (Kavanagh et al., 2020; Siwatu, 2011) in a safe space through mastery experiences or *approximation of practice* in low-risk experiments in acting out the practice of teaching.

Local universities could also engage in communities of practice (COPs), in which students seeking administrative credentials are immersed in education labs and pedagogical feedback seminars through actionable learning. In addition, we'll uncover some missing links, such as leveraging funds to build an African American teacher pipeline with extended learning agencies and after-school networks. From a practical standpoint, the community school model can create synergy focused on the disparities in academic achievement for Black and other underserved student populations.

LOCAL CONTROL FOR CULTURALLY RESPONSIVE PEDAGOGY

Under the guidelines of ESSA, school districts nationwide have been poised with local flexibility through the LCFF to further strengthen teacher effectiveness under the three-pronged approach to foster *academic success* for all students, strengthen teachers' *cultural competence,* and create schoolwide *sociopolitical consciousness* (Ladson-Billings, 2009). Clearly, student demographics and academic outcomes indicate a unique opportunity for educators to leverage the diverse sociocultural strengths of students, their families, and the community at large. In galvanizing this opportunity, educators can work in unison to dismantle the disparities of academic achievement.

Building capacity for teachers through critical self-reflection and pedagogical reasoning (discussed in chapter 5) upon the enactment of culturally relevant pedagogy is paramount for better student outcomes. By utilizing cultural referents to foster knowledge, skills, and positive self-belief, culturally responsive teaching empowers students intellectually, emotionally, and sociopolitically (Ladson-Billings, 2009; Young, 2010).

Currently, however, most teachers and school leaders continue to utilize instructional techniques and curricular frameworks tied to the NCLB *teach to the test* mentality, negating (if not ignoring) pedagogical practices centered in cultural responsiveness and affirming racial identities (Kohli, 2009; Zoch, 2017). The dominant instructional practice became and continues to be focused at the acquisition level: multiple-choice questions and packets resembling test worksheets that replace more authentic, adaptive, and collaborative learning (Daggett, 2008; Hammond, 2015; Zoch, 2017).

Presently, inequities in schooling are often the consequence of continued adherence to the assimilationist approach and race-neutral epistemologies of the past—stifling student voice and social interactions and devaluing the collaboration exemplified by Ladson-Billings's culturally responsive approach. Bringing meaningful learning structures into play allows for classroom teachers and site leaders to consider the diverse backgrounds and sociocultural needs of students of color (Zoch, 2017). Moll et al. (1992) asserted that teachers rarely draw on the funds of knowledge of students' world outside the context of the classroom.

Culturally responsive pedagogy can help teachers in designing rich curriculum that promotes students' intellectual capacity and the transition from dependent to independent learners (Hammond, 2015). Chan (2007) and Kohli (2009) argue that culturally sensitive curriculum can contribute to shaping the ethnic identity of a child and, therefore, can create an extension between the students' world, theirs, and their family's funds of knowledge.

> It [culturally responsive pedagogy] is a student-centered approach—I think it's very important. The root of it is not only identifying but also nurturing the differences of our students and to use that background knowledge to promote student achievement. (Lisa, first-grade teacher)

There is an abundance of research indicating that teachers are able to articulate both successes and areas for growth within their individual experiences with Black and underserved students of color (Gutierrez, 2002; Ladson-Billings, 2009). As Chan (2007) points out, once teachers realize and become willing to accept student differences as a mechanism for higher levels of learning, the movement away from the Eurocentric approach becomes easier. In making the necessary shifts from the high-stakes testing classroom framework to a deeper inquiry-based and culturally responsive mindset, educators begin to set the stage for greater depths of knowledge.

Perhaps more importantly, at its core, schooling can become equitable and inclusionary for our most vulnerable student populations by improving socioeconomic mobility and social capital. Imagine educational investments explicitly targeted for a teacher preparation pipeline built on the foundational model of culturally relevant teaching. It can be done. Yet educators, specifically site principals, must be aware of deep-rooted philosophies and political views when it comes to attempting to shift the current culture of their schools.

> I realized that in order to have the students go through this [culturally responsive pedagogy], I have to be self-aware of some perceptions or stereotypes that I have and how to build that self-worth with my students—that empowerment. (Suzanne, fifth-grade teacher)

THE MARGINALIZATION OF CULTURALLY RELEVANT PEDAGOGY

Throughout the sectors of education, attention to cultural responsiveness, social justice, and bilingual approaches to teaching have constantly been replaced by efforts to standardize curriculum and annual tests (Sleeter, 2012). In fact, some argue that standardization in schools mirrors the nation's individualistic mindset, where performance is tied to a business-type model (David & Cuban, 2010; Morrison et al., 2008).

This narrowed conception of education holds that human capital can advance only within a structure of competition, ignoring the collaborative learning frameworks so vital to culturally responsive teaching (Howard, 2001; Ladson-Billings, 2009; Sleeter, 2012). In education, if not mitigated by a lens of equity, this individualist mindset overshadows the socially just system, which not only marginalizes culturally responsive pedagogy but trivializes social injustices (National Equity Project, n.d.).

Moreover, Sleeter (2012) argued that due to the *high-stakes* reform approach based on standardization, "teachers have less time to research and develop curriculum that students can relate to, [and] non-tested curriculum disappears under pressure to raise test scores" (p. 577). By denying the core principles of professional learning for teachers, as well as contextual frameworks of culture and racism, the *business model* works to reverse the potential empowerment for educators (Sleeter, 2012) and perpetuates academic disparities for culturally and linguistically diverse students (Ladson-Billings, 2009).

Teachers in our public school system tend to navigate accountability pressures by teaching a canned curriculum adopted without considering culture as an asset for learning. Others remain "in their comfort zone," often inundated with random "other duties as assigned," negating any opportunity to effectively design lessons. Therefore, at the site level, teachers must be allowed the time to familiarize themselves with effective tactics and to engage in safe conversations on cultural responsiveness.

More importantly, administrators must model the progressive nature (dependent to independent learning) of the lessons they expect to see in the classroom. This can only be done in an adaptive-gradual manner, where teachers begin to see the correlation between instruction and positive results. This is critical on two fronts. First, without sustainable measures surrounding effective feedback, pedagogical shifts always fail to live up to desired student proficiency and therefore disappoint. Second, in the impatient (and rightfully so) world of educational equity, which promises academic success for Black and underserved students, disappointment leads to cynicism and apathy (David & Cuban, 2010).

If culturally responsive pedagogy is perceived by teachers as just another mandate or reform effort, most principals will have failed before they've even begun the work. When done effectively, pedagogical shifts toward *good teaching* become part of the climate—"it's what we do!"

> I don't really use it [cultural responsiveness] just because it's another thing. It was just for a couple years. It was like, okay here's this, here's this, here's this, and you know it was just kind of overwhelming. (Julie, fifth-grade teacher)

Unfortunately, however, the statement above crystallizes much of the attitudes surrounding the potential power of culturally responsive teaching. In later chapters, we'll discuss the role of school leadership in creating coherence around the transformational nature of the practice. The promotion of culturally responsive teaching also requires "political work to combat its marginalization due to persistent simplistic conceptions of what it means, and backlash prompted by fear of its potential to transform the existing social order" (Sleeter, 2012, p. 563). In actuality, it's the sociopolitical work that is necessary to reshape the existing *rote* learning mode of operation, to a more *reasoned* level of knowledge.

School district leaders must be willing to "call out" and perhaps critique their own systemic forms of oppression, which challenges individualistic thinking and interrogates the complex interactions of people, the novel forms of dominant pedagogical practices, and the ideologies that perpetuate educational inequity (Bourdieu, 2003; National Equity Project, n.d.). Principals must detoxify the space that interrupts their students' ability to see themselves as equal—if that is sociopolitical work, then so be it.

CHALLENGES TO CONCEPTUALIZING CULTURALLY RELEVANT PEDAGOGY

Although culturally relevant pedagogy is widely espoused and applied in educational experimentation and classroom practice, little research examines the elements of academic success, cultural competence, and sociopolitical consciousness (Ladson-Billings, 2009) from a conceptual framework. To define, implement, and assess the practice of culturally relevant pedagogy, Young (2010) performed a critical case study combined with action research. Essentially, the study was an attempt to form a collaboration with educators who were committed to social justice and to engage in debate, application, and analyzation of the theory of culturally relevant teaching in practice. Young found three critical challenges in this area:

1. Illuminating the race consciousness of educators while confronting their cultural biases.
2. Addressing systemic origins of racism in school policies.
3. Adequately equipping preservice and in-service teachers with the skills to implement culturally relevant pedagogical theories into practice.

Overall, Young's study found that deep structural issues related to teachers' cultural biases, the makeup of racism in school settings, and the lack of support by district-level and site-level leaders to adequately implement their day-to-day practice only marginalized the efforts to sustain culturally responsive teaching.

For example, the teachers tended to regard the students' *academic success* as a means to build learning on their personal experiences but not to promote academic learning using culture as a vehicle. Missing from district documents was the tenet of *cultural competence*, which looks to help students to honor their own cultural beliefs while acquiring access to wider power structures. Teacher participants' understanding of cultural competence equated to "knowing your students," merely reflecting the feel-good curricula that Ladson-Billings (2009) sought to dispel. In terms of *sociopolitical consciousness*, the district's promotion of cultural sensitivity had more to do with students meeting grade-level proficiency on tests than with creatively crafting lessons to illuminate social inequities and current unjust affairs.

Young (2010) found that teachers were often unprepared to discuss issues of social and racial inequity, mainly because they lacked awareness of the larger sociopolitical issues that continued to permeate their students' lives. What essentially unfolded was a fragmented misinterpretation of the theoretical framework of culturally responsive teaching, adding to teachers' inability to see its true potential for positive academic outcomes.

Many misconceptions have emerged as major factors within research, in particular, the depth of knowledge needed to create a comprehensive culturally responsive school. District-level initiatives add to the barriers teachers and site leaders have regarding the implementation of culturally responsive structures. In many districts, especially coming off the heels of the pandemic, social-emotional learning is taking precedence over culturally responsive learning. In others, both teachers and principals are inundated with behavioral outbursts, shifting priority toward restorative justice practices. Although these approaches are necessary, teachers' time is taxed and dedication is lost in developing expertise in the art of designing culturally responsive lessons tied to higher-order learning.

In speaking to Zaretta Hammond, Jennifer Gonzalez (2017) uncovered four common misconceptions educators have about the implementation of culturally responsive teaching at the school site. These misinterpretations,

> **Misconception 1: It is not multicultural or social justice education** – Although celebrating diversity can foster an enriching climate, it does not pertain to the cause and effect of students cognitive learning at the adaptation level. Similarly, social justice education broadens students' world view (on injustices), however, it does not tap into students' cognitive abilities in relation to the fidelity of pedagogical tactics tied to rigor.

> **Misconception 2: Must begin with addressing implicit bias** – This area can overshadow (and sometimes overwhelm) the priority of understanding inequity, specifically in designing lessons that build depths of knowledge.

> **Misconception 3: It's all about relationships and self-esteem** – Often over-emphasized as a districtwide initiative and although highly important, social emotional learning does not equate to higher levels of proficiency.

> **Misconception 4: It's a menu of the "right" strategies** – As mentioned, it is not a script or 'toolkit' of activities. Culturally responsive pedagogy allows teachers to creatively design lessons that build up students' processing skills, collaboratively network, and use their cultural experiences to reach proficiency.

Figure 2.1. Four Common Misconceptions of Culturally Responsive Teaching
Source: Adapted from Gonzalez (2017). Copyright 2022 by Cult of Pedagogy.

as illustrated in figure 2.1, can stifle the actual work involved in designing the instructional piece that equates to student learning. As mentioned in *Misconception 2*, rather than grapple with implicit biases, teachers can validate students' cultural contexts and racial identities in knowing the *whole child*—sometimes simply by showing up as their authentic selves. Students are keen to recognize teachers' joy and love of the art of teaching. With this joyous energy, learning collusions between teacher and students occur readily, as we'll discuss in the next chapter.

Specific pedagogical tactics, such as mining for students' funds of knowledge or eliciting prior knowledge within the anticipatory set, break the deficit discourse regarding students' lack of cultural knowledge (Bernal, 2016). As a strand of implicit bias, the issue of perceived cultural normalcy becomes a significant barrier in the teacher's ability to see value in building positive relationships with students and their families. By illuminating race consciousness, Hyland (2009) found one teacher's "discomfort was rooted in her sense that her cultural frame was 'normal,' and her students' cultural frame was inferior and abnormal" (p. 106).

Although the teacher was able to make change and improve her practice, she struggled with creating the kind of community relationships vital to building the alliances found among effective culturally responsive teachers (Hyland, 2009). Similar to what was seen by Young (2010), the teacher's unpreparedness for holding interactions with the community based on hidden biases became a critical factor in her struggles to sustain her enactment of culturally responsive teaching.

Some of these scenarios demonstrate the misconceptions teachers face in addressing academic success, cultural competence, and sociopolitical awareness (Ladson-Billings, 2009), specifically the need for more inquiry-based discourse mediated by school leaders. In doing so, teachers begin to see that developing powerful relationships with families, along with creating community-based pedagogical experiences, simply accentuates learning for Black and underserved students. Once this transition occurs, it becomes liberating for both the teacher and the students they serve.

JUST GOOD TEACHING

So what does it mean to employ culturally responsive pedagogy in the classroom? A loaded question to say the least, but the answers may surprise you. As noted, it is not a content playbook or a scripted step-by-step set of curricular prompts, but rather a relational piece that allows educators to tap into the whole child, securing learning through students' inherent cultural powers.

It is not a "cheap fix" framework or set of benchmarks for "poor students," but a pedagogical practice that speaks to students' power languages, much like relational love languages build trust and connectivity. Culturally responsive pedagogy is dependent on positive teacher-student relationships, but it cannot remain stagnant in the relational realm—high levels of cognitive development must be embedded within that trust. It should be stressed that culturally responsive teaching is not "one more thing I have to do." *It is just good teaching.*

In chapter 3, we'll take a deep dive into the intricacies of culturally responsive pedagogy and illuminate some of the missteps educators often make. For example, through speaking with district leaders and teachers it becomes apparent that culturally responsive pedagogy too often is looked at as a way to enhance *multiculturalism* or enlighten a *social justice* mindset in the school setting. In other schools, it's misconstrued with training students about positivity, ethnic appreciation, or character. As mentioned in chapter 1, culturally responsive teaching is designed to force educators to *own results* and to ensure lessons are built around the *Apex of Student Learning*.

The beauty is this: *you*, the educator, have the power to liberate a child from their current circumstances and to gain the promises and riches this land proclaims for everyone. If you hold that sacred—no matter if you are an educator at year one or you've been in the profession for many years—your career is about to change for the better. If by now you've guessed that the only true *reform effort* is the relational effect of classroom instruction and leadership described in this book—you're correct.

So let's bridge this gap together and examine exactly how culturally responsive pedagogy and the leadership that supports it create a culturally responsive school climate—and the ultimate academic success for Black and historically marginalized students.

Chapter 3

Culturally Relevant Pedagogy
Capacity over Contention

> "True intelligence is the ability to gain information, develop knowledge, hone skills, and apply knowledge and skills to meeting individual or collective goals that emerge in the moment."
>
> —Christopher Emdin

For decades, educational goals have focused on the consistent underperformance of Black and socioeconomically disadvantaged students of color compared to White students, spawning various terms to describe the relationship between culture and teaching (Ladson-Billings, 1992). To address academic disparities and social needs, scholars have applied educational research to inform pedagogical frameworks that embrace a belief in students, with culture being the mechanism for transformational success (Gay, 2010; Hattie, 2012; Howard, 2003; Ladson-Billings, 2009). Gloria Ladson-Billings's theory of culturally relevant pedagogy centers on a "three-pronged paradigm" of criteria consisting of building students' academic success, cultural competence, and sociopolitical consciousness (Ladson-Billings, 2009).

The theory originally served as a pedagogy that ensured that Black students would be empowered intellectually, socio-emotionally, and politically through the educator's ability to leverage cultural strengths to secure high levels of learning. Ladson-Billings (1992) asserted, "The primary goal of culturally relevant pedagogy is to empower students to examine critically the society in which they live and to work for social change" (p. 314). More importantly, the culturally relevant educator takes personal accountability for critically examining and then infusing these components into the classroom, schoolwide, and in community settings.

Culturally relevant teaching is seen as a multidimensional pedagogical approach, addressing curricular content, learning context, classroom culture, teacher-student relationships, and individual pedagogical procedures (Emdin, 2021; Gay, 2010; Hammond, 2015; Ladson-Billings, 2009; Moll et al., 1992). When practiced effectively, culturally responsive pedagogy requires that teachers tap into the multitude of cultural proficiencies, lived experiences, historical perspectives, and relationships that students possess. In doing so, students are empowered and believe *their* beliefs, ethnic values, and cultural heritages are *assets* to learning, rather than *deficits*. Fundamentally, academic success and cultural affiliation are developed in unison, as culturally responsive pedagogy instills pride and self-efficacy for students of color (Gay, 2010).

Educators highly skilled in a culturally relevant pedagogical approach understand that explicit knowledge about racial injustices and cultural diversity are imperative to meeting the educational needs of students (Gay, 2002; Darling-Hammond & Darling-Hammond, 2022; Wright, 2022). As such, it is vital for educators to appreciate the cultural characteristics and contributions of students and their families within the school community. Because culture is multifaceted, some elements play a more direct role in teaching and learning. For example, cultural values, communications, and learning styles can be leveraged for cultivating classroom structures, thereby affecting motivation and task performance (Hammond, 2015; Hattie, 2012). Similarly, Gay (2010) pointed out that culturally responsive teaching "builds bridges of meaningfulness between home and school experiences as well as between academic abstractions and lived sociocultural beliefs" (p. 31), which validates and affirms students' cultural identity. This is important to keep in mind, as practitioners need not become experts overnight—trial and error in this pedagogical framework must be nurtured (in safe settings) by site principals.

As mentioned, despite its effectiveness, teachers continue to struggle to enact culturally relevant pedagogy in the classroom, often held back by a myriad of factors. For example, instructional planning time is overtaken by a reprioritization of other schoolwide initiatives, such as restorative justice and trauma-informed practices. The newly appointed site leadership may have little expertise in coaching or mentoring teachers who need support. Teachers' lack of instructional experience is often coupled with lesson observation checklists or evaluative metrics that are not congruent with the components of culturally responsive structures.

As we'll discover in chapter 4, district and site leaders must interrupt these obstacles that work, either implicitly or explicitly, to perpetuate educational inequity for diverse learners. Both leaders and teachers must use a racial equity lens to analyze the current context at the individual, institutional, and structural levels, bringing clarity for sustainable equitable change (Khalifa, 2012; National Equity Project, n.d.; Paris & Alim, 2014).

In the case of enacting culturally responsive pedagogy, it is crucial to cultivate a climate of positive relationships, focus on the *Apex of Student Learning*, prioritize pedagogical reasoning, and secure accountability (Fullan & Quinn, 2016; Kavanagh et al., 2020; Leithwood & Sun, 2018), thereby creating a framework for capacity—the shared depth of understanding about the purpose of equitable learning outcomes.

The various components presented in this book, both surface level and highly effective, should compel district- and site-level leaders to model instructional practices and then reprioritize professional development surrounding all aspects of culturally responsive pedagogy.

SETTING CULTURALLY RELEVANT PEDAGOGY IN MOTION

Educators (both Black and White) who effectively engage in culturally relevant pedagogy possess positive conceptions of themselves and others, foster enriching social interactions in their classrooms, and promote conceptions of investigative knowledge for students (Hattie, 2012; Ladson-Billings, 2009; Young, 2010). In these teachers' classrooms, learning is facilitated by leveraging students' culture when implementing cooperative activities and developing personal relationships with Black and underserved students (Siwatu, 2007).

In fact, without validating culture, educators align with the assimilationist role of teaching, which carries low expectations for students, accepts failure as a part of systemic outcomes, and shifts accountability to others (Ladson-Billings, 2009). Conversely, the culturally relevant educator believes all minoritized students are capable of academic excellence, by way of classroom procedures that ensure learning gradually progresses to the adaptation level (Daggett, 2008; Hammond, 2015; Hyland, 2009; Ladson-Billings, 2009). Such a teacher takes ownership of the practices set in place, never blaming failure on the student.

In essence, the expert culturally responsive teacher is a *high-impact* teacher, which generally equates to one's beliefs, attitudes, and expectations around what to teach and to what degree learning is possible. Hattie (2012) suggests the difference between a *high-impact* teacher and a low-effect teacher is about $d = 0.25$, meaning students gain nearly a year's advantage in a *high-impact* classroom. To sustain these areas of instructional effectiveness, site leaders must address teachers' "theories about race, culture, learning, development, and students' levels of performance" (Hattie, 2012, p. 26), as these pertain to implicit biases and beliefs.

When practicing culturally responsive teaching, *high-impact* instruction often equates to building trusting relationships, providing constructive feedback, and fostering independent practice that allows students to authentically showcase their talents. These dimensions act as launching points in conceptualizing what novice teachers as well as highly experienced teachers enact in their classrooms. Analyzing lesson design, holding collaborative discussions, and practicing site observations and interviews are three distinct components.

As a principal (the instructional leader), think of these three components as building blocks that set a foundation to connect learning to culture and build sustainability during professional development (discussed in chapter 5). Figure 3.1 gives insight to these *high-impact* actions, allowing current educators to find commonalities (a starting point, if you will) among what they may already be practicing in their classrooms on a *subconscious* level.

As you'll find throughout this book, effective culturally responsive pedagogy is a much more intricate approach than the actions listed in figure 3.1—but not that far off. Where do we start? Culturally responsive pedagogy begins with one's willingness to reject the status quo and to fully analyze, then critically self-reflect on, one's own approach, and through this critical self-reflection, exhibit the vulnerability to take risks, try and then reassess, and accept colleagues' different levels of understanding throughout.

Long-lasting equitable climates start with honest conversations, in which staff can voice their authentic self—the culture, values, and approaches

---

Focused on improving the learning capacity of diverse students and building students' confidence through trusting relationships.

Concentrated on monitoring students' cognitive routines and providing constructive feedback that allowed for deeper levels of learning.

Set challenging goals for students and provided independent practice that tapped into a personalized approach to authentic learning.

Figure 3.1. Common Culturally Relevant Teacher Actions
Source: Commissioned by author.

they bring to the table. In essence, this book aims to move pedagogical connections founded on students' cultural strengths to the teacher's *conscious* level—multiplying the impact on learning.

As Ladson-Billings (2009) identified, classroom teachers must develop specific behavioral dimensions that provide a deeper understanding of the methods required for automaticity in practice. To perform to the fullest, teachers need to analyze *conceptions of self and others*, holding themselves accountable and seeing themselves as catalysts for transformational change. This dimension requires that teachers take a stance in believing that all students, no matter their race or circumstances, are capable and deserving of the highest levels of learning.

In essence, this dimension invites a platform for educators to envision a new stance, a *just cause* (Sinek, 2019) for how the future must look in advancing equitable educational attainment. The descriptions below provide a glimpse of contrasts within the three dimensions of a cultural relevance ideology versus one with an assimilationist approach.

Conceptions of Self and Others

Culturally Relevant: Teacher helps students make connections among their cultural, community, and national and global identities.

Assimilationist: Teacher homogenizes students into one "American" identity.

Enriching Social Relations

Culturally Relevant: Teacher-student relationship is fluid, humanely equitable, and extends to interactions beyond the classroom and into the community.

Assimilationist: Teacher-student relationship is fixed and tends to be hierarchical and limited to formal classroom roles.

Conceptions of Investigative Knowledge

Culturally Relevant: Knowledge is continuously re-created, recycled, and shared by teachers and students. It is not static or unchanging.

Assimilationist: Knowledge is static and is passed in one direction, from teacher to student.

Teachers who develop *enriching social relations* with their students continually use the students' language or culture to validate intellective capacity. Finally, *conceptions of investigative knowledge* promote the engagement of the student voice and view knowledge development as a fluid teacher-student process. The assimilationist (or individualistic) approach to teaching acts as a barrier to the necessary ecosystem of culturally responsive learning.

CONCEPTIONS OF SELF AND OTHERS

In your journey to become an effective culturally responsive educator, this aspect of your behavioral inner work may be the most vital in meeting the needs of your Black and historically marginalized students. Ladson-Billings (2009) notes that educators who practice culturally relevant strategies not only distinguish themselves as professionals in their craft but work to empower their students to become professional learners. In this manner, teachers hold themselves accountable and see themselves as catalysts for transformational change in the communities they serve.

Paramount to this notion is the teacher's ability to critically self-reflect, examining all forms of racism and giving attention to the teacher's own realities and tendencies, which allows meaning to be made that informs future pedagogical decision making (Hattie, 2012; Howard, 2003; Lopez, 2014). This shift in critical consciousness, sometimes referred to as one's *lens of equity*, is vital to culturally relevant teaching.

In her experience with White teachers, both preservice and veteran, Ladson-Billings (2009) mentioned that many teachers are reluctant to acknowledge racial differences. The teachers in my research were all keenly attuned to their own self-awareness, and when it came to race and color blindness, they understood it was an ever-evolving practice surrounding racial inequalities. Gay (2010) and Hattie (2012) made extremely clear that it is essential for teachers to examine their own beliefs and attitudes before considering their instructional actions.

> I've never been subjected to racism. I've never felt that. And so, I was kind of almost color-blind. And that's a form of racism and so that was something I really had to analyze and say, well, I need to do something about this. (Suzanne, fifth-grade teacher)

Therefore, culturally relevant pedagogy requires that *high-impact* teachers possess a critical stance against any structural racism or institutional racism that creates inequities within the schoolyard. For example, teachers of all races must confront their own racial viewpoints and question the *hidden curriculum*. One underlying element that most teachers face today is the concept of race-neutral or standardized curriculum. The idea of fairness through neutrality relies on the fallacy that if curriculum reflects no one, then it is equally fair for everyone (Faulkner-Bond, 2022).

Color blindness accepts the concept of removing all racial and culturally diverse perspectives and lived experiences from curriculum in the name of neutrality. More directly, "by claiming not to notice [color], the teacher is saying that she is dismissing one of the most salient features of the child's identity and that she does not account for it in her curricular planning and instruction" (Ladson-Billings, 2009, p. 36). Essentially, the individual's "commitment to color blindness creates the illusion of progress" (Wright, 2022, p. 11), while the gaps in academic achievement based on racial inequities continue to plague our public school system.

Culturally responsive teachers, no matter their race or ethnicity, respond to the *color-blind* colleague with, "Not only do I see color, but it's also what I value most about my students. We can't afford to fail." If you truly believe in this behavioral inner work (mind shift), then you truly believe in the power of students' cultural strengths to propel higher levels of learning.

Schmeichel (2012) refers to Ladson-Billings's culturally relevant teaching as an instructional approach that fosters students' ability to achieve academically and demonstrate cultural competence, thereby empowering students to analyze and understand the existing social order. By embracing this approach, educators shifted their mindset from the deficit approach to continually building self-efficacy by enacting these skills in the classroom. As mentioned, a critical first step for teachers is to understand that their own cultural values and stereotypes often shape or dictate learning expectations.

Creating Capacity over Contention

Never in our nation's history has there been a more pressing need to prepare students to thrive in a democracy filled with people from different racial backgrounds, holding political beliefs, and having various interests, in order to solve problems and build collective capacity (Rogers et al., 2022). Our public schools are the cornerstone to this goal. Research indicates that the pandemic has permeated nearly all aspects of schooling, including systemic inequities, such as race, racism, or implicit bias (Rogers et at., 2022; Woo et al., 2022).

In fact, a recent poll found that nearly 70 percent of principals reported their students had made at least one demeaning or hateful remark toward classmates for expressing political viewpoints (Rogers et al., 2022). The same principals also reported that their districts have provided less professional development for their teachers related to teaching about controversial issues. Although these tensions have compounded postpandemic, "research evidence suggests that classroom discussions about racial inequalities can enhance students' self-efficacy, academic outcomes, and appreciation for racial fairness and diversity" (Woo et al., 2022, p. 3). But are these discussions happening?

Because educating youth for a more diverse democracy is paramount, these findings suggest the need for school leaders to facilitate and sustain critical professional development (Kohli et al., 2015) centered on the school's vision of equity—in essence, advancing a *just cause* (Sinek, 2019). Within a high-impact culturally responsive school, teacher inquiry groups and racial affinity spaces focus on the future capacity of the vision and clearly define a commitment based on academic success, cultural competence, and sociopolitical consciousness (Ladson-Billings, 2009).

Overall, the *just cause* can be looked at as a moral obligation, awakening a new social structure within a school. In advancing a *just cause*, cultural stereotypes, social structures, and implicit biases can be addressed, and teachers and educators are invited to share in a brave space (Sinek, 2019). Implicit biases, for example, simply hold that even racial minorities (along with Whites) are unconsciously predisposed to associate positive attributes with Whites and have negative assumptions about minorities. As humans, we all "draw on racial ideas at the implicit level, sorting those we meet and forming early judgements virtually automatically, long before our conscious minds have a chance to recognize, let alone object to, the errors" (Lopez, 2014, p. 44).

Failing to examine one's own bias and expectations for the academic learning of Black and historically marginalized students plays a key role in the trivialization of culturally responsive teaching (Ladson-Billings, 2009; Sleeter, 2012) and student success. Collectively, redesigning systems through a lens of equity and through critical self-reflection is the key to advancing the culturally responsive school's *just cause*. Perhaps most importantly, these efforts are led by the culturally responsive *prepared* leader, one who shifts and adapts (many times in crisis), empowering the school to rebuild (James & Wooten, 2022).

> I think [in] our drive to teach through a culturally responsive lens, we first must understand our own biases and be aware of our own beliefs. We need to have a lens of compassion. (Lisa, first-grade teacher)

White teachers can, as Ladson-Billings (1995a) demonstrated in her seminal research, teach in ways that minimize the impact of cultural biases on students when they possess positive *conceptions of themselves and their students*, foster enriching classroom *social interactions*, and promote *conceptions of investigative knowledge* for students of color (Ladson-Billings, 2009). The fact is, teachers need not share the same ethnic background as their students, but they must demonstrate high levels of expertise in culturally responsive practices—the through line in equitable academic outcomes.

Do we need more Black teachers in urban and rural school districts? Absolutely, we do, and in chapter 9 we'll explore best practices in the recruitment, preparation, and retention of Black educators. In addition to Black teachers, however, we also need teachers willing *to do right* by our Black and historically marginalized student populations. And since we will not wake up tomorrow morning with complete alignment in racial composition of the Black teaching force, we need collective thinkers, not individualistic mindsets.

Adding to Ladson-Billings's analyses, thinking collectively to foster cultural responsiveness is the clear antidote to the assimilationist (individualistic) way of teaching (Real, 2022). It's a shift from "everything is fine in *my* classroom" to "I want everything to be fine in *our* (students and teacher) classroom." If this is not happening, school leaders must ask themselves, "What should we do about it?" If the collective is happening authentically, the work comes in bringing that to scale in all public schools. The culturally responsive leader ensures that it does and builds a culture to sustain it.

These schools, starting in prekindergarten, are the cultural cocoon for a more diverse teacher workforce. So *today*, our American public education system needs the collective group to teach through a lens of equity, be *caring*, establish a *familial classroom setting*, make learning *fun*, secure focus, and utilize each students' *power languages*—centered on students' cultural strengths (Hammond, 2015; Howard, 2001; Jha, 2021; Ladson-Billings, 2009). In other words: Are we building schools that compel future Black teachers to seek and embrace the profession and give back to their communities?

A System of Belief

The culturally relevant teacher believes culturally diverse students can learn at the highest levels and, in believing so, rejects the deficit-approach mentality (Gay, 2002; Howard, 2003; Ladson-Billings, 2009). One example of a distinct teaching trait is having high expectations and a belief that diverse learners have the capability to learn rather than holding on to lowered expectations (Hyland, 2009; Ladson-Billings, 1992). In turn, supported by effective teachers, Black and historically marginalized students have high expectations of themselves within a structured academic culture.

A second strategy is designing learning opportunities that provide social capital for students within their own community. For example, connecting curricular knowledge with students' lives in the form of social activism, university internships, panel discussions, and oral sociopolitical dialogue (Hyland, 2009; Ladson-Billings, 1995a). In real time, teachers can cultivate change by allowing students to research a community social justice issue (such as homelessness) and work side by side with government officials to create change.

The assimilationist, however, believes teaching is a technical task that rarely taps the imagination, while adhering to unrelatable subject matter. Possessing positive conceptions of themselves and their students allows teachers to build trusting relationships and then see students rise up to meet expectations at the adaptation level. Lesson design, however, must be intentionally built to do so.

Vulnerability

What does vulnerability have to do with culturally relevant teaching? As much as teaching is an art of social interaction, it is equally an art of self-examination *within* social interaction. Vulnerability is at the heart of fostering courage, yet as educators, we forget that without vulnerability there is no creativity (Brown, 2018). Without creativity, there cannot be culturally relevant teaching. Educators must ponder the following areas of vulnerability when employing culturally responsive pedagogical practices:

- Understanding one's own identity and how one is empowered to ensure the academic success and identity formation of students (Gist et al., 2021).
- A willingness to be comfortable in "working behind the scenes" and sharing responsibility with parents, community members, and the students themselves in facilitating academic excellence (Gist et al., 2021; Ladson-Billings, 2009).
- Securing a school climate in which frequent listening, paying attention, and positive connections with teachers, students, and parents are the cornerstone of trust building (Brown, 2018).
- Understanding that taking risks involves trust and that trust requires vulnerability. Leaders' instructional feedback is a shared vulnerability with teachers in real time, just as teachers' employment of culturally relevant practices is a shared vulnerability with students in real time (James & Wooten, 2022; Kavanagh et al., 2020).
- Seeing teaching as an infinite game. However, the assimilationist forces a pedagogy of "control"—one that is finite. In finite teaching, some students will win (learn), while some students *must* lose (fail). Finite games are predicated on winners and losers (Sinek, 2019). Culturally responsive teachers live in an infinite game, where they "give up control" and rely on textural practices (invisible behaviors), the interplay of

thought, identity, and knowledge (Kavanagh et al., 2020), understanding that learning is centered on continuous improvement.
- Vulnerability for self-trust and trust in leadership to see positive results, not as an immediate endgame but as a process where knowledge is continuously re-created, recycled, and shared between the teacher and historically marginalized students (Ladson-Billings, 2009; Sinek, 2019).
- A realization that teaching is a craft of interpersonal structures. Therefore, embracing our emotions through vulnerability allows for more powerful decision making, critical thinking, creativity, and self-compassion—all necessary traits for culturally responsive teachers and leaders (Brown, 2022; Hammond, 2015).
- Knowing that the culture of individualistic self-protection (assimilationist teaching) is marked by dominance and invulnerability (Ladson-Billings, 2009). Accepting both these conditions erodes the relational connection of cultural responsiveness (Real, 2022).

Because teaching is filled with uncertainties that evolve from checking for understanding, learning progressions, and perhaps redirecting pace, teachers are constantly in a state of vulnerability. When leaders build trust with their teachers, new standards and expectations for higher academic performance for Black and underserved students can be achieved. Through this relational component, teachers and leaders can move curriculum and pedagogical practices forward, where vulnerability becomes a metaphorical coteacher in every classroom.

ENRICHING SOCIAL RELATIONS

Developing positive relationships with students not only enhances their ability to succeed academically (Ladson-Billings, 2009) but creates a channel for teachers to understand motivational factors for learning (Edwards & Edick, 2012). Enriching social relations in the classroom opens up a learning exchange where teachers see a student's culture or language as a means to validate learning. Culturally relevant teachers get to know their students as a "whole" person (Moll et al., 1992), while extending learning interactions beyond the classroom and into community contexts (Ladson-Billings, 2009).

This concept builds on creating equitable learning relationships, which Moll et al. (1992) refer to as the teacher's ability to recognize and capitalize on students' *funds of knowledge*. In contrast, educators with an assimilationist mindset rarely draw on resources from students' outside worlds, and cultural relationships are limited to knowledge gained from isolated classroom interactions (Ladson-Billings, 2009; Moll et al., 1992).

I pride myself on relationships with my students because in this community, if a kid doesn't trust you, or doesn't have a good relationship, they're not going to learn anything. (Julie, fifth-grade teacher)

In supporting equitable relationships, teachers embrace the social history of households and accept sociopolitical contexts as contributing to the knowledge that diverse learners possess in school. Too often, however, schools are satisfied with "multicultural" events and remembrances, such as Cinco de Mayo or Black History Day. The true equitable relationships that support learning happen when teachers move past "one-time" trivialized diversity events and "orchestrate learning so it builds student's brain power in culturally congruent ways" (Hammond, 2015, p. 19).

Tapping into a student's prior learning or lived experiences brings their *funds of knowledge* into the learning forefront. For example, household management and religion can offer insight into cultural wisdom, spanning areas such as morals and cultural customs to childcare and budgeting (Moll et al., 1992). In terms of school success, developing an understanding of a family's ability to develop social networks that connect them with their social environments can reshape lesson design (discussed in later chapters) and enhance students' ability to learn.

Doing this, however, takes skillful consideration and reflection when ensuring Black and marginalized students of color become valued members of the teacher-student learning partnership. Classroom social environments and learning structures, built on equitable teacher-student relationships, are essential to the enactment of effective culturally responsive teaching. Leveraging the cultural strengths of students allows teachers to broaden enriching social relations and sustain a more collaborative environment in the classroom (Hammond, 2015; Ladson-Billings, 2009).

Teachers with an understanding of the positive cultural knowledge students come equipped with from home will likely challenge the deficit discourses that label students as deficient (Kinney, 2015). Moll et al. (1992) explained that "this view of households [as asset filled] contrasts sharply with prevailing and accepted perceptions of working-class families as somehow disorganized socially and deficient intellectually" (p. 134). Culturally responsive teachers take the time to know students and their families on a personal level, uncovering complex social networks, hopes, and goals, along with terms of behavior, values, and educational aspirations. For example, if respect in a child's household is shown by looking down at the floor when being disciplined, but the teacher expects respect to be shown by looking them in the eyes, strife is unavoidable.

If a child's voice is not valued in the home, teachers must be considerate when demanding participation—vulnerability to verbally engage must be celebrated and inviting. In illuminating a family's *funds of knowledge*, teachers immerse themselves in a familial connection, tied to bilingualism, social networking and media, instructional design, and technology (Kinney, 2015). Most importantly, teachers build an inner belief system based on an asset-based framework, which compels them to design lessons around deeper knowledge acquisition—the *Apex of Student Learning*.

CONCEPTIONS OF INVESTIGATIVE KNOWLEDGE

Wide research depicts the acquisition of knowledge as a social construction (Kinney, 2015; Ladson-Billings, 2009; Moll et al., 1992), which effective teaching fosters by examining student perceptions and building cultural competence (Howard, 2001; Milner, 2011). As such, learning must be cultivated by cooperation, collaboration, and mutual responsibility for gaining knowledge among students and between student and teacher (Gay, 2013). Unfortunately, in many classrooms across America, the assimilationist approach tends to see knowledge as static, passed on in a hierarchical structure from teacher to student. Conversely, effective culturally responsive teachers engage student voice and view knowledge development as a continuous process of creation.

Milner (2011) examined a White science teacher's experience in building cultural competence in order to maximize student learning opportunities. Revealing was the teacher's ability to secure a learning environment that invited students to critically examine the content through a culturally competent lens. This is highly important in culturally relevant teaching, as it allows students to move beyond spaces where they are merely consuming knowledge (acquisition) to higher levels of thinking (adaptation). In culturally responsive practice, effective teachers use students' culture in their curriculum planning and implementation, allowing students to develop the skills to question how power structures are created and maintained.

Three areas surfaced regarding this teacher's mindset and experiences in relation to building a culturally responsive learning environment. Milner (2011) concluded that the teacher was able to (1) build and sustain meaningful and authentic relationships, allowing him to build cultural competence and foster students' conceptual knowledge; (2) recognize the multiple layers of identity among his students; and (3) perceive teaching as a communal affair. Howard (2001) mentions that when teachers secure a safe learning space for students through positive relationships, their ability to learn at high levels is also secured.

Teachers' efforts to create positive interactions, taking diversity into account or *seeing color*, along with clearly communicating, allow students to feel safe. When students feel safe, they are more likely to be vulnerable in sharing their voice, allowing funds of knowledge to drive learning. Howard (2001) noted, "The attribute most frequently mentioned by the students about what created an optimal learning environment was their teachers' willingness to care about them and their ability to bond with them" (p. 137). Like Howard (2001), Milner (2011) found that building and sustaining caring relationships with students not only deepened teachers' knowledge of students' cultural identities but forged learning collisions that allow for the necessary cognitive shifts or progressions of learning (figure 3.2).

Think of this as a molecular collision in a learning analogy, where teacher-to-student interactions release new energy through a *caring, fun,* and *familial* community. Put differently, high-impact culturally responsive teachers "believe that knowledge is continuously re-created, recycled, and shared by teacher and students alike" (Ladson-Billings, 2009, p. 28).

In building your own lens of equity, it's important to reflect on the original theory of culturally relevant pedagogy—one that ensures diverse students are empowered intellectually, socio-emotionally, and politically through the teacher's ability to leverage cultural referents to impart knowledge. This chapter and the chapter that follows demonstrate the intricate yet reflective knowledge necessary to build cultural competence in ways that allow educators to effectively engage culturally and linguistically diverse students.

As mentioned, there is no order of operations that explains the complexities or explicit approaches to leveraging students' cultural strengths. The power of your teaching comes from the reflective piece:

Student Perspective - Howard	Teacher Experience – Milner
• Caring teachers are extremely important • Teachers establish a community or "family environment" in the classroom • The teacher makes learning entertaining	• Builds and sustains meaningful and authentic relationships with students, which builds cultural competence and fosters students' conceptual knowledge • Recognizes the multiple layers of identity among students and connects race matters with them • Perceives teaching as a communal affair, continually learning from students in the classroom

Figure 3.2. Student-to-Teacher Learning Collisions
Source: Commissioned by author.

- Can you *see color* and allow students' cultural genius to inform your pedagogical moves?
- Are you able to recognize some teaching habits that may be leaning toward the assimilationist approach?
- How well are you balancing your ability to critically examine conceptions of self and others, foster social relations, and develop students' deep investigative knowledge?
- Are your lessons explicitly built to scaffold and then progress learning goals to the adaptation level?

THE PARADIGM SHIFT

Although researchers have formulated pedagogical theories to make teaching and learning more responsive to the cultural practices of diverse learners (Gay, 2010; Ladson-Billings, 2009; Moll et al., 1992), Paris and Alim (2014) argued that culturally sustaining pedagogy "seeks to perpetuate and foster—to sustain—linguistic, literate, and cultural pluralism as part of schooling for positive social transformation" (p. 1). Therefore, culturally sustaining pedagogy requires that teaching be more than *responsive* to the cultural experiences and practices of students of color. Instead, culturally sustaining pedagogy demands that teachers support their students in *sustaining* their cultural identity and linguistic competence, while continually focusing their practice for racial justice and positive transformation (Paris, 2012).

Culturally Sustaining Pedagogy

Prior to the 1960s and 1970s, the dominant language, literacy, and cultural practices demanded by the school fell in line with White, middle-class norms and positioned diverse cultures that fell outside those norms as unworthy of legitimacy in U.S. schools and society (Paris, 2012). In essence, schooling largely forwarded the assimilationist approach (Ladson-Billings, 2009), asking students of color to deny their cultures and histories in order to achieve academically, and schooling continues to do so today. Many educators described culture as the key to understanding what was inhibiting the academic success of children of color—the perceived difference between mainstream culture and the culture of children of color was described in terms of a gap that must be filled (Schmeichel, 2012).

Over the years, this *deficit-based approach* to students' cultural and linguistic richness has had and continues to have devastating effects on their educational attainment (Paris & Alim, 2014). As our society continues to experience massive demographic changes, coupled with continued socioeconomic inequities, the more pressing question becomes this: What is the purpose of schooling in a multicultural, pluralistic society?

Paris and Alim (2014) advocated for educators not only to focus on and examine educational spaces that disrupt a schooling system centered on White assimilationist ideologies, but to strive for racial justice and positive social transformation built on *asset-based approaches*—essentially, building bridges from the classroom to community social justice efforts, where students are empowered in real-world scenarios.

Learning Climates

Cultural themes and practices pertinent in many diverse students' home experiences could be used to enhance academic achievement in classroom settings (Gay, 2010; Moll et al., 1992). However, interactions between White middle-class teachers who expected "the norm" and students who were not the perceived norm have been described as unsolvable—marking academic failure as a concept where *culture* equated to *disadvantage* (Schmeichel, 2012). To that end, learning, or lack thereof, was not blamed on pedagogical practice or teacher belief, but rather on the students.

Within the classroom, Schmeichel (2012) argued that for teachers with an assimilationist perspective, there was little interest in making a distinction between concerns about a particular cultural group. Rarely did teachers with an assimilationist perspective make a distinction between the needs of African American students and those of Latinx students and how their needs differed from those of the dominant White narrative being taught in schools, according to Schmeichel. The consequence is a learning climate that does not support students from backgrounds that differ from the dominant White mainstream culture.

The colorblind assimilationist might say (or you may have heard directly), "I don't see color, I treat all my students the same."

Doucet (2017) examined the learning climate for students at the intersection of students' immigration status, disproportionality, and teacher perceptions, making a case for instructional settings that are humanizing and more culturally sustaining. Built on the conceptual frameworks of Freire's (1985) *humanizing practice* and Paris and Alim's (2014) *culturally sustaining pedagogy*, Doucet (2017) asserted these provided "a deep awareness of the matrix of power and privilege that shapes society, centering the experiences of White middle and upper-class individuals" (p. 196).

These sociocultural frameworks have implications for teachers' work in maximizing the life chances of Black and underserved students by fostering critical awareness—empowering students to face an inequitable society.

Developing the ability to foster students' critical awareness is an ongoing process, by which teachers allow diverse students agency in learning. Both in-service and preservice teachers must commit to increasing knowledge about diversity and building their classrooms as communities of trust.

For example, teachers must have an understanding and be prepared to discuss issues of social and racial inequity (Hyland, 2009; Young, 2010). In addition, classroom structures should be built on trusting teacher-student relationships, allowing students to cultivate a positive mindset and a sense of self-efficacy (Doucet, 2017; Hammond, 2015). Effective culturally sustaining teachers combat prejudice and discrimination as well as address student diversity in its full complexity. Doucet (2017) asserted that combating racial injustice means "explicitly teaching young children about how prejudice and discrimination operate in the world and engaging young children in critical conversations about the world around them" (p. 199).

In addressing diversity, teachers engaged and recognized the humanizing practice of teaching, whereby the many strands of students' cultural knowledge and identities were respected and weaved into rich teacher-student relationships (Doucet, 2017; Kinney, 2015; Moll et al., 1992). Paris and Alim (2014) advocate for pedagogical practices, like those advocated for by Schmeichel (2012) and Doucet (2017), that recognize the continual shifts and cultural reworkings in our pluralistic society, while equipping students with opportunities to survive and prosper. Effective teachers validate and honor the languages, literacies, and cultural practices of students and communities, creating learning frameworks that sustain higher levels of learning (Hammond, 2015; Paris, 2012).

A FRAMEWORK FOR TEACHER CAPACITY

Making classroom instruction more consistent with the cultural orientations of students of color, while recognizing the importance of racial competencies, is vital to putting culturally responsive pedagogy into practice (Gay, 2010). This viewpoint moves teachers past traditional interpretations of "multiculturalism" and into an inquiry stance, wherein culture validates greater depths of knowledge. In doing so, pedagogical decisions drive equitable opportunities for Black and underserved students to develop learning habits and cognitive capacity.

For too long, however, students of color have been stifled by an achievement gap that transcends the schoolyard, creating disparities into adulthood (Hammond, 2015; Williams, 2011). Effective culturally responsive pedagogy allows students to become better prepared to do higher-order thinking, engage in creative problem solving, and develop skills in analytical reading and writing (Hammond, 2015; Hattie, 2012; Daggett, 2008).

Proponents of culturally responsive pedagogy suggest that, without teaching these advanced cognitive skills in a way that leverage students' cultural identities, the achievement gap will not only be maintained but continue to grow within our American educational system.

In her seminal work, *Culturally Responsive Teaching and the Brain*, Zaretta Hammond (2015) compels the reader to examine the achievement gap from two angles: (1) the American public school system's creation of dependent learners who are unprepared to do higher-order thinking, problem solving, and deep analysis of texts, and (2) the phenomenon that culturally responsive teaching focuses on improving the learning capacity for more independent learning.

Hammond (2015) defines culturally responsive teaching as an educator's ability to recognize students' cultural displays of learning while responding constructively by using students' cultural knowledge as a scaffold for effective information processing. As shown by Ladson-Billings (2009) and Paris (2012), these pedagogical innovations look to move teaching further from the *deficit approach*, which negates home languages, literacies, and cultural ways of interacting that differ from the mainstream White culture, toward a sustained effort, viewing culture as an *asset to learning*.

In the classroom setting, these structures demonstrate that diverse learners thrive when teachers give affirmation, validation, and constructive feedback and allow for Black intellectual thought (Hammond, 2015; Howard, 2001; Milner, 2011; Thomas, 2023). Although rudimentary, these simple principles are often not intentionally built into lesson design. We'll explore those features in later chapters.

According to Hammond (2015), there are four key classroom learning structures: (1) teachers developing an *awareness* of their own cultural lens of equity in interpreting and evaluating students' knowledge and skills, (2) creating socio-emotional *learning partnerships* that build capacity for and establish an authentic connection with students to foster mutual trust, (3) creating a *community of learners and a learning environment* that is intellectually and socially safe, and (4) strengthening students' intellective capacity and *information-processing* skills in order to engage in high-leverage social and instructional activities.

Hammond (2015) provides constructs that prove necessary for active student engagement and socially cooperative learning while at the same time fostering students' ability to learn independently. Advocating for these learning structures is no longer about equally valuing all communities of color; it is also about the skills, funds of knowledge, and concepts needed for sustainable success in the present and future (Moll et al., 1992; Paris & Alim, 2014).

As figure 3.3 illustrates, each frame of teacher capacity is not an isolated construct; rather, practitioners should become adept at navigating in and around each pedagogical practice. For example, within my research, effective teachers were fluid in simultaneously integrating elements in each area, such as *knowing their own cultural lens* and supporting students' use of code switching, which built a culture that was *socially and intellectually safe for learning* (Gutierrez, 2021; Hammond, 2015). Figure 3.3 provides a framework of culturally responsive pedagogical constructs that prove necessary for guiding students toward more independent critical thinking at the adaptation level. This framework stresses how teachers must be fluid in bringing each construct into play while practicing culturally responsive teaching.

In the next chapter, you'll see how related components serve as foundational pieces within current research, depicting practices that remain on the surface, versus deeper instructional undercurrents.

Awareness

Effective culturally responsive teachers develop a sociopolitical consciousness and an awareness of the role that schools play in perpetuating unearned disadvantages due to race, gender, and class (Hammond, 2015). From a social justice perspective, culturally responsive teachers are keenly aware of the impact of their own cultural lenses in judging students' learning capabilities and how these lead to underestimating the cognitive capabilities students bring to the classroom (Gay & Kirkland, 2003; Hammond, 2015; Moll et al., 1992).

By fostering critical sociopolitical awareness, teachers begin to reimagine the implications of their own work for empowering and maximizing the life chances of Black and marginalized students (Doucet, 2017). As Hyland's (2009) study demonstrated, effective teachers improved their sociopolitical lens of equity by engaging in external workshops on multicultural education, antiracist and diversity pedagogy, and school community arts projects led by university doctoral students.

Through her own knowledge and awareness in using students' culture to propel learning, the teacher became highly skilled in structuring her classroom in such a way that students felt important, accomplished, valued, and empowered (Hyland, 2009). Furthermore, the teacher became adept at scaffolding and supporting her students to view knowledge critically. After attending a seminar on antiracist teaching and diversity, the teacher became comfortable incorporating a more project-based style of teaching centered on issues of race and gender (Hyland, 2009).

With stronger awareness of self and the students they serve, teachers are able to go against a school culture that encourages rote, teacher-directed

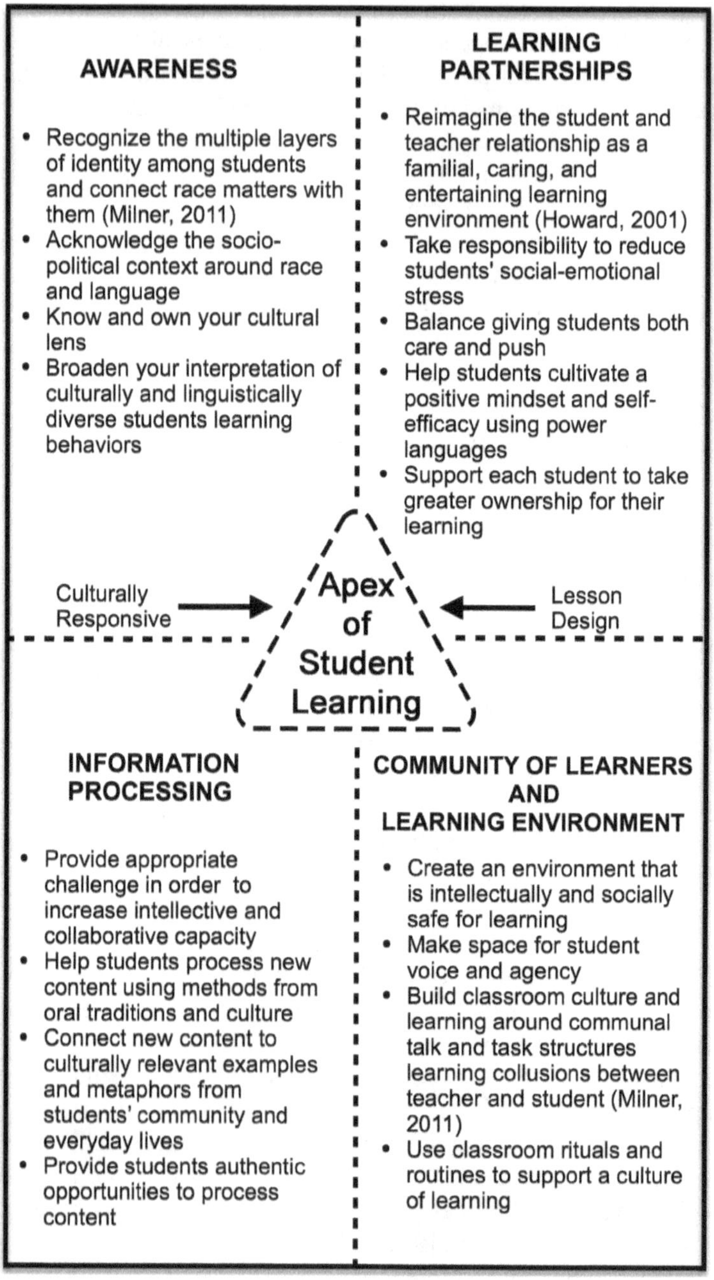

AWARENESS	LEARNING PARTNERSHIPS
• Recognize the multiple layers of identity among students and connect race matters with them (Milner, 2011) • Acknowledge the sociopolitical context around race and language • Know and own your cultural lens • Broaden your interpretation of culturally and linguistically diverse students learning behaviors	• Reimagine the student and teacher relationship as a familial, caring, and entertaining learning environment (Howard, 2001) • Take responsibility to reduce students' social-emotional stress • Balance giving students both care and push • Help students cultivate a positive mindset and self-efficacy using power languages • Support each student to take greater ownership for their learning
INFORMATION PROCESSING	COMMUNITY OF LEARNERS AND LEARNING ENVIRONMENT
• Provide appropriate challenge in order to increase intellective and collaborative capacity • Help students process new content using methods from oral traditions and culture • Connect new content to culturally relevant examples and metaphors from students' community and everyday lives • Provide students authentic opportunities to process content	• Create an environment that is intellectually and socially safe for learning • Make space for student voice and agency • Build classroom culture and learning around communal talk and task structures learning collusions between teacher and student (Milner, 2011) • Use classroom rituals and routines to support a culture of learning

Culturally Responsive → Apex of Student Learning ← Lesson Design

Figure 3.3. Key Areas of Culturally Responsive Teacher Capacity to Promote the Rigors of Learning

Source: Adapted from Hammond (2015, p. 17). Copyright 2015 by Corwin.

pedagogy, finding resources built on students' cultural proficiencies, experiences, and historical perspectives to support learning (Gay, 2010; Ladson-Billings, 2009; Milner, 2011). Schmeichel (2012) noted that as teachers shift their perspective from deficit thinking toward positive self-efficacy and creativity, the enactment of culturally relevant pedagogy empowers students to analyze and further understand the existing sociopolitical order.

Continual self-critique of one's beliefs is crucial to improving educational opportunities for students of color, yet teachers use various measures to avoid engaging with racial issues within the field. Gay and Kirkland (2003) warn that, too often, teachers "confuse reflection with describing issues, ideas, and events; stating philosophical beliefs; or summarizing statements made by scholars" (p. 182).

For example, when discussing achievement among students of color, many teachers merely refer to current trends or conventional deficit mindsets for disparities, without examining their own accountability or personal positions. *Remember the assimilationist?* Another obstacle is that both preservice and in-service teachers rarely have high-quality opportunities for guided practice in self-reflection (Gay & Kirkland, 2003), suggesting the need for more explicit professional development on the issue in order to develop teachers' awareness. Sustaining efforts to build teachers' beliefs in their capabilities as culturally responsive educators can positively influence learning outcomes for students of color.

Learning Partnerships

Creating social-emotional learning partnerships for deeper learning involves concerted efforts in building trust with one's students (Hammond, 2015). Gutierrez (2002) notes that effective teachers take the opportunity to get to know their students, then develop their pedagogical practices around relationships and cultural knowledge. Moll et al. (1992) asserted that positive social relations were achieved when minoritized students become valued members of the learning partnership, which fosters higher levels of engagement and learning.

Klem and Connell (2004) examined the relationship between teacher support and student engagement and between student engagement and academic achievement. Developed using principles of Connell's Self-System Process Model, the authors examined students' individual experiences in a social context, their self-system processes, their patterns of action, and actual outcomes of performance.

Two forms of engagement were defined and measured: *ongoing engagement* refers to student behavior, emotions, and thought processes during the school day, while *behavioral engagement* includes time spent on work, intensity of effort, tendency to stay on task, and propensity to initiate action when given the opportunity. Depending on whether the students were elementary or secondary, Klem and Connell (2004) asked student respondents to rate the degree to which they believed they exerted effort on schoolwork, paid attention in class, prepared for class, and thought that doing well in school was personally important—regarding ongoing engagement and reaction to challenge.

The same rating survey structure was completed by teacher participants regarding student engagement, measuring the extent to which teachers believed students were attentive, came to class prepared, and did more than required. As reported by both teachers and students, Klem and Connell (2004) concluded that teacher support is important to student engagement. Students who identified teachers as creating a caring, well-structured learning environment with high and fair expectations were more likely to report engagement in school.

More significantly, high levels of student engagement were linked with higher attendance and test scores, which strongly predict graduation outcomes and college attainment. Elementary students within the study sample with high levels of self-reported engagement were 44 percent more likely to achieve high levels of academic performance, suggesting strong teacher-student relationships and a well-structured classroom (Klem & Connell, 2004). Teachers indicated behavioral factors such as paying attention, staying focused, and doing more than required as strong measures of engagement.

Like the findings of Milner (2011) and Gay (2010), the findings of Klem and Connell (2004) demonstrate that positive relationships exemplified as *caring* are one of the key components of culturally responsive teaching. Within a community-based classroom, relationships or learning partnerships are the foundation of all sociopolitical and cognitive endeavors (Hammond, 2015; Ladson-Billings, 2009).

Community of Learners and Learning Environment

Within the construct of socially and intellectually safe learning environments, Hammond (2015) advocates for building a sense of community and connection in the classroom setting. Ladson-Billings (2009) asserts that empowerment through validation and positive relationships is a critical component of culturally responsive teaching, as it restores a sense of hope and self-worth for diverse students.

Through establishing trust and gaining rapport, teachers can offer positive ways to propel stronger learning identities and a sense of confidence for diverse learners (Hammond, 2015). When schools *adapt*, and do not adopt, a system of belief, they accept that knowledge is embedded in students' culture and can therefore be leveraged for greater depths of knowledge. Culturally relevant pedagogy mirrors a community platform, which fosters a learning environment where Black and underserved students can thrive not only academically but psychologically (Cholewa et al., 2014; Griner & Stewart, 2012).

Building on Ladson-Billings's (2009) theory of culturally responsive pedagogy, Cholewa et al. (2014) examined culturally responsive education (CRE) practices through the lens of relational cultural theory (RCT) to further understand how CRE may be associated with enhancing the psychological well-being of diverse learners. Specifically, within a professional development setting, the study examined the interactions of a culturally responsive female teacher and how she developed relationships with her low-income, Black students at a Title I school in the southeastern United States.

With the multicultural education movement as the catalyst, CRE, like culturally relevant pedagogy, looks to integrate and build on the culturally based lived experiences of diverse students (Gay, 2010; Ladson-Billings, 2009; Moll et al., 1992). The authors noted, "RCT asserts that misinterpretations, misunderstandings, and denial of life experiences result in emotional and relational disconnections" (p. 578). The teacher within the study mitigated these areas by incorporating many culturally responsive practices centered on her experiences with her students, namely, familial routines, integrating music and dance, and utilizing familiar communication styles (Cholewa et al., 2014). We'll further explore these tactics in later chapters, specific to culturally responsive lesson design.

> I feel like the students need to make that connection. I can't just force it. That happened to me too, so I definitely allow them to code switch from Spanish to English. Right now, I do have a student who speaks English, but every now and then he'll just look at me and then the code switching just happens. I've seen other students become more comfortable using their home language because of my interaction with this student. (Victoria, second-grade teacher)

Cholewa et al. (2014) found that the learning environment was enhanced when the teacher capitalized on the skills that emanated from the students' lived experiences, like the findings of Moll et al. (1992). In addition, the study illuminated the importance of promoting self-worth and connection to students—showing the psychological benefits that may arise for Black students taught through a culturally responsive lens.

Like Ladson-Billings (2009), the authors advocate for creating learning environments that include high expectations and beliefs in students' abilities, capitalizing on opportunities to demonstrate the value of African American–centered learning experiences.

Information Processing

In addition to creating supportive learning environments, teachers must pedagogically scaffold or build bridges from prior learning to facilitate learning (Young, 2010). In doing so, effective teachers build intellectual capacity through information processing, which is a student's ability to take mundane facts and concepts and leverage them into sustainable and meaningful learning (Hammond, 2015). The ability to process, store, and use information, scaffolded by teacher feedback, allows students to perform more complex thinking at the adaptation level—often required in high-stakes testing.

As we know, current Smarter Balanced standardized exams measure proficiency by testing students' ability to respond constructively in unpredictable scenarios. Zoch (2017) conducted a study to understand teachers' instruction that is responsive to students' backgrounds (Ladson-Billings, 2009; Moll et al., 1992) amid expectations to prepare students for high-stakes testing. Developed using principles of Paris's theory of culturally sustaining pedagogy (CSP), various practices were used to support diverse learners in sustaining the cultural and linguistic competence of their home community while simultaneously affording access to dominant cultural competence (Hammond, 2015; Zoch, 2017).

Participants were four English as second language (ESL) bilingual teachers at a school in the largest Latinx community in Texas. The primary focus of analysis was to describe the teachers' pedagogical literacy practices and demonstrated efforts to sustain students' cultural competence within a test-driven context. Zoch (2017) found that the teachers used a variety of techniques to promote information processing. For example, the teachers employed the use of code switching (switching between English and Spanish), which, although not delineated in CSP, allows students linguistic flexibility within guided reading instruction.

Perhaps more importantly, Zoch (2017) discovered that effective teachers supported students' understanding of a wide variety of texts and reading strategies, while also addressing issues of social justice. Finally, critical thinking skills were fostered through teachers' engaging in dialogue that encouraged critical consciousness and access to the academic demands of school reading while supporting students' cultural identities. Important to note is that the teachers were doing this within a climate that prioritized students' achievement on high-stakes assessments. Consequently, the findings demonstrate that teachers need not feel limited in their teaching.

In fact, the teachers were able to leverage the information-processing skills of students from diverse backgrounds while also addressing their sociocultural needs and responding to the demands of the high-stakes assessments (Hammond, 2015; Ladson-Billings, 2009; Zoch, 2017). While keeping learning goals centered on the adaptation level of cognition, Hammond's (2015) four frameworks, when used in daily interactions with students, also broaden teachers' interpretations of student learning behaviors.

In essence, learning becomes a communal partnership (Ladson-Billings, 2009), thereby helping students become independent learners by processing new content through positive feedback, cultural and linguistic strengths, and cognitive routines (Gay, 2010; Hammond, 2015). What needs to be added to Hammond's insight is that lesson design coincides with the environment. Think of the classroom structure as the implicit (unconscious order), while the explicit learning is derived from intentional culturally responsive lesson design (conscious planning). Paramount to lesson design are the elements of *input*—a student's ability to decipher what information is important and worth storing. Equally important is the intentional planning to ensure input translates to *elaboration*, where the student's brain is stimulated to categorize information. Once the information is meaningful, the brain must *apply* that knowledge in real-world tasks and unpredictable scenarios.

As we'll see in the next chapter, expertise can span a continuum of surface-level implementation while discovering tactics that allow for deep instructional undercurrents. Through the support of site leadership, movement toward more complex tactics can be developed to meet the needs of diverse learners. Teachers and principals must work in unison to adapt to the needs of their students and, most importantly, must be unapologetic in moving pedagogical tactics toward the *Apex of Student Learning*.

Chapter 4

The Surface-Level Examination

"Nothing about education is about just making you feel comfortable. Sometimes we learn the most in the midst of discomfort."

—Gloria Ladson-Billings

As mentioned in chapter 1, it's important to highlight the necessary elements or *requirements* for sound culturally relevant pedagogy. In the previous chapter, some essential and evidenced-based approaches of culturally responsive pedagogy were provided. It's equally important to make real-world connections where theory drives actual classroom practice.

This chapter offers practical examinations from teacher interviews and classroom observations from six teachers and two site administrators, using academic success, cultural competence, and sociopolitical consciousness as anchors. Six themes emerged, illuminating specific actions at the school site, with subthemes supporting each (see table 4.1). What became clear and directly supported prior research were the categories that live within the surface level, versus those demanding more deep instructional undercurrents (or practices).

Although surface level in nature and not directly tied to culturally responsive instructional tactics, three *central components* emerged within the interviews and observations, as teachers and site leaders reflected on their practices in implementing culturally responsive pedagogy. In fact, each component acts as a marker of *capacity in practice* along the continuum of experiential knowledge at the school site. In building capacity and expertise, practitioners can reflect on their own actions and schoolwide structures pertaining to the two arrays of culturally responsive teaching.

In this case, *learning partnerships* and *awareness* were important; however, they remained shallow within the continuum toward sociopolitical consciousness (as seen in figure 4.1). The third category, *social-emotional*

Two Arrays of Culturally Responsive Pedagogy

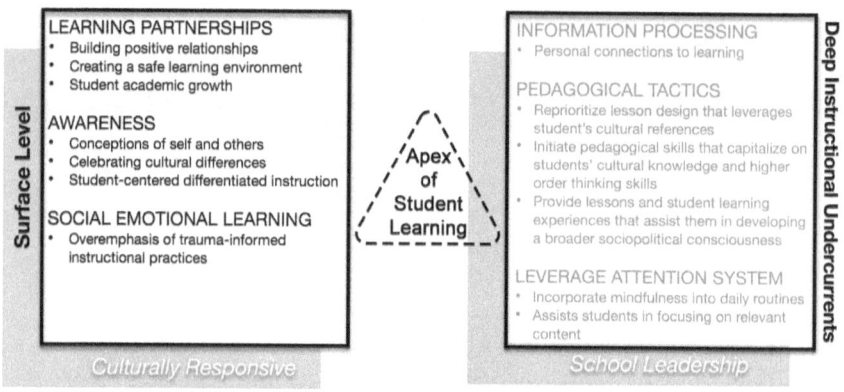

Figure 4.1. Surface-Level Themes of Learning Partnerships, Awareness, and Social-Emotional Learning

Source: Adapted from Hammond (2015, p. 17). Copyright 2015 by Corwin. Two Arrays of Culturally Responsive Pedagogy adapted from Gutierrez (2021, p. 151).

learning, became the overpowering root cause in shifting pedagogical attention away from cultural responsiveness.

However, *information processing* showed promise as a category that truly spoke to the tenets of culturally responsive teaching, especially pertaining to shaping students' ability to critique social inequities—or *centering* student identity within the curriculum (Ladson-Billings, 1995a). Within this section, I'll discuss the tenets that emerged at the surface level and that, although acting as building blocks, did not reach the true pedagogical tactics necessary for deeper learning.

CULTURALLY RESPONSIVE PEDAGOGY IN ACTION

Participant reports of their implementation of culturally responsive pedagogy carried similar themes, yet how they described their actions varied depending on their experience and conceptualization of the approach (Gutierrez, 2021). Table 4.1 represents an overview of findings related to culturally relevant pedagogy as described by Ladson-Billings (1995a).

All eight participants (each given a pseudonym) openly shared their experiences and conceptions in practicing culturally responsive pedagogy. Each participant was interviewed twice, once at the beginning of the school year and again just before the winter break. Their responses showcased their enactment

Table 4.1. Overview of Findings Related to Learning Partnerships, Awareness, and Information Processing

Themes	Academic Success	Cultural Competence	Sociopolitical Consciousness
Learning Partnerships			
Building Positive Relationships	9 Participants (73 References)	0	0
Creating a Safe Learning Environment	8 Participants (14 References)	3 Participants (4 References)	0
Student Academic Growth	6 Participants (17 References)	1 Participant (1 Reference)	0
Awareness			
Conceptions of Self and Others	3 Participants (6 References)	8 Participants (41 References)	0
Celebrating Cultural Differences	2 Participants (2 References)	3 Participants (9 References)	0
Student-Centered Differentiated Instruction	6 Participants (21 References)	0	0
Information Processing			
Personal Connections to Learning	2 Participants (2 References)	3 Participants (3 References)	1 Participant (1 Reference)

in the classroom and the support they received from the site administration. Each response offered a unique perspective of the participants' experiences in addressing the tenets of academic success, cultural competence, and sociopolitical consciousness (Ladson-Billings, 2009).

Interestingly, the participants conceived academic success as a product of the development of positive relationships, offering validation and affirmation, and creating an inclusive learning environment. The contextualization of pedagogical actions in relation to culturally responsive teaching was not mentioned within participant interviews and will be a major focus in chapter 5.

As seen in table 4.1, however, seven themes emerged in relation to Ladson-Billings's (1995b) three-pronged paradigm of academic success, cultural competence, and sociopolitical consciousness. Most prominent were the participants' statements related to the concept of *learning partnerships*, containing subthemes pertaining to aspects of social-emotional learning, such as building positive relationships.

Learning Partnerships

In enacting culturally responsive pedagogy, participants within this study overwhelmingly reported fostering and building positive relationships with their students and using classroom rituals to solidify an inclusive learning environment (Hammond, 2015). In addition, they associated creating a safe learning environment with the ability to foster learning and sustain a shared purpose. Participants also predominantly equated academic success with students making individual incremental gains in both English language arts and mathematics. The *learning partnerships* that took place within their classrooms on a daily basis are vividly described below.

Building Positive Relationships

Hammond (2015) asserted that culturally responsive educators build a trusting relationship with their students, leveraging a caring and supportive partnership for learning. Participants within this study capitalized on building mutual trust and took pride in their efforts to sustain positive relationships as a way to support academic success. However, none of the comments made by participants linked building positive relationships with developing cultural competence or sociopolitical consciousness.

Looking across the interviews, there were seventy-three comments from participants that aligned with the subtheme *building positive relationships*. In the enactment of culturally responsive pedagogy, both teachers and site administration spoke to the importance of this tenet in fostering student *academic success*.

For Dora, enacting culturally responsive pedagogy meant creating an environment where students felt loved and supported. When asked about the development of her personal knowledge on culturally responsive pedagogy, Dora commented:

> I think students really want to know about you and they want to feel important, and they want to be loved. Well, they want you to love them, and they want to be loved, especially our kids. They want to feel that love because they might not be feeling it at home.

Dora's viewpoint substantiated the importance of reimagining the teacher-student relationship as a partnership, one that fosters trust and respect. Within her two-decade tenure at the school, Dora realized that students thrived in a loving environment, and she correlated this with preparing students to succeed academically. As a precursor to academic success, Dora facilitated a caring and nurturing environment within her classroom.

Similarly, Victoria alluded to the learning partnerships built within her classroom, which in turn set a foundation for the ability to create a culture built on relationships:

> So, for me, it was building relationships. I think that's the most important thing because you're creating your own culture in your classroom. So you have to get to know the students in your classroom. Getting to know them has helped me.

In building positive relationships with her students, Victoria often affirmed the academic success of her students, which she believed in turn helped students cultivate a positive mindset. In her mind, getting to know her students on a personal level helped facilitate a sound learning environment that was conducive for academic success. Victoria felt that academic success was enhanced through a culture of positive praise and student recognition. Like Dora, Victoria felt creating this type of classroom culture was a necessity for enacting culturally responsive pedagogy.

Similar to Dora and Victoria, Marisol also built positive relationships with her students through mutual trust in the classroom. However, for Marisol, these relationships with students began with first developing relationships with the students' families:

> Number one, I have to instill trust, so the kids have to trust me. After the kids trust me, actually number one, I have to get trust from the parents. Without parental trust, I don't think that I'd be able to have student trust.

Marisol felt that parental trust was paramount, as it often equated to teacher-student trust. In turn, Marisol used this *familial* connection to secure a classroom culture conducive for academic success, which for her also included building relationships among the students: "They (students) need time to build relationships, not only with their teacher, but with their peers, and if their peers don't make them feel safe, then I have to create that culture."

In capitalizing on her efforts to forge positive relationships with the students' families, Marisol looked to ensure students felt trusted among their peers. Like the other teachers, her enactment of culturally responsive pedagogy included holding herself accountable for creating such a safe, supportive environment in the classroom.

Suzanne also shared that, within her classroom, the enactment of culturally responsive teaching was founded on a positive teacher-student relationship. When asked how she saw herself enacting culturally responsive pedagogy, Suzanne commented:

> Like I said, building relationships is huge for me. I really try to take the time to get to know my students and let them get to know me so that we have this trust

within each other and get to know each other so they feel comfortable to talk about themselves and their cultures.

Suzanne's comments illuminated her belief in the importance of creating a trusting teacher-student relationship, which remained a catalyst for her ability to secure a culturally inclusive learning environment. She felt that fostering mutual respect and trust within her classroom allowed students to excel academically. In addition, the trust built in her classroom allowed students to embrace the ability to share about their own cultures.

The quotes highlighted here from Dora, Victoria, Marisol, and Suzanne were indicative of the comments made by participants overall: establishing positive relationships with students was a necessary precursor to enacting culturally responsive pedagogy. More importantly, utilizing students' *power languages* was prevalent in each conversation with the teacher participants.

As mentioned in chapter 1, effective culturally responsive teachers must be keen in utilizing each student's *power language*, which orbits the *Apex of Student Learning*. As shown in figure 4.2, teachers can use power languages (nonexhaustive list) both inside and outside of the classroom in meaningful ways.

Like communicators of love, we know that verbal appreciation or words of affection are powerful both in the classroom and in life in general (Chapman, 2015; Howard, 2001). For example, the effective teacher understands that *words of praise* or *visual clout* can cultivate students' commitment and motivation to excel academically. Ultimately, its use drives the teacher's ability

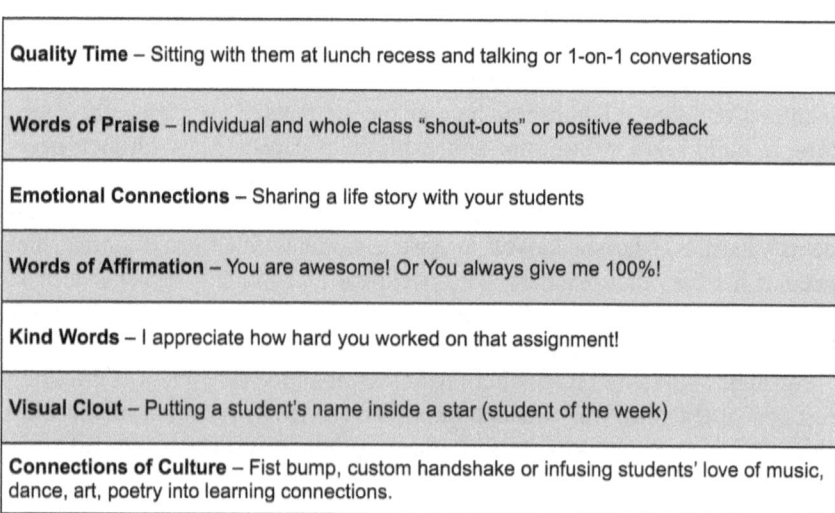

Figure 4.2. Examples of Teachers' Use of Power Languages
Source: Commissioned by author.

(if planned accordingly) to sustain positive relationships, which enhances students' information processing skills to succeed when faced with more rigorous content.

There is no one-size-fits-all power language, as each student may thrive from a completely unique set of connectors. The more practitioners get to know the whole child, the more they'll understand each student's power languages. The most effective culturally responsive teachers know each student's primary and secondary power language, instinctively, for example, knowing when to create a connection using *kind words* initially or by spending *quality time* with a student. More importantly, teachers must be willing to recognize and accept students' vulnerability and bids for connection. When power languages are used effectively, emotional synchronization (Real, 2022) is fostered between teacher to student and student to student.

These daily connections are small wins, and if a small win is like a raindrop, then our Black and historically marginalized students need a hurricane of wins in our classrooms every single day. Positive connections are built when small wins are deposited as if into a bank account; when the account is full, there is no desire to act out on the part of the student.

Creating a Safe Learning Environment

Establishing positive relationships with their students allows teachers to create safe learning environments that would enable academic success. In all, eight participants referenced the need to create a safe learning environment, the second subtheme highlighted in table 4.1. Within *creating a safe learning environment*, fourteen references fell within the area of academic success and four references aligned with cultural competence.

Participants within this study made concerted efforts to foster an emotionally and intellectually safe learning environment to support academic success and cultural competence. However, none of the comments made by participants leveraged the creation of a safe learning environment with a system that built students' sociopolitical consciousness inside or outside of the classroom.

Examples of safe learning environments that promote *academic success* were documented from the first interviews with Marisol and Julie.

Marisol reiterated the importance of a safe learning environment yet was cognizant of student well-being beyond the classroom. When asked how she fostered a learning environment with enriching social relations for all students, Marisol commented:

So I have to create a safe learning environment by letting them know it's okay, I will help you with anything you need. All I need you to do is try your best. So just being able to instill that trust with the kids by doing certain activities that are fun. Kids need to be kids. They need time to explore. So definitely, creating a culture that is safe within the classroom and beyond, because again, it doesn't stop here. Once the kids get home or their parents get home, they still need to be able to trust me and be able to reach out to me.

Marisol built mutual trust with her students through her understanding of specific student needs, such as the ability to freely explore with *entertaining* educational activities. Facilitating an environment where students could create allowed Marisol to prioritize learning while simultaneously sustaining trusting relationships with her students. In addition, Marisol understood the importance of classroom safety extending to the home, which allowed for open communication between her and her students beyond school hours.

Julie explained that building a safe learning environment was important in the initial development of her classroom culture. When asked what strategies she used to promote learning partnerships among her students, Julie commented:

We do a lot [trust building] like in the beginning of the year. I tried to do a lot of partner-like activities, not so much academic, but we do a partner drawing thing, where they face opposite directions, and they have to direct each other. So they have to learn to trust each other first before I can set them down and say, "Explain to your partner what you did academically," or "Collaborate on this."

Julie found that setting the tone for a trusting social-emotional environment preceded the development of an academic culture between students. Like Marisol, Julie accepted the responsibility to reduce students' social-emotional stress through *entertaining* activities. Julie felt her efforts to foster a trusting relationship among students were a precursor to their ability to succeed academically.

In fostering a safe learning environment, teachers within this study recognized their lens of equity in supporting *cultural competence* within the classroom. Within the learning partnerships facilitated in their classrooms, curricular content was used in relation to students' culture. Lisa made the following statement as it pertained to creating an environment that was intellectually and socially safe for learning:

Number one for sure is building that safe place. I think that's the most important. And when we put on the lens of being culturally responsive and having that empathy and know our students and their background, I think that we understand that it's our job to create that climate in our classroom. I think that learning should also be entertaining and relatable to students' culture and that basic needs must be met in order for students to be ready to learn.

Lisa placed high importance on securing a safe learning environment in her classroom, which stemmed from her ability to show empathy and to understand students' backgrounds. In her opinion, the learning readiness of her students was dependent on her ability to meet their basic needs. Making sure that learning was enjoyable and relevant to students' culture was also seen as an important foundation for student learning.

Overall, the statements highlighted here from Marisol, Julie, and Lisa are indicative of the comments made by participants overall: creating a safe learning environment for students was a vital component to enacting culturally responsive pedagogy. The participants felt that creating a socially and emotionally safe environment fostered both academic success and cultural competence within the learning environment.

Student Academic Growth

Capitalizing on building positive relationships and ensuring a safe learning environment allowed for students to make growth academically. In all, seven participants referenced fostering student academic growth, the third subtheme under *learning partnerships* in table 4.1. Within *student academic growth*, seventeen comments from participants fell within the realm of academic success and one reference aligned with cultural competence.

Participants saw student academic growth as a catalyst to support academic success and cultural competence, closely related to social-emotional and relational factors. As with the previous subtheme, none of the comments made by participants associated academic growth with guiding students to critique the community norms or racial issues around them.

Throughout the study, teachers continually referred to and defined *academic success* as students making incremental growth, neglecting to connect pedagogical structures in mastering grade-level content standards in English language arts and mathematics. As shown in table 4.1, *student academic growth* is the third subtheme highlighted within the major theme of *learning partnerships*.

Dora spoke about the balance between having high expectations for all students while knowing and recognizing the effort her students put forth:

> We always want to be doing our best, and I know what's your best, so when you're not doing it even online, I know what's your best. But when you're not doing it, yes, I'm going to push you. We're always down to that [academic success], and I'm not going to let you do any less than your best, because as a teacher, you know when they're giving and when they're really doing. It's like, "No, go do it again. I know you better."

Dora's comments reflected her belief that all students can succeed academically, along with the importance of maintaining a balance of both care and push to help them realize that success (Hammond, 2015). Being attuned to the metrics of student ability allowed Dora to leverage high expectations for her students. Along with creating a caring learning environment, Dora felt pushing students to give maximum effort was a component of her enactment of culturally responsive pedagogy.

Angelo, like Dora, relied on student effort as he articulated what academic success entailed. Although he praised students for meeting challenges, Ladson-Billings (1995a) warned that "culturally relevant teaching requires that teachers attend to students' academic needs, not merely make them feel good" (p. 160). Angelo referred to academic success as a symbol of self-confidence and lent recognition and affirmation to students' accomplishments. Although keen to use students' *power languages*, Angelo did not articulate or reference his own pedagogical practices in relation to academic success:

> Right there—not even words, it's the smile and self-confidence a child shows when they're done with something. So I want them to feel, "Hey, if you tried your best because it's the effort you put on and you smile about it, I'm smiling with you." So it's the individual success that we learn their [the student's] challenges on what they accomplished. It's a lot of praise. It's a lot of praise and integrity. I think my students know that when I talk, even though I repeat myself, I'm being genuine. Like I tell the kids, "Once you're in the heart, you're always going to be in the heart forever."

For Angelo, academic success was fostered by the high importance he placed on emotional deposits and building his students' self-confidence, displaying an authentic belief and connectedness with his students (Ladson-Billings, 2009).

Like Dora, Angelo's attunement to student effort and commitment to learning shaped his ability to provide continual praise. In referencing his practice of culturally relevant pedagogy as a means for academic success, Angelo placed more value on the teacher-student relational factor than on the academic outcomes based on instruction.

Suzanne felt that social-emotional learning fostered students' ability to regulate their own behavior, which would then allow them to succeed academically, and substantiated Angelo's sentiment. When asked how she defined academic success for her students, Suzanne said:

> There's a lot of ways behaviorally I want success—I know that's not academic. But that's something huge, emotionally [for students]. I need those socio-emotional needs met; they need to be successful emotionally to be academically successful. That's why a lot of this stuff [social-emotional learning]

is important, building their own behavior and emotional aspects of their success, and then the academic success can come through that.

Suzanne's comments equated academic achievement with positive social-emotional attainment. In fact, within the arena of academic success, rather than using student culture as a tool for learning, Suzanne felt social-emotional learning remained primary to achieve success. For her, the ability to achieve academically was preceded by students' ability to regulate their emotional well-being, rather than by her pedagogical strategies that leveraged culture.

For the most part, participants felt academic success hinged on securing strong emotional deposits, which in turn developed resiliency within their students. Participants also felt responsible for maintaining and sustaining students' ability to succeed through providing a balance between high expectations and a caring nature within the school setting.

Vital to the enactment of culturally responsive pedagogy is the ability of teachers to support students' *cultural competence* as they grow academically.

Among the teachers interviewed, Lisa made the sole comment that explicitly related to supporting students' cultural competence in the learning environment:

> I do collaborative group structures like Think, Pair, Share, which gives them the opportunity to build those cultural connections and common interests and just being very aware and intentional with the way that I group students up.

Through the use of routine learning structures, Lisa gave students an opportunity to actualize their cultural knowledge with their peers. Furthermore, she made collaboration among students intentional within the learning environment to enhance academic dialogue. Allowing students to interact with each other in a culturally inclusive academic setting allowed Lisa to enact culturally responsive pedagogy.

The statements highlighted from Dora, Angelo, Suzanne, and Lisa were indicative of the comments made by participants overall: student academic growth and incremental individual achievement defined academic success, leaving aside cultural knowledge as a conduit for academic success. In employing instructional modifications with individualized and group accommodations, participants' reports of their pedagogical efforts touched on learning growth, spanning the tenets of academic success and cultural competence.

Implications for academic growth suggest professional development could heighten teachers' expertise in guiding students to develop a critical lens to see the inequities around them in their communities (Ladson-Billings, 2009).

Awareness

In supporting cultural competence, the teachers I worked with built capacity through their *awareness* of their own cultural lens and experiential knowledge. In doing so, the teachers found it necessary to strengthen their own self-awareness, celebrate cultural differences, and maintain a student-centered approach to teaching (Hammond, 2015). In addressing students' needs, teachers reported reflecting on, and then capitalizing on, students' lived experiences to make learning more relevant. Most significant, students were allowed to use their home language when processing new content, opening a cultural conduit for learning.

Conceptions of Self and Others

Culturally relevant teachers continually self-reflect and then adapt to students' needs, opening an awareness to engage students in high levels of learning built on their cultural strengths (Ladson-Billings, 2009). Overall, there were forty-seven statements pertaining to the theme of conceptions of self and others coded in participants' responses. Within the subtheme *conceptions of self and others*, six references pertained to academic success and forty-one references were associated with cultural competence.

Teachers recounted their experiences in addressing their own cultural awareness and biases pertaining to student learning. Participants within this study leveraged their own experiences and made concerted efforts to develop their own lens of equity to support academic success and cultural competence. Again, however, none of the comments made by the teachers linked conceptions of self and others with the possibility of creating further self-empowerment through social action.

Within the framework of culturally relevant pedagogy, teachers assist students in making connections between their own identities in order to show *academic success*. Victoria shared her experience as an English language learner and how, through the support of her parents, she learned the importance of self-awareness as it pertained to instructional guidance:

> So I feel like in order for us to be able to celebrate and everything as far as culturally for our students, we need to first love ourselves and understand where we come from and you know growing up. I feel like I did—my parents at least did a really good job of teaching me who I am and what I'm capable of. Now I'm able to bring that to my kids. So I think that's where it all began. It's like finding who you are, accepting who you are. Before you can accept everybody else.

Victoria explained that being secure in her own identity, as it pertained to her upbringing, was a valuable component of using culturally responsive pedagogy with students. Along with acknowledging the strength of her own upbringing, Victoria elaborated on providing students authentic opportunities to process content as well as to maintain cultural competence using code switching:

> I feel like the students need to make that connection. I can't just force it. That happened to me too, so I definitely allow them to code switch from Spanish to English. Right now, I do have a student who speaks English, but every now and then he'll just look at me and then the code switching just happens. I've seen other students become more comfortable using their home language because of my interaction with this student.

Through her development of cultural competence, Victoria was able to utilize students' home language as a tool for learning. Academically, she leveraged students' cultural knowledge in the form of their home language through *code switching* to foster success. More importantly, she was able to capitalize on her own experiences in order to make learning more relevant for her students. Through this, Victoria felt she created a *caring* teacher-student learning environment, based on students' cultural strengths.

Participants felt that the development of self-awareness aided in their ability to enact culturally responsive pedagogy and in turn build students' *cultural competence*. For Suzanne, professional development (from an outside agency) in culturally responsive pedagogy shaped her realization of key areas, such as self-reflection and its relation to student outcomes. Suzanne felt she became more equipped to see her own potential stereotypes and biases, as well as find teaching techniques that fostered self-worth within her students:

> Basically, a lot of it [professional development] was a self-reflection of myself. Self-awareness was really, and it was one of the big takeaways, because I really realized that in order to have the student's kind of go through this [culturally responsive pedagogy] that I have to be self-aware of myself and some perceptions or stereotypes that I have. And so that was something that was a really big takeaway and then just some strategies on how to build that self-worth within my students, that empowerment.

Suzanne's acceptance of the concept surrounding self-awareness allowed her to make personal meaning in respect to cultural competence. In turn, she looked to build experiences that validated students' cultural experiences and instilled a sense of self-worth.

Lisa also recalled the ways the professional development (from an outside agency) propelled her to self-reflect as it pertained to her approach to culturally responsive pedagogical practices. She thought about her own background and how it shaped her ability to support diverse students:

> I think [in] our drive to teach through a culturally responsive lens, we first must understand our own biases. I think that we must be aware of our own beliefs, and I think that we just need to have the lens of compassion and empathy in order to be a culturally responsive educator. We must have cultural competence, and we must look within ourselves and our own stories and backgrounds and how that affects our overall teaching.

Lisa shared that in order to enact culturally relevant pedagogy, she needed to be aware of her own lens of equity, therefore understanding her own implicit biases. Without doing so, Ladson-Billings (2009) warned that educators perpetuated the trivialization and misconceptions of culturally relevant pedagogy. For some, such as Lisa and Angelo, personal experiences played an integral role in their development of cultural competence. Along with self-awareness, Lisa believed compassion and empathy for her students enhanced her enactment of culturally responsive pedagogy.

Most poignant within the theme of conceptions of self and others was Angelo's recollection of being the victim of a racial slur at the age of eleven. Subsequently, like Lisa, Angelo was able to self-reflect on cultural differences within himself. When asked how he has developed his knowledge of culturally responsive pedagogy, Angelo reflected on his past:

> But then when that one year being very young called a [racial slur], I said, hey wait a minute, I'm bicultural, as are others. So it just made me more aware of other people's background because suddenly I realize I'm biracial.

Through this experience, Angelo gained an ability to critically self-reflect on diversity, which gave him a unique perspective on the cultural differences among his students. Angelo used this experience to better empathize with the lived experiences of the students of color within his classroom. For Angelo, the awareness of students' cultural backgrounds and multiracial ethnicities assisted him in developing his conception of culturally responsive pedagogy.

The quotes highlighted here from Suzanne, Lisa, and Angelo were indicative of the comments made by participants overall: the development of conceptions of self and others remained a vital component of enacting culturally responsive pedagogy. Personal experiences and aspects of professional development aided in their enactment of culturally responsive pedagogy in the area of cultural competence.

Celebrating Cultural Differences

The ability to establish positive conceptions of self and others enabled teachers to celebrate the cultural differences of their students. In all, five participants referenced various approaches to celebrating students' cultural differences. Within the subtheme *celebrating cultural differences*, two references fell within the area of academic success and nine references pertained to cultural competence. Participants within this study established a celebratory mindset pertaining to their students' differences and character traits as a way to support academic success and cultural competence. Participants neglected to associate celebrating cultural differences as a means to building bridges to sociopolitical consciousness within their daily instructional practices.

As the school principal, Sandra's conception of celebrating cultural differences equated to celebrating *academic success*, as she believed students were empowered through their cultural strengths. In her viewpoint, culturally relevant pedagogy tapped into the background knowledge of diverse students and, therefore, utilized those strengths to promote academic success. When asked how she defined culturally relevant pedagogy, Sandra commented:

> For me it's always been more about the culture of empowering students to be able to utilize their voice and their beliefs and their experiences and bring those into the classroom and for them to be able to see that in their classroom. Also, to be able to use their gifts and talents. Teachers should know their kids, know their background, and utilize that within the classroom to help kids feel that comfort and feel like it's a place that's like home where they can take risks.

As the school leader, Sandra associated cultural responsiveness with a teacher's ability to leverage students' diverse experiences to cultivate learning. In turn, Sandra believed that getting to know one's students' strengths could be used to foster authentic learning. For her, teachers' efforts to secure an empowering classroom setting, where student voice was valued, allowed teachers to foster resilient risk-taking learners.

In defining culturally responsive pedagogy, participants believed student culture must be represented and celebrated within the classroom, fostering students' *cultural competence*.

In describing her takeaway from the professional development she received in culturally responsive pedagogy, Victoria described using academic success to make students feel celebrated, regardless of their cultural background:

> Being able to celebrate their culture, but I think also academically for many of my students, our curriculum adapts to differing levels, so even kids that are performing low academically feel celebrated, so I'm able to celebrate that. Maybe they haven't had the opportunity to talk about that in other classrooms, which is just celebrating some academics, aside from, oh, they're just a really nice student.

Victoria's conception of celebrating cultural differences was directly tied to celebrating the academic success of her students. She felt celebrating academic success was more substantial than acknowledging positive character traits. For Victoria, it was important that her students felt a deeper level of celebration, tied to academic achievement, rather than being looked at as being well mannered.

In contrast to what Victoria shared, Lisa expanded on the individuality and differences associated with students' cultural backgrounds:

> So I think that it's a student-centered approach. I think that it is all about celebrating the uniqueness and differences of students. I think that it's very important that when using this [culturally responsive] type of teaching, I think that the root of it is that we are not only identifying but nurturing the differences of our students and just celebrating those and being culturally intelligent. And to use those differences, to use that background knowledge, to promote student achievement.

Lisa built her teaching around celebrating student diversity, as well as using her students' differences as a tool for tapping into background knowledge. At its core, Lisa conceptualized her role as a culturally responsive pedagogue as being able to nurture the differences students brought to her classroom. In doing so, she was able to capitalize on students' cultural knowledge to promote academic success.

When asked how she promoted a student's ability to make connections between their culture and the greater school community, Suzanne intentionally built lessons that fostered shared cultural interest among students:

> Having them [students] share stories with each other, having them share their strengths with each other and their cultures and what they do. Then just establishing that interest in showing the kids, "Well, I'm interested in what you do, so that they can maybe show some interest within each other and other peoples' cultures."

Suzanne's comments revealed the priority she placed on creating a foundation for supporting students' cultural competence within her classroom. For her, intentionality in allowing for communal dialogue among students became a valuable tool for teaching.

From a pedagogical standpoint, teachers who commented within this area were intentional in celebrating the cultural differences within their students. Overall, eleven statements were made that spanned academic success and cultural competence; however, no comments were made supporting sociopolitical consciousness regarding celebrating cultural differences.

Student-Centered Differentiated Instruction

Looking across the interviews, there were twenty-one statements from participants that aligned with the subtheme *student-centered differentiated instruction*. Participants within this study attempted to provide learning accommodations and structures as a way to support academic achievement. However, none of the comments made by participants linked providing student-centered differentiated instruction with developing cultural competence or sociopolitical consciousness.

In describing their enactment of culturally relevant pedagogy, six teacher participants in this study elaborated on their attempts to foster *academic success* while providing differentiated instruction and learning modifications. However, in enacting those instructional differentiations, the utilization of students' cultural knowledge and background remained hidden, while teacher instructional strategies focused on equitable outcomes for *all* students.

When asked how she defined culturally responsive pedagogy, Dora reflected on her students' needs based on her own upbringing as a migrant student living in poverty, which allowed her to show empathy and seek an equitable learning experience for her students:

> To me it's just basically thinking about how I grew up and how I learned and my experiences as a kid, using those experiences as a teacher to help kids that might be in the same position that I was growing up. I'm just trying to make things equitable for all kids, any way that I could, and just trying to do what I need to do to make it successful no matter what their background is, what their struggles are, whether they're struggling or whether they're not.

Dora's ability to use a lens of equity remained central to her conscious efforts to differentiate and facilitate learning for all students. She relied on her own childhood experiences to provide a clearer picture of the potential diverse learning needs among her students. Interestingly, Dora remained focused on wanting all students to be successful *despite* their background, rather than leveraging that very background to engage in culturally responsive pedagogy.

When asked how she used a lens of equity when preparing students for academic success, Lisa explained the importance of differentiating instruction based on learning needs. For Lisa, the realization that lesson accommodations meant differing learning outcomes for students became apparent, yet she never explicitly used the term *cultural responsiveness*:

> I think that we as educators just know that it is so important to differentiate based on the students' learning needs and just understanding that the end product may look different. So, when accommodating students and their needs, one knows that at the end of a project or a lesson, it may look different from child

to child. Just making sure that you are setting them up for success and it's not about everyone being equal, but providing that equity so that we can make sure that they have what they need in order to succeed.

Although Lisa recognized the need for equity in intentionally scaffolding lessons, taking students' culture as a direct and explicit tool for learning was absent. Her frame of reference regarding equity shaped the ability to give students the necessary tools to be successful, without taking culture into account. Setting students up for academic success was based on Lisa's ability to target the individual needs of her students, rather than using their cultural knowledge as a tool to facilitate learning.

Similar to Dora, Victoria acknowledged that she often planned and adjusted lessons in order to meet the needs of her diverse students:

> Especially with our curriculum constantly changing, I feel like they give you an idea of where the kids should be, but unfortunately that's not where they are. So my job is to try to find ways to help them at the level that they are currently at, and one way that I've done that is when we do stations. I try to pull my small groups and work with them on a skill that they need before they can move on to the next step.

Like others, Victoria consciously planned instructional time and learning structures based on the differing needs of her students. Based on proficiency levels, small group instruction was provided to enhance students' ability to master skills. For Victoria, this instructional practice was used in order to ensure learning is scaffolded for students to move on to the next competency level.

Suzanne's approach to differentiated instruction was mostly based on students' specific needs, consisting of a variety of accommodations:

> We know not all of our students learn the same. That is not true in education. There's no one size fits all. So I think about what my students are going to need, whether that's additional support, additional time, maybe they need some extension throughout that lesson, whatever it may be. And then I like to have the students kind of give me some feedback on what they would like within a lesson and try to create it that way. I want to hear what they liked from the lesson, what they struggled with, and then when I'm creating my lessons, trying to make sure that I'm hitting those things that are interesting to them and trying to make sure that I'm supporting them [the individual student] and not just the whole class as one.

Suzanne's conception of differentiated instruction was unique in that she concertedly took student feedback into consideration when planning both new and follow-up lessons to meet her students' needs. In making lessons more interesting, she legitimized student voice, which was an integral component of differentiating instruction. For Suzanne, supporting the individual student through various accommodations was intentionally prioritized.

Although intentional instructional practices responsive to student culture remained elusive, teachers' attempts to respond to individual and group needs were readily reported. The quotes highlighted here from Dora, Lisa, Victoria, and Suzanne were indicative of the comments made by participants overall: providing student-centered differentiated instruction was, in their minds, a necessary and commonly practiced component of enacting culturally responsive pedagogy.

Social-Emotional Learning as an Instructional Practice

In addressing childhood trauma, my conversations with practitioners illuminated a third category related to an overemphasis on trauma-informed practices and social-emotional learning. Although creating an environment that is intellectually and emotionally safe remains a focus of culturally responsive pedagogy (Hammond, 2015; Young, 2010), participants were overly dependent on social-emotional learning, which lacked the cultural affirmation and real-time tactics in developing students' cognitive ability in relation to the *Apex of Student Learning* framework.

Overuse of Daily Conferences

Throughout the interviews for this case study, both teacher and site administration participants continually commented on their use of various activities surrounding social-emotional learning as a component of their enactment of culturally relevant pedagogy. As a clear misconception, trauma-informed practices were referenced synonymously with culturally responsive instructional tactics. Sandra, the school principal, spent a concerted amount of time providing teachers with instructional strategies to foster social-emotional well-being inside and outside the classroom. When asked how she supported teachers in developing their skills in their enactment of culturally responsive pedagogy, Sandra commented:

> We came away with how powerful daily conferences could be, and so last year, we did a big focus on having daily conferences with our kids and really giving them a chance to [connect with the teachers], so the approach kind of all encompasses with our social-emotional learning stuff that we're doing. A student who's grown up in trauma, we need to combat that, so bringing in some of those best practices is essential.

Sandra's experiences seeing student trauma led her to implement a schoolwide instructional refocus on social-emotional learning. The perceived learning loss tied to trauma became embedded in the teachers' minds as an instructional focus. This belief prompted Sandra to address social-emotional learning schoolwide to offset student trauma, which unintentionally left a gap in the deep instructional tactics tied to cultural responsiveness.

Due to the instructional focus set forth by the site administration, teachers regularly mentioned the promotion and allocation of instructional time for assessing the social and emotional well-being of students. Although vital to establishing a conducive learning environment, trauma-informed practices are not built on foundations of cultural responsiveness, nor are they indicators of higher levels of proficiency. This misconception was also highlighted as Lisa talked about her efforts to incorporate daily conferences as an element of culturally responsive pedagogy within her classroom:

> So I incorporate daily conferences every single morning, no matter what. So we come in and we take attendance. We have our little morning routine, and then we go to the carpet—it is my number one intention, because it is so important that I know where each child is [emotionally] at the beginning of every new day. So that is my number one thing.

Lisa's viewpoint pinpointed the priority she placed on intentionally keeping a pulse on students' social-emotional well-being. She routinely used daily conferences to set foundational routines of positive discourse and to promote a social-emotionally safe classroom environment. For Lisa, the use of instructional time to gauge the social-emotional well-being of her students was meaningful.

However, culturally responsive teaching calls for more in-depth lessons that use cultural referents to cultivate students' depths of knowledge. Daily conferences used to check in on students' well-being fell far short of the deep curricular connections to students' academic success, cultural competence, and sociopolitical consciousness that are necessary in culturally responsive teaching. If Lisa practiced these deeper learning tactics, they were not mentioned as part of her pedagogical routines.

When asked how she developed her ability to enact culturally responsive pedagogy, Julie referred to using daily conferences to foster trust and relationships:

> I pride myself on relationships with these kids because, in this community, if a kid doesn't trust you, or doesn't have a good relationship with you, they're not going to learn anything. So we do daily conferences and in class we usually incorporate a morning message and then an activity. So that could be something

fun or it could be something educational. Typically, I try to do a game just because the kids love it.

Like Lisa, Julie commented on the importance that daily conferences (a construct of trauma-informed practices) played in building relationships with her students. In fact, Lisa asserted that without trust and a solid relationship with their teacher, students at the school were not going to learn. Within her expertise of enacting culturally responsive pedagogy, Lisa relied on securing a trusting relationship, rather than citing lesson design crafted to leverage students' culture as a conduit to higher levels of learning or rigor.

Similar to Julie, Dora shared that she developed her knowledge of culturally responsive pedagogy using daily conferences, which supported positive teacher-student relationships:

> Daily conferences became something really big in my classroom last year, that I feel really helped build relationships with my kids. The love in our classroom last year was just amazing. And that's where our daily conferences were about just, "How are we feeling today? Do you want to share about it? If you're feeling good [or] you're not feeling good today." [And] "I hope your day gets better" kind of feel and then just we'd also practice on greeting each other, saying hello to each other and stuff.

Dora reflected on her use of daily conferences to evaluate students' social-emotional well-being in real time. Although this practice allowed her to build and maintain relationships with her students, Dora did not embed components that would assist students in embracing or accepting their cultural identities. In addition, she did not mention leveraging her relationships with students in cultivating deeper learning.

In all, participants regularly referred to teaching and addressing social-emotional learning as a central framework for their enactment of culturally responsive pedagogy. All participants elaborated on elements of relationship building along with social-emotional learning within the classroom. Misconceptions over poverty equating to trauma resulted in a shift from the core tenets in culturally responsive pedagogy to social-emotional learning. More importantly, a focus on the actual pedagogical planning, which speaks to moment-to-moment teacher moves, was not mentioned by the practitioners I worked with.

In summary, all participants openly shared their experiences and conceptions in enacting culturally responsive pedagogy both in the classroom and broadly at the school site. As displayed in table 4.1, seven themes emerged, representative of the findings related to culturally relevant pedagogy as described by Ladson-Billings (1995a). Most prominent was the concept *learning partnerships*, which encapsulated the subthemes of building positive relationships, creating a safe learning environment, and student academic growth—all highly dependent on the social-emotional well-being of students.

Participants' comments leaned heavily on ensuring academic success, shying away from constructs of cultural competence and sociopolitical consciousness. In fact, only a single comment was made in the arena of sociopolitical consciousness, which fell within the concept *information processing* under the subtheme *personal connections to learning*.

As mentioned, participants expressed that accountability and pedagogical approaches were linked to students' social-emotional well-being, rather than using their culture as a catalyst to secure depths of knowledge and higher levels of cognition. While participants embraced the concept of culturally responsive pedagogy, their comments indicated a surface-level adoption of the approaches rather than a deep, pedagogical approach that informed their instruction toward the *Apex of Student Learning*, in the ways intended and advocated for by Ladson-Billings and Hammond.

From a practical standpoint, three categories emerged pertaining to challenges or misconceptions in enacting culturally responsive pedagogy. Participants readily spoke about aspects of social-emotional learning in their daily instruction and acknowledged that most of their students experienced trauma and lived in generational poverty. Amber, the guidance specialist, mentioned that the school was inundated with an increase in behavioral issues the previous year, which prompted the implementation of the school's character development curriculum.

Character development, which we'll discuss in later chapters, became a schoolwide priority, which took up time that could have been dedicated to pedagogical development and subsequent coaching. From a relational standpoint, built between students and parents, centered around the philosophy of mutual trust, the administration and teachers have laid the foundation for a school that is poised to become highly proficient in the deep dive of schoolwide culturally responsive practices. In the next chapter, we take a deep dive into the essence of this book: the deep instructional undercurrents of culturally responsive teaching.

Chapter 5

Deep Instructional Undercurrents

"I find the culture of poverty discourse so disturbing because it distorts the concept of culture and absolves social structures—governmental and institutional—of responsibility for the vulnerabilities that poor children regularly face."

—Gloria Ladson-Billings

Below the surface-level elements of culturally responsive pedagogy, such as supporting students' social-emotional well-being, lie the explicit culturally responsive instructional practices aligned to grade-level standards and core curriculum guidelines. At deeper instructional undercurrents, effective practitioners look to deliver instruction "that not only addresses student achievement but also helps students to accept and affirm their cultural identity while developing critical perspectives that challenge inequities that schools (and other institutions) perpetuate" (Ladson-Billings, 1995b, p. 469).

Lesson design capitalizes on cultural strengths and ensures students reach higher levels of knowledge. More importantly, teachers leverage mindfulness practices to ensure students' attention system is at optimal levels for learning. Figure 5.1 illustrates the categories of deep instructional undercurrents—the necessary practices that pertain to the tangible aspects of culturally responsive teaching.

INFORMATION PROCESSING

In allowing students authentic opportunities to process information, culturally responsive teachers connect new content to students' cultures in relevant learning experiences (Hammond, 2015). In the teacher interviews, participants reported making minimal attempts to facilitate this area regarding supporting sociopolitical consciousness (Gutierrez, 2021). Although limited,

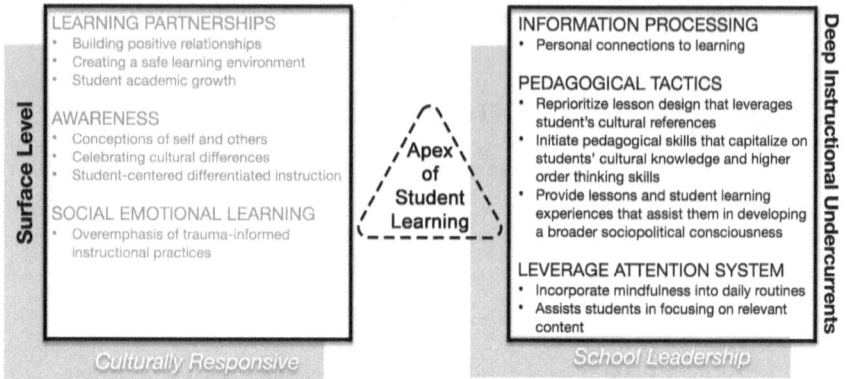

Figure 5.1. The Deep Instructional Undercurrents of Culturally Responsive Teaching
Source: Adapted from Hammond (2015, p. 17). Copyright 2015 by Corwin. Two Arrays of Culturally Responsive Pedagogy adapted from Gutierrez (2021, p. 151).

this area lives in the realm of deep instructional undercurrents as shown in figure 5.1.

Personal Connections to Learning

There were six references pertaining to the theme *information processing*, with *personal connections to learning* being the prevalent subtheme captured through the views of the participants (see chapter 4, table 4.1). In all, two references pertained to academic success and three references were associated with cultural competence. Only a single reference, made by Victoria, related to supporting students' development of sociopolitical consciousness. Overall, the teacher participants recounted their experiences in supporting students to make attempts at sociopolitical consciousness based on intellectual affirmation or behavioral development.

Establishing Personal Connections for Academic Success

When asked about encouraging students to make personal or cultural connections to the curriculum, Lisa felt that the teacher-student relational factor was a precursor to facilitating deeper levels of learning and *academic success*:

> I would make personal connections, just because with kids, relationship building is important and feeling connected is the most important. Once you know your kids and you know their background, then teaching just becomes that much

more deep because it's not just teaching to teach, it's teaching your students that are sitting in your classroom that personal connection. Teaching students to apply their knowledge to any subject matter, just using personal connections that I know about them as examples in different subject areas.

Leveraging the background knowledge of her students was manifested by Lisa's ability to build rapport and positive relationships. For Lisa, relationship building also allowed students to have a sense of connection to the classroom learning environment. In building relationships, she focused on teaching students to apply their background knowledge across the curriculum. In fact, Lisa paralleled teacher-student connectivity to students' self-efficacy for academic success.

Outside World Connections in Support of Cultural Competence

Other participants' comments pertained to their ability to support students in connecting their home experiences (*cultural competence*) to classroom learning. Marisol expressed the value of tapping into background knowledge at appropriate levels of discourse, along with extending partnerships with students' families:

> So when it comes to bringing the outside world into my kindergarten classroom, I just try to have them make connections with what we're learning. So inviting them to share about their home life or what they know. They have these little minds, but everybody has some type of experience, so I always give them a chance to talk about it. So we have these classroom discussions as much as we can at their level.

Marisol noted the value in ensuring that students make personal connections to learning, along with respecting the individuality within her students. Classroom discussions often involved the sharing of student personal experiences, which allowed for a more inclusive and welcoming classroom environment.

Dora's concept of fostering students' development of sociopolitical consciousness revolved around the development of personal character traits. Although classroom curriculum was used, it was dependent on the newly adopted character development framework rather than on grade-level standards:

> So, developing as a person, their character would help out their community. Culturally, it would just be inviting them to share, in daily conferences, to like maybe just right now to especially like their holidays, traditions,

foods—especially, with the Mexicans, the *tamales* and *posole*. And then just the different traditions, because like even with us, we never hung up stockings. We always put out our shoes. I think our kids, at this level, would be probably where they would connect best [with the curriculum], but just trying to do good.

Dora made use of the character development curriculum to attempt to connect students' personal development in the broader sociopolitical construct. In her use of whole-group daily conferences, students were allowed to share cultural experiences and customs.

Some Attempts at Developing Sociopolitical Consciousness through Personal Connections

Overall, participants' understanding of *sociopolitical consciousness* as a means to guide students to engage and question structural inequities that exist in society (Ladson-Billings, 1995a; Young, 2010) was minimal as they looked to promote social and civic engagement with their students. As reflected in figure 5.1, the theme *information processing* houses the subtheme *personal connections to learning*, in which participants commented on the various components of their enactment of culturally responsive pedagogy related to developing sociopolitical consciousness.

Victoria's comment was the single most related to Ladson-Billings's (1995a) concept of sociopolitical consciousness, which she defined as the teacher's ability to assist students in developing "a broader sociopolitical consciousness that allows them to critique the cultural norms, values, and institutions that produce and maintain social inequities" (p. 162). Victoria referenced the use of grade-level curriculum to develop students' concept of societal norms and citizenship. Although she felt the explicit development of sociopolitical consciousness was lacking within her classroom, she made attempts to guide students to make a connection with school rules:

> I don't think I've done anything to promote that [sociopolitical consciousness]. The only thing that would possibly fall into that area would be in our curriculum for the reading benchmark. The first unit is all about our government laws, and we do the story in there about our government and laws. We talked about rules, just because it's a great way for us to introduce the rules in the classroom and what we expect in the classroom and outside of the classroom with our school rules, because one of our things is positive behavior interventions and supports, so I think that's the most I've done as far as that.

Victoria was able to connect grade-level curriculum to students' development of societal norms, rules, and policies. More importantly, she was able to guide students to better understand the concept of behavioral norms both in the classroom and in the broader school community. For Victoria, preparing students for behavioral expectations outside of school allowed students to evaluate their own behavior in relation to the values of society. In her mind, this aligned, at least somewhat, with developing their *sociopolitical consciousness*.

The quotes highlighted here from Victoria, Marisol, Dora, and Lisa were indicative of the comments made by participants overall: making personal connections to learning was a necessary component in their attempts to prepare students to develop a broader sociopolitical consciousness, a process that lived in the realm of deep instructional undercurrents.

PEDAGOGICAL TACTICS

Within this study, both teacher and administrator participants reported that instructional feedback lacked intentionality regarding moving from surface-level to more in-depth frameworks of culturally responsive pedagogy (Gutierrez, 2021). As illustrated in figure 5.1, specific areas of pedagogical tactics must be reprioritized to ensure culturally and linguistically diverse students are learning at higher levels of cognition. As described in chapter 1, learning must not remain stagnant at the acquisition level but gradually progress to the adaptation level of complex thinking (Daggett, 2008).

- *Acquisition:* Students gather and store bits of knowledge and information. Students are primarily expected to remember and understand this knowledge.
- *Application:* Students use acquired knowledge to solve problems, design solutions, and complete work. The highest level of application is to apply knowledge to new and unpredictable situations.
- *Assimilation:* Students extend and refine their acquired knowledge to be able to use that knowledge automatically and routinely to analyze and solve problems and create solutions.
- *Adaptation:* Students have the competence to think in complex ways. Even when confronted with perplexing unknowns, students can use cultural knowledge and skills based off lived experiences to create solutions across disciplines.

As mentioned, when designing sound culturally responsive lessons, practitioners must shift learning progressions to the *adaptation* level at the *Apex of Student Learning*, which remains central when moving toward deep instructional undercurrents (see figure 5.2).

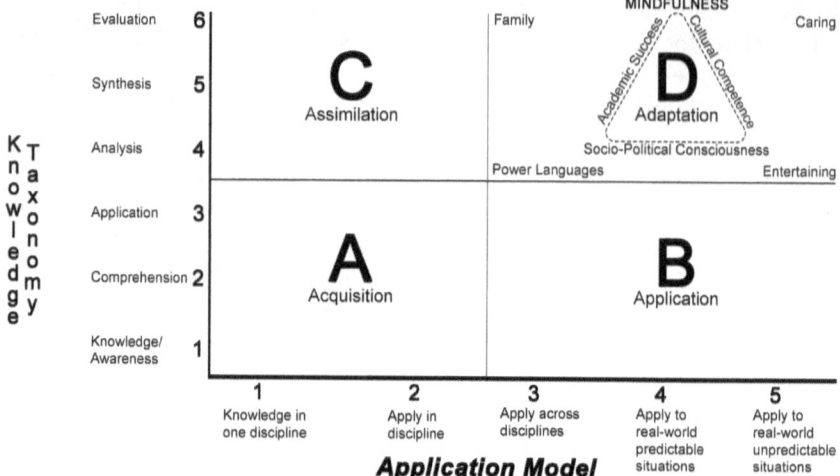

Figure 5.2. The Apex of Student Learning
Source: Adapted from Daggett (2008, p. 42). Copyright 2008 by International Center for Leadership in Education. The *Apex of Student Learning* adapted from Gutierrez (2021, p. 151).

Achievement gaps, proponents of culturally responsive pedagogy argue, are merely information processing gaps, where Black and historically marginalized students are deprived of opportunities to develop key cognitive skills that are culturally meaningful to them (Hammond, 2015; Ladson-Billings, 1995a). In this case, lessons must be written to reflect equal parts cultural experience and curricular content. In other words, teachers must intentionally allow students to culturally relate to the content, thereby guiding them to synthesize and apply information in real-world problem solving.

The beauty of this concept is that higher-level learning expectations are built into the lesson design, thereby holding teachers and principals accountable for academic success.

Culturally Responsive Lesson Design

When designing culturally responsive lessons, *high-impact* teachers increase racially diverse students' interest by allowing them to create self-agency in setting mastery goals tied to academic success, cultural competence, and sociopolitical consciousness (Goodwin et al., 2022; Ladson-Billings, 2009). Embedded guiding questions that ensure mastery goals progress toward the *Apex of Student Learning* must leverage students' cultural strengths, skills, and lived experiences (Daggett, 2008; Hammond, 2015; Knight, 2013; Ladson-Billings, 2009).

Hammond (2015) reports that culturally responsive teachers are also extremely intentional in "expanding students' intellective capacity so that they can engage in deeper, more complex learning" (p. 19). Guiding questions, when infused with engagement activities and checking for understanding, essentially become a critical component of students' ability to process essential information tied to content standards. In real-time classroom instruction, the teacher ensures that engagement activities are tied to students' learning strengths (cultural or linguistic), which creates authentic dialogue and learning outcomes.

Because culturally responsive teachers prioritize this within the design process, exposure to daily higher-level thinking develops *predictable cognitive processing* in the face of unpredictable standardized exams. In other words, well-prepared Black students can make well-prepared responses when presented with the rigors of interim and summative assessments or Smarter Balanced exams. Students' cognitive preparedness is solely based on teachers' intentional planning, critical consciousness, and lens of equity when teaching to content standards.

High-impact culturally responsive teachers intentionally plan for and are critically conscious to include Black students' voices when making real-time judgments, considering alternative progressions, and using instructional decisions that ensure success. Furthermore, *high-impact* teachers "pay special attention to the way in which students define, describe, and interpret phenomena and problem-solving situations" (Hattie, 2012, p. 112). This allows the teacher to be culturally responsive in real time, ensuring that Black students' engagement is linked with facts, skills, and procedures that forge new facets of higher-level thinking. This invisible work involves navigating the balance of learning progressions that might produce an unpredictable outcome and the ability to make rapid professional decisions that yield student success.

Being vulnerable to this deviation is also part of culturally relevant pedagogy, as *high-impact* teachers embrace students' ability to demonstrate mastery through rich teacher-to-student interactions and intellectual thought that spawn learning collusions (Howard, 2001; Knight, 2013; Milner, 2011; Thomas, 2023). Kavanagh et al. (2020) suggest that effective culturally responsive teachers plan for and develop automaticity for the rapid and reasoned moves (invisible behaviors) that connect new content to students' lived experiences and racial identities (Hammond, 2015; Moll et al., 1992). Although highly important, the (visible) behaviors, such as scanning the room, using nonverbal cues, or giving praise, merely serve as surface-level routine-type teacher moves.

As mentioned in earlier chapters, the relational aspects between teacher and student are foundational in securing learning that highly affects students' cognitive abilities, taxing knowledge at the evaluation level as it is applied in real-world unpredictable scenarios (Daggett, 2008). This is meaningful from the standpoint of what is considered the *efficiency of cognition*. In other words, if higher levels of taxonomy tied to cultural strengths are explicitly planned for and connected to students' power languages, then learning at those higher levels is more likely to occur.

Powell and Chambers Cantrell (2021) report that "intentionally connecting instruction to students' backgrounds, experiences, and cultural identities affects their learning; thus, creating a classroom environment that views students' cultural knowledge as an asset and affirms students' racial, ethnic, and gender identities is an important part of culturally responsive instruction" (p. 110). Although prescriptive standards across content areas and grade levels can differ greatly, culturally responsive lesson planning can capitalize on students' cultural knowledge, engagement, and higher-order thinking skills (Marzano et al., 2001; Powell & Chambers Cantrell, 2021; Reeves et al., 2023).

High-impact culturally relevant teachers are intentional in incorporating rigorous guiding questions based on information processing with higher-order skills directly into independent practice (Hammond, 2015; Knight, 2013). When designed properly, culturally responsive teachers' lessons are a gradual-release model, embedded with higher-order guided questions—ultimately leading to independent and more personalized learning.

The following section can be used by practitioners as a blueprint to build sound culturally responsive lessons that can be adapted to any grade level or subject matter. Each section of the template is dissected to provide detailed theory-to-practice concepts, as well as to help keep practitioners focused on essential learning progressions. It's important to keep in mind that culturally relevant pedagogy is based on learning and is not a set of activities or frameworks. It's equally important that teachers become vulnerable to the learning collusions that take place, for an overemphasis on control can negatively impact learning (Adelman & Taylor, 2018).

A fundamental element of delivering a culturally responsive lesson involves the critical awareness of how students of specific cultural groups have thought about, engaged with, and experienced academic success. In other words, teaching to who students are, or the *whole child*, involves a recognition of their realities—issues of race relations, self-belief in intellectual power, and stories of cultural pride (Emdin, 2016). Coupled with this critical awareness, Hammond (2015) and Hattie (2012) describe the intellectually and socially safe classroom climate as one of the more essential factors that secures learning.

The culturally responsive teacher holds an infinite mindset for student learning, innovatively adapts to new ideas amid ambiguity, and accepts multiple measures of learning based on validation, respect, care, and a spirit of familial collaboration (Hammond, 2015; Hattie, 2012; Howard, 2001; Marzano et al., 2001; Sinek, 2019). The following components are vital in shaping the continuum of dependent to more independent learning.

Introduction/Opening

Within the introductory section of lesson design (see figure 5.3), teachers must keep in mind that this is students' first opportunity to culturally connect to the content that is tied to the essential standard. Equally important, the *input* stage of learning lives in this arena. Students' ability to connect to relevant information is crucial at this stage. Therefore, learning targets built from English language arts standards, such as "integrating information presented in different media or formats (e.g., visually or quantitatively) as well as in words to develop a coherent understanding of a topic or issue," must contain metrics toward achieving academic success, cultural competence, and sociopolitical consciousness (Ladson-Billings, 2009).

Because this may be students' first experience engaging with the standard, infusing music, storytelling, or hip-hop can stimulate intellective connectivity, while serving as a motivational factor in setting mastery goals for learning (Goodwin et al., 2022; Hammond, 2015). This *anticipatory set* allows teachers to expose students to the lesson objectives in a fun manner that is tied to cultural strengths and lived experiences. More importantly, in these beginning stages of learning, teacher clarity, or the *why* of learning, is critical, meaning

---

Introduction/Opening

1. Learning Targets (Ladson – Billings, 1995a) tied to content objective. Learning goals must be explicit to:
   - Academic Success
   - Cultural Competence
   - Sociopolitical Consciousness

2. Anticipatory Set (Teacher infuses music, storytelling, hip-hop, video, poetry)
   - Engagement activity connects to students' cultural competence (identities and lived experiences)
   - KWL Activity

3. Build Learning Partnerships – Communal talk tied to students "funds of knowledge," Think-Pair-Share strategy – Students share thoughts around cultural connectivity/communal talk

Focus on Attention (see section: Find Your Flashlight)

4. Facilitate mindfulness exercise at teacher discretion
   (Could be performed before Introduction/Opening)

Figure 5.3. Introduction/Opening
Source: Commissioned by author.

practitioners are explicit with students on learning intentions and success criteria (Reeves et al., 2023).

In culturally responsive teaching, the *why* becomes the main factor, as it is tied to cultural relevance. In the anticipatory set, *high-impact* culturally responsive teachers allow students to engage with the *why* of learning through their own funds of knowledge. One of the foundational activities is the teacher's ability to leverage students' prior knowledge by using a KWL activity—in essence, it's a question–response–feedback exercise (see figure 5.3).

Through this exercise, teachers can immediately build self-confidence through validating students' background knowledge, as it "explicitly retrieves pertinent information from long-term memory and places it into working memory so students are now consciously thinking about it" (Hollingsworth & Ybarra, 2009).

KWL Activity Chart

In this activity, presented as an example, teachers preplan a short film or read a short book that is culturally engaging and tied to the content (see figure 5.4). Before introducing students to a short reading or film, the teacher asks questions about the topic and students respond based on what they already know (What I Know). At this point, it's important to *elicit* students' existing knowledge rather than *testing* knowledge on new content (Hollingsworth & Ybarra,

K-W-L Chart

K (What I Know)	W (What I want to Learn)	L (What I Learned)
		☐ Academic Success ☐ Cultural Competence ☐ Sociopolitical Consciousness

Figure 5.4.   KWL Activity Chart
Source: Commissioned by author.

2009). Furthermore, the teacher introduces the *elaboration* stage of learning here, where the material is based on prior knowledge (Hammond, 2015).

For example, if a lesson on *integrating information presented in different media* pertains to a central figure such as Jackie Robinson, students should not be asked to write down all the statistics they know about him. This may not activate much prior knowledge of a historical figure or the content desired. Rather, students' prior knowledge will be activated by something they know about baseball players and iconic athletes in general. The teacher (and students, depending on the grade level) then writes different responses in the "K" column.

More importantly, the teacher now can use students' *power languages*, immediately creating an environment where students gain confidence and see their funds of knowledge as assets (Moll et al., 1992). Now, the teacher-student or student-to-student interactions can be bolstered by additional engagement activities after the short film, such as Think, Pair, Share (Boyko et al., 2016) in a relational setting of talk and task structures (Hammond, 2015) as the teacher makes notes within the "W" section (What I Want to Learn).

- *Think, Pair, Share:* Used as quick processing activities or checks for understanding. The Think (i.e., brainstorming) step is critical in allowing students to process their understanding in preparation to share.

Within this communal talk activity, students may be allowed to share multiple times. Once the overall lesson reaches the *closure* phase, the teacher returns to the KWL activity (What I Learned) so that learning ("L") is acknowledged from the core tenets of academic success, cultural competence, and sociopolitical consciousness.

The final component, the "L," is key, as instructional leaders perform observations, engage in coteaching, or provide critical feedback. At the end of the introductory phase, teachers can take the opportunity to help students regulate the mind and build attentional capacity (see the section "Leverage Attention System" below) to focus on the upcoming complexities of learning (Jha, 2021).

Direct Teaching

Zaretta Hammond (2015) contests that *high-impact* culturally responsive teachers "have a particular duty to help dependent learners build their intellective capacity so that they are able to do more independent learning and higher order thinking" (p. 89). In the direct teaching phase (see figure 5.5), the teacher immediately models learning tasks that live in the acquisition

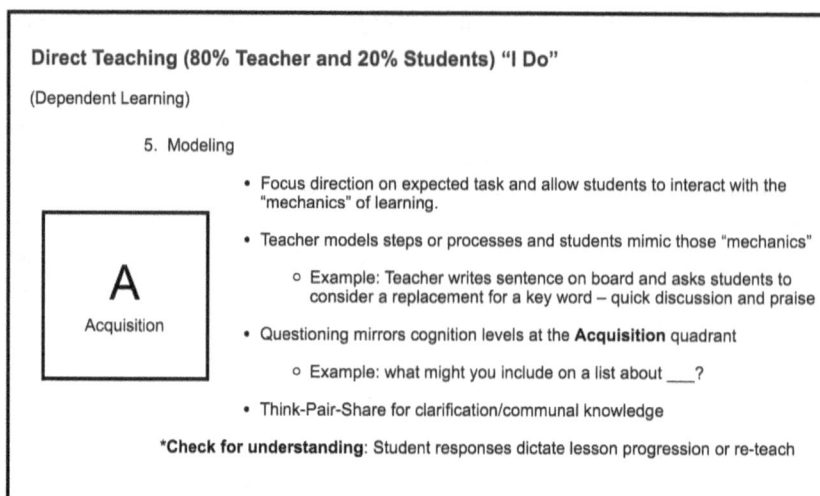

Figure 5.5. Direct Teaching
Source: Commissioned by author.

quadrant, while not abandoning student-to-student interaction. At this part of the lesson, students deliberately find success through an ability to remember or understand an aquired piece of knowledge (Daggett, 2008).

For example, a graphic organizer might be used to categorize *on-the-surface* or literal-level facts, such as who, what, where, or when, that can be pulled directly from the text. Although simplictic in fashion, this phase is critcal as high-impact teachers model the *strategic thinking* used in solving problems (Hollingsworth & Ybarra, 2009). Checking for understanding is equally crucial, for building students' cognitive power sets the stage for deeper learning.

Although the teacher is modeling most of the cognitive tasks or processes, students must be allowed to interact in a collective community (Hammond, 2015; Powell & Chambers Cantrell, 2021), with engagement secured in a *fun* fashion. However, because modeling is so critical, throughout this phase of intensive-explicit instruction, teachers must provide detailed feedback and determine if scaffolding is needed for culturally and linguistically diverse students.

This occurs with sound checking-for-understanding strategies, which verify that students understand the process of strategic thinking (Hollingsworth & Ybarra, 2009) and are engaged within their lens of learning. Within direct teaching, teachers make learning intentions transparent and guide students' progression based on further learning *elaborations* and cultural knowledge tied to mastery goals (Goodwin et al., 2022; Hammond, 2015; Hollingsworth & Ybarra, 2009; Knight, 2013).

Guided Practice One

Within culturally responsive lesson design, it is important to build in two phases of guided practice as it relates to teacher negotiation of learning interactions (see figures 5.6 and 5.7). During this phase, teachers lead discussions on making meaning of the content and decide on whole-group interactions versus small-group isolations. Depending on mastery goals, guided practice is supervised delicately as teaching often requires checking for understanding to ensure learning at the application quadrant is being met. In fact, guided questions throughout checking for understanding should mirror those in the application level of thinking.

For example, teachers might model their own information processing by demonstrating how they might address a quick-write prompt. Then, in assigning a quick-write question to students, the application quadrant can be embedded in the prompt and students' answers can be scaffolded in real time. Guiding questions provide culturally responsive teachers a "firm foundation for thinking about how and where to differentiate learning" (Knight, 2013, p. 33).

Depending on whole-group discussion or small-group interactions, guided practice must ensure that the intended knowledge (in this case, application) is being met. In working step by step with students during this phase, high-impact culturally responsive teachers also begin to incorporate student voices into their declarative knowledge (Hollingsworth & Ybarra, 2009). Graphic organizers help leverage students' cultural strengths, declarative

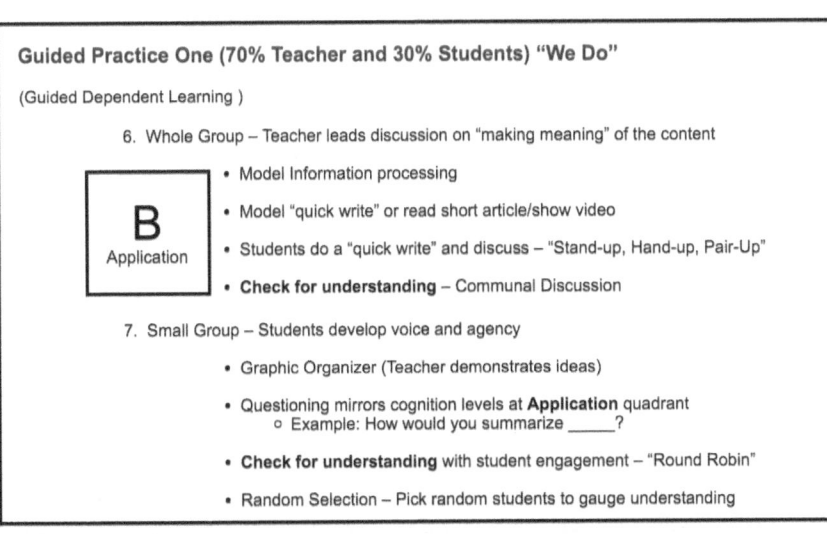

Figure 5.6. Guided Practice One
Source: Commissioned by author.

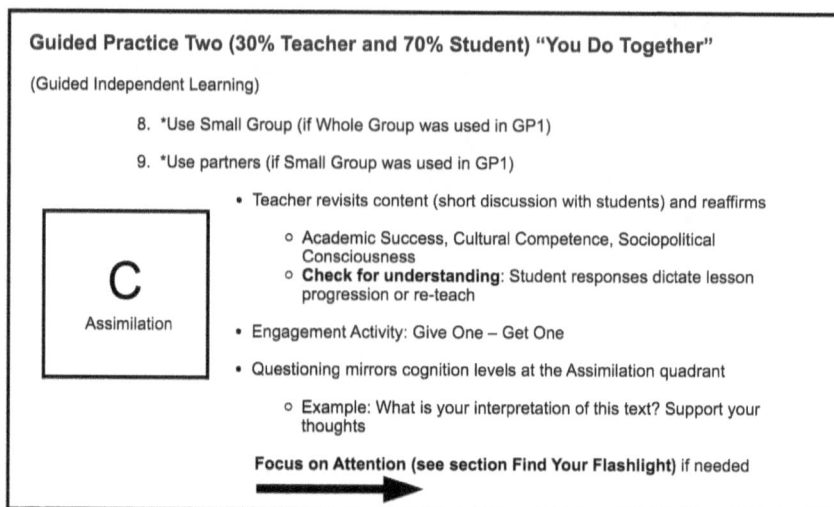

Figure 5.7. Guided Practice Two
Source: Commissioned by author.

knowledge, and learning modalities using tools that combine nonlinguistic modes (symbols and arrows) and linguistic modes (words and phrases) in visually appealing formats (Marzano et al., 2001).

Again, throughout Guided Practice One, high-impact teachers can model making meaning of the content by demonstrating ideas that fulfill the completion of graphic organizer descriptors. Most important to Guided Practice One is the fun and entertaining nature of the planned guided questions tied to students' cultural strengths, coupled with the teacher's ability to make reasoned decisions if scaffolding is needed.

High-impact teachers leverage these learning collusions, in which spontaneous teacher-to-student interactions release new energy through a *caring*, *fun*, and *familial* community (Howard, 2001; Milner, 2011). The lesson cannot progress to Guided Practice Two unless students (especially the most vulnerable) are able to demonstrate mastery of learning targets at the application phase.

Guided Practice Two

Many of the elements of Guided Practice One can be scaffolded within Guided Practice Two; however, the goal within this phase is to shift learning toward student independence. In fact, students begin to showcase the skills and concepts they are learning, while the teacher uses their power language in giving actionable feedback. In Guided Practice Two, culturally responsive teachers have the autonomy to revisit and reaffirm learning as it pertains to students' academic success, cultural competence, and sociopolitical consciousness (Ladson-Billings, 2009).

Planning in this phase also entails students learning cooperatively and completing tasks in small groups or in partner fashion, with the teacher assessing and providing explicit feedback. Because this phase of the lesson is anchored in cooperative learning structures, teachers must have a lens of equity in fostering positive interdependence for Black students. Culturally responsive teachers believe in their students' ability to carry out academic leadership roles such as encourager, timekeeper, and lead questioner, while also giving them an empowering identity (Knight, 2013).

During Guided Practice Two, high-impact culturally responsive teachers shift the cognitive load to students by allowing more personalized approaches to mastery. When students are provided authentic opportunities to process content, they are more likely to make the leap into self-directed learning and free to *apply* knowledge where they feel a sense of belonging within the lesson (Hammond, 2015; Rebora, 2022).

Because student learning agency is based on this gradual release framework of teacher feedback and content scaffolding, socially relevant tasks tied to mastery goals are more likely to be reached independently. Student cooperative grouping must be based on individual interests, cultural strengths, intellectual thought, and the highest probability of engagement (Thomas, 2023). According to Adelman and Taylor (2018), high-impact culturally responsive teachers use three types of groupings to maximize student independent learning:

- *Needs-Based Grouping:* Short-term groupings are established for students with similar learning needs (e.g., to teach or reteach them skills and in keeping with their current interests and capabilities).
- *Interest-Based Grouping:* Students who share a personal interest to pursue an activity usually can be taught to work together well on active learning tasks.
- *Designed-Diversity Grouping:* For some learning goals and objectives, it is desirable to combine sets of students who come from different backgrounds and have different abilities and interests (e.g., to discuss certain sociopolitical topics, foster certain social capabilities, and allow for mutual support in learning).

Based on the assimilation target of learning, "small learning groups are established for cooperative inquiry and learning, concept and skill development, problem solving, motivated practice, peer- and cross-age tutoring, and other forms of activity" (Adelman & Taylor, 2018, p. 23). Student learning partners, or what Emdin (2016) describes as "cosmo-duos," ensure that students (in some cases, those that underperform) support each other academically and allow for spaces of vulnerability.

Ladson-Billings (2009) describes cooperative learning as a means "to prepare students for collective growth and liberation" (p. 65). When culturally and linguistically diverse students experience familial support from peers or their teachers, they are more likely to take ownership and excel toward higher levels of learning (Hammond, 2015; Howard, 2001). Again, the critical component within Guided Practice Two is guiding questions within the assimilation level of higher learning. Learning structures, such as Give One, Get One or Stand Up, Hand Up, Pair Up are critical as they allow learning to become communal, ignite learning collusions, and empower student self-agency (Howard, 2001; Milner, 2011; Rebora, 2022).

In real time, scaffolding depends on the teacher's ability to make rapid and reasoned decisions dictated by questioning and learning progressions targeted toward academic success, cultural competence, and sociopolitical awareness. As students begin to select how they will demonstrate independence of learning mastery, the lesson must not progress until checking for understanding ensures the assimilation quadrant has been met. At the teacher's discretion, Guided Practice Two can loop back to reteach Guided Practice One or revisit elements within direct teaching.

Independent Practice

Within the independent practice phase of culturally responsive lesson design (see figure 5.8), teachers are essentially allowing students the autonomy to explore learning relative to their cultural strengths. Tasks based on maximizing academic success, cultural competence, and sociopolitical consciousness foster independence not isolation. So what exactly does that mean? High-impact culturally responsive teachers, through a lens of equity, plan for the development of intrinsic motivation and students' ownership in learning (Reeves et al., 2023). In this phase, students "apply new knowledge through deliberate practice and real-life application" (Hammond, 2015, p. 126).

However, throughout the independent practice phase, the teacher remains responsible for offering reflections and extensions, ensuring that the adaptation quadrant of high-level learning is reached. Again, guided questions relate to students' ability to investigate and draw conclusions in real-world, unpredictable scenarios. Although this phase leads to student independence, learning discussions and cooperative learning must be tied to adaptational rigor.

The elements of independent practice, or developing students' ability to become *expert* learners, are dependent on motivational factors. Personalized learning has clear connections to culturally responsive teaching, as it

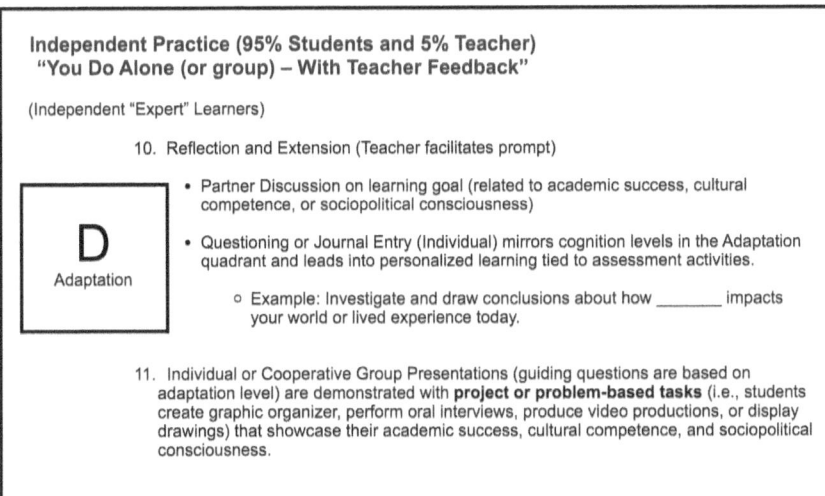

Figure 5.8. Independent Practice
Source: Commissioned by author.

adheres to the learner's perceptions of how well classroom structures match their cultural strengths and lived experiences (Adelman & Taylor, 2018; Ladson-Billings, 2009). As I discovered throughout my research, the most elusive aspect of culturally responsive teaching is developing students' sociopolitical consciousness, specifically in the application phase of learning.

High-impact teachers design learning demonstrations (and assessments) based on multiple means of action. Fisher and Frey (2015) propose project-based learning (PBL) tasks and problem-based tasks, both of which can be infused with progressions that display students' academic success, cultural competence, and sociopolitical consciousness. Here are brief descriptions of both, showcasing students' *application* of learning:

- *Project-Based Learning Tasks:* Engaging students in a highly (culturally) relevant assignment to acquire deep knowledge of a topic. These tasks contain two categories, investigation (deeper inquiry) or performance (publicly displayed end product).
- *Problem-Based Learning Tasks:* Engaging students in problem solving that is not focused on a single answer. These tasks are designed to foster the development of adaptive thinking, which can be tied to sociopolitical (unjust) issues, promoting academic success and cultural competence within the continuum of learning.

By allowing students, whether independently or in small groups, to demonstrate adaptive levels of knowledge through multiple means, personalized learning can be leveraged to secure academic success, cultural competence, and sociopolitical consciousness. With this, "even when confronted with perplexing unknowns, [Black] students are able to use extensive knowledge and skills to create solutions and take actions that further develop their skills and knowledge" (Daggett, 2008, p. 45). When planning and developing culturally responsive lessons, *this* is the key element—the unapologetic stance that all culturally and linguistically diverse students can learn at the highest of levels.

Closure

In order for students to reach the *Apex of Student Learning*, culturally responsive lessons must embed a final checking for understanding that explicitly readdresses the goals of content mastery. Although traditional lesson design does not allow for independent practice without students proving they learned the content, in culturally responsive lessons the teacher holds him- or herself accountable to revisit the KWL chart's last component. Revisiting the "Learned" category is essential in validating student success. The lesson closure in this case becomes a final checking for understanding on what was learned in the realm of academic success, cultural competence, and sociopolitical consciousness (see figure 5.9).

Closure

12. **Check for understanding** – Ticket out of class (teacher checks responses for scaffolding or continuous learning)

- Gallery Walk (students' critique and evaluate others' projects in small groups and offer new solutions)
- Ticket out of class (quick evaluation of learning – verbal response, electronic survey, or quiz)
- Teacher returns to KWL chart to ensure teaching and learning are accountable for student academic success, cultural competence, and sociopolitical consciousness.

Figure 5.9. Closure
Source: Lesson design adapted from V. Alterwitz at T4 Learning.

In many classrooms, teachers neglect to ensure that Black students have secured proficiency before leaving the class. This allows for the necessary scaffolding to be glossed over without truly evaluating student learning. Lesson closure must include quick ticket-out-of-class chats, in which teachers self-evaluate their content delivery based on student responses that might contain misconceptions and simple errors (Hollingsworth & Ybarra, 2009). Essentially, the lesson closure is the final check for understanding and, when overlooked, can become a small barrier, leading to larger gaps in reaching the *Apex of Student Learning*.

Collaborative Engagement Strategies

Foundational to culturally responsive teaching are the collaborative and communal learning structures that facilitate dialogue, build cohesion, and stimulate different opinions among students. These strategies also serve as processing routines—movement, dialogue, and routines that serve memory capacity. At various junctions within the lesson, teachers can incorporate specific engagement strategies to elicit specific skills and secure the elaboration phase of learning (Hammond, 2015; Klem & Connell, 2004). For example, a Gallery Walk provides opportunities for reading, talking, and listening (at high levels of taxonomy) as small groups share the findings from a project-based task. In this structure, students join small groups and visit others' project posters and demonstrate a different solution to share with their peers. The following strategies coincide with the lesson design provided above (Boyko et al., 2016; Kagan & Kagan, 2009).

- *Think, Pair, Share:* The teacher announces a topic (new or previously discussed) and assigns students in pairs. This structure can be used as a quick processing activity or to check for understanding. The "think" or brainstorming time is critical in allowing students to process their understanding in preparation for sharing. This can be used within KWL, as mentioned.
- *Stand Up, Hand Up, Pair Up:* Students stand up and keep one hand raised until they find a partner that is not from their desk group. Paired students give a high five and put their hands down. The teacher poses a guiding question (assimilation level) or gives a task. Students interact by taking turns in sharing their understanding.
- *Round-Robin:* Students take turns (within their desk team) responding orally to a guiding question or sharing their opinions on a sociopolitical issue. There may be multiple responses, and opinions should be affirmed.
- *Give One, Get One:* After students have gathered information on a topic, they are put in pairs or teams to gather information from other students

or teams. As one speaks and "gives" information, the listener adds insights to their original thoughts. Roles reverse, and the other student now "gets" new information from the opposite student.
- *Gallery Walk:* This activity allows individuals or groups to investigate and approach solutions from a new lens by critiquing others' work in a socially safe and celebratory manner. It can be done in various ways; however, it is often done as a culminating activity once students' project-based or problem-based learning is completed. In small groups, students walk around the room (in rotation) and spend one to two minutes viewing and discussing each project poster. The main task is to give praise and suggest an alternative solution before it is time to visit the next poster.
- *Quick Write:* A quick write is a fluency activity in which students write nonstop for two to five minutes on a specific topic that they are studying. The purpose is for students to find out what they know about the topic, to explore new ideas, and to find out what they need to learn about the topic. Once the allotted time is up, students can engage in collaboration and share their writing through activities such as Round-Robin.

As these strategies are used throughout the lesson to promote student engagement, the teacher must promote fun and allow students to experience joy in collaboration. It is also important to use students' responses or dialogue to adapt to new learning in real time. At times, these strategies may pose a pedagogical dilemma, and professional judgments may dictate scaffolding or reteaching. In striving for deeper learning, all instructional moves should center on academic success, cultural competence, and sociopolitical awareness.

LEVERAGE ATTENTION SYSTEM

Students' ability to concentrate during instruction allows them to better engage with instructional content (Fuller et al., 2020). Observable practices within culturally responsive pedagogy reflect students' ability to engage in active, hands-on, meaningful skills-based tasks, including inquiry-based and real-world unpredictable learning (Powell & Chambers Cantrell, 2021). Savvy teachers understand that everything in and around their classroom is competing for students' brain activity—every millisecond of the day.

Incorporating mindfulness strategies at the beginning of and at intervals within lessons equates to higher odds of student's paying attention, which stimulates neuron activity, bringing clarity to learning (Jha, 2021). This matters when looking at the driving force in helping Black and marginalized students reach learning progressions at the adaptation level. Jha explains that "attention biases brain activity and gives a competitive advantage to the information it selects" (p. 33). *Why does this matter for underperforming students?* It's about tapping into students' innate abilities to be receptive, curious, and present in the moment, while simultaneously fighting off external stressors.

Find Your Flashlight

It's important to keep in mind that mindfulness is not an *intervention* as it pertains to the true nature of culturally responsive teaching. In fact, as we saw in previous sections, when mindfullness is used as an *intervention or stand-alone curriculum*, teachers rarely see its true benefits in accentuating learning. The true essence of mindfulness, when properly infused into lesson design, helps regulate the mind and build attentional capacity (Zenner et al., 2014). According to Jha (2021), the fundamental practice is breath awareness, which allows students to pay attention to their attention. With proper training and usable techniques, breath awareness can be done in three- to four-minute intervals within a fifty-five-minute lesson or class period. Figure 5.10 shows an oversimplified version of the three simple steps of a breath awareness exercise.

As mentioned, students' ability to focus on cognitively taxing learning is enhanced when their internal "flashlight" secures attention to the content. Leveraging attention within the actual act of teaching and learning serves as a filter to trauma and other stress agents. This is especially crucial in the *input*

Step 1. Students sit in an upright, stable, and alert posture: Students' hands are rested on top of their laps. Students close their eyes (preferably) or soft gaze. Have students begin to breath and follow their breath. Follow breath at natural pace – do not try and control breath.

Step 2. Tune in to breath and the accompanying sensations: Students may recognize their lungs filling up with air or their stomach moving in and out. Key in on one of those sensations in the body and focus in on the breath as it relates to that sensation for the rest of the exercise. Direct your focus here like a flashlight with a strong and bright beam of light.

Step 3. If you notice your flashlight move – move it back: Once students have chosen the target for their flashlight, paying attention to what happens next is important. When students' thoughts arise that pull their flashlight off target, such as a memory or something on their "to-do" list, they must redirect their flashlight back to their breath. Nothing major, just a gentle mental nudge to move their flashlight back to their breath.

Figure 5.10.   Find Your Flashlight
Source: Adapted from Jha (2021, pp. 117–18). Copyright 2021 by HarperCollins.

phase of information processing. In the input phase, "the brain decides what information it should pay attention to" (Hammond, 2015, p. 125). Think of this as instant enlightenment. Practitioners should keep this in mind, as the pandemic has enticed district leaders to invest in stand-alone mindfulness curriculum and schoolwide mandates based on trauma-informed practices. Not necessarily bad, this focus has nonetheless meant at times that the true art of teaching and culturally responsive lesson design have been given less priority.

Crafting lessons tied to lived experiences and cultural strengths should allow students to engage in conscious experiences that automatically complement attention and working memory. A few minutes of mindfulness can play a significant role in developing students' mental model toward academic preparedness and proficiency.

Although well attuned to social-emotional frameworks, the educators I worked with did not infuse the mindfulness techniques described above in their lesson design. It became evident that an inordinate amount of time was spent on communal talk based on relational connections between teacher and student. In working with site administrators, both felt that shifting toward relationally authentic learning experiences could enhance culturally responsive pedagogy. Although highly supportive in many areas, administrators did not engage in learning partnerships that guided teachers to become skilled in making rapid, reasoned, and in-the-moment instructional decisions (Kavanagh et al., 2020).

This learning partnership (pedagogical reasoning), which will be discussed in later chapters, has the potential to support decision making informed by knowledge about historical and ongoing structures of oppression or students' cultural funds of knowledge within the teaching context (Kavanagh et al., 2020; Moll et al., 1992; Paris & Alim, 2014). Explicit pedagogical reasoning entails connecting the dilemma—in this case, real-time shifts in instructional delivery—with a cultural purpose, engaging in relevant learning, and ensuring instructional goals are connected to the *Apex of Student Learning* (Gutierrez, 2021; Kavanagh et al., 2020).

CULTURALLY RESPONSIVE TEACHING IN ACTION

To understand the critical components we are working toward, we'll look at culturally responsive teaching in practice, focused on deeper levels of personalized learning in one urban elementary school in California. The school, and in particular this individual teacher, has worked to develop racially inclusive learning centered on students' racial identity and linguistic diversity.

***

Walking into Mr. Garcia's classroom, one cannot help but notice a prominent poster hanging in the middle of one wall that reads "TEAM—Together Everyone Achieves More."

In Mr. Garcia's sixth-grade classroom in California's Central Valley, twenty-six racially, ethnically, and linguistically diverse students are excited to continue learning more about Jackie Robinson. After a guided reading exercise, the students were well versed in the trials and tribulations of Robinson's journey in breaking the color barrier in Major League Baseball. Purposefully, Mr. Garcia acknowledged Jackie Robinson as an early powerful figure in the fight for equality. While some teachers might introduce a Black figure such as Jackie at the superficial level, Mr. Garcia elaborated on the social context of Brooklyn at the time, made up of racially segregated boroughs. "Jackie's presence on the team helped shape unity within the greater Brooklyn area, and he was looked at as a role model for many young Black students—just around your age," he explained to the class.

The previous day, students viewed a slideshow of national and local Brooklyn companies that endorsed Jackie's image for advertisement and subsequent profits (Wheaties, Bond Bread, Lindsay Laboratories and Pharmacy, and even Lee's Chinese Restaurant). Today's task is for small groups to research a current African American figure or role model (sports related or not) who shares some of Jackie Robinson's qualities. This prompt is crucial in allowing students to connect cultural competence (lived experiences) and relatable context to curricular goals. Because this portion connects to their current reality, it allows for more ease in orally presenting during the culminating activity. Once a short research session was completed, the class engaged in a Give One, Get One activity, sharing who they chose as a role model and why. Mr. Garcia explained that each group would use a Venn diagram to compare their person to Jackie.

After a ten-minute recess, Mr. Garcia led a discussion on public media, and students learned about systems that deliver information, communication, or entertainment. The class discussed ways peoples' daily lives are affected by the media. As a whole class, students analyzed examples of commercials that promoted goods and services as well as the methods used by marketers and advertisers.

The following point was made: The content of publications, programs, and films *shapes peoples' opinions.*

Two guiding questions were presented to the students:

1. If Jackie Robinson were alive today, what products might he be asked to endorse?

2. Which of his qualities would advertisers want the public to associate with their product?

The students immediately thought of products that would fit the description. Nike, Gatorade, and Apple came to mind almost immediately among student responses. Students felt that the three brands reflected grit, excellence, and a sense of coolness! They felt Jackie had all three of these characteristics that advertisers would love.

Students were then divided into cooperative learning groups. The focus was to analyze one advertisement to gain an understanding of the possible impacts these commercials had on the public. Each group was assigned an iPad with a different commercial. The students were prompted with the following: "What is the message of the advertisement? Who are they targeting? Find the qualities of the product or service." Every member in the group was responsible for making sure that all team members could answer the focus questions. Walking around the room, you could sense excitement and engagement. Conversations and discussions over what each member interpreted were powerful.

Mr. Garcia encouraged the groups by verbally praising their collaborative work as he checked on their progress. The safe and positive learning environment was conducive to reaching learning at the adaptation level. Each student felt that their voice mattered. A Black student by the name of Vince (pseudonym) was taking a lead role in his group. Mr. Garcia was quick to provide praise as he recognized Vince's communication skills and love of the topic. There was an aura of extra motivation in the classroom, tied to a sense of validation in their learning. In walking through the classroom, one could immediately notice the familial vibe among the students.

Using chart paper, each group put together their thoughts and ideas to share with the class. After writing and drawing their analyses, students then presented the advertisement to the class and explained orally what the commercial was trying to get consumers to buy or believe.

Vince raised his hand and bluntly asked, "Can we do the Give One, Get One again?"

Mr. Garcia responded, "We'll do the Gallery Walk, and I'll have you lead the class in the activity."

In small groups, students rotated around the room evaluating others' posters and reflecting on the presentations. Many students shared and explained their thoughts on the unpredictable manner in which consumers would be compelled to buy a product. Also, many of the kids felt as though they could someday be able to create their own advertisements to sell ideas with power, persuasion, and charisma.

When each group was done presenting, Mr. Garcia talked about how the media and Major League Baseball promoted Jackie Robinson as a hero and role model for African American youth. "Media can impact society, but it's up to us to decide, decipher, and analyze information to find connections," explained Mr. Garcia. On this day, students evaluated and applied their voice in making decisions on what attributes inspired them from the past and present.

Mr. Garcia is in Room 42 (Jackie's jersey number), and posters throughout the room depict Black pride, perseverance, and unity. The entire theme of Room 42 is centered on Jackie's powerful attributes, but, more importantly, Mr. Garcia fosters self-belief and intellectual fearlessness in all students. Vocabulary posters, artwork, and mathematical batting averages carry throughout the room. Mr. Garcia has embraced the art of collectiveness, and students from all racial identities are affirmed, continually learning at high levels.

It's important to note that at the end of the 2023 school year, Mr. Garcia's class cohort showed a 35% increase in students meeting or exceeded standard on the ELA SBAC and a 27% increase in mathematics from the 2022 assessment (62% in ELA overall and 46% in mathematics). On district diagnostic exams, all students showed over one and a half year's worth of growth in both ELA and mathematics.

***

This short vignette illustrates how Mr. Garcia's class is grounded in culturally responsive learning progressions, intentionally planned for higher levels of learning. Students' cultural strengths and lived experiences are leveraged along the continuum from dependent learning to and through independent *personalized* learning. Mr. Garcia's ability to shift the cognitive load within the guided practice phases is based on his ability to make rapid and reasoned decisions built on intentional guiding questions. Cooperative learning structures infused with checking for understanding and communal learning accountability are constant within the classroom culture.

Too often, lessons remain stagnant at levels of acquisition, where the gap widens primarily when learning becomes stagnated on a dependent foundation (knowledge and awareness are gained in simplistic, rote fashion). Providing students with short, intentional mindfulness techniques allows for improved focus on learning goals—stretching toward adaptation. Ultimately, in Mr. Garcia's culturally responsive setting, students were able to demonstrate academic success, along with the ability to develop critical awareness and a sociopolitical mindset (Darling-Hammond & Darling-Hammond, 2022; Hammond, 2015).

Mr. Garcia's practices guarantee students are engaged, with the opportunity to bridge the gap when cultural assets are used and cognitive abilities are taxed at the evaluation level and knowledge is applied in real-world unpredictable scenarios (Daggett, 2008; Gay, 2010; Klem & Connell, 2004; Ladson-Billings, 2009). More importantly, he places Black students at the center of learning goals and leadership experiences. In seeing their cultural strengths and investment in learning, Mr. Garcia's lens of equity continually validates Black students' ability to learn at high levels.

Developing instructional intentionality using students' culture as a vehicle for learning is a major key in enacting culturally responsive pedagogy. Implications for a more critical professional development tied to deep instructional undercurrents and teacher inquiry groups were highly evident. In taking theory to practice, educators may reflect on the individual needs of their students and prescribe the necessary components for rich levels of learning as it pertains to the learning outcomes of students. In the following chapters, we'll take a deep look at the macro level and micro levels of culturally responsive leadership that shape the all-inclusive culturally responsive school.

Chapter 6

Culturally Responsive School Leadership

"The paradox of education is precisely this; that as one begins to become conscious, one begins to examine the society in which he is being educated."

—James Baldwin

Over the last three decades, school leadership and the body of work it entails has shifted with equal urgency to that of teacher performance and its effects on student achievement. Yet today's school leader is also accountable for school safety, building infrastructure, community relations, driving buses, providing therapy, and navigating reform efforts dulled out by the district office and state agencies.

All equal, school leadership is second only to classroom instruction among the factors that contribute to what students learn at school (Darling-Hammond & Bransford, 2005; Grissom, et al., 2021; Hattie, 2012). Perhaps the most compelling question is this: *What leadership actions bring about the highest degree of academic performance for Black and historically marginalized students?*

The complexity of culturally responsive pedagogy raises more questions for instructional leadership as teachers look to gain automaticity in making adaptive, effective, and informed instructional decisions. Particularly, what kind of guided experiences do teachers need to become skilled in making rapid, reasoned, and in-the-moment instructional decisions (Kavanagh et al., 2020) based on equitable academic success, cultural competence, and sociopolitical awareness (Ladson-Billings, 2009)?

In order to lead teachers' efforts and secure a more culturally responsive school climate, site principals must develop the skills inherent to culturally responsive leadership. In other words, you cannot expect culturally responsive teaching to permeate or be sustained without a culturally responsive instructional leader. That said, Khalifa et al. (2016) spell out distinct culturally responsive school leadership (CRSL) approaches to improve schoolwide cultural responsiveness for diverse student populations. Figure 6.1 offers an overview of the four major strands of CRSL (Khalifa et al., 2016).

ESTABLISH CRITICAL SELF-AWARENESS SCHOOLWIDE

Self-reflection and cultural critical consciousness are vital to raising educational outcomes for students of color (Gay & Kirkland, 2003; Hammond, 2015; Kohli et al., 2015; Ladson-Billings, 2009; Matschiner, 2022). Like the teachers in their schools, culturally responsive school leaders reflect on their awareness of self and their values, beliefs, and dispositions when it comes to educating socioeconomically disadvantaged and minoritized students (Khalifa et al., 2016).

From a leadership standpoint, the ability to critically self-reflect with a lens for racial equity mirrors the critical piece required of teachers in culturally responsive classrooms (Howard, 2003; Ladson-Billings, 2009; National Equity Project, n.d.), which influences how one responds to the needs of diverse learners (Hammond, 2015). Leadership decisions, like pedagogical reasoning in practice (Kavanagh et al., 2020), must be developed from a contextual belief that all students—and all teachers—can succeed at high levels.

Gooden and Dantley (2012) advocated for educational leadership frameworks that specifically addressed the issue of race within a broader context

Establishes critical self-awareness in the continuous learning of cultural knowledge
Leads professional development opportunities to ensure teachers are continuously culturally responsive
Promotes a culturally responsive and inclusive school environment for minoritized students
Engages students and parents in positive community contexts

Figure 6.1. Culturally Responsive School Leadership Approaches
Source: Adapted from Khalifa et al. (2016). Commissioned by author.

of social justice. The authors outlined five critical areas of such a framework, which included self-reflection as the motivation for transformative action, a prophetic and pragmatic voice, a grounding in a critical theoretical construction, a pragmatic edge that supports praxis, and the inclusion of race language.

At the core of culturally responsive leadership is critical self-reflection that leads to transformative action (Gooden & Dantley, 2012). The development of transformative action includes developing constituents' ability to reflect on and deeply analyze systemic inequities, coupled with awareness of community contexts. In today's educational arena, this transformational component may be the most vital in securing a culturally responsive school.

Kelly and Brandes (2010) asserted that principals' actions premised on equity are better equipped to link beliefs to action, specifically assisting teachers to recognize and analyze social and institutional inequities. More importantly, principals can assist teachers to be more explicit in the inquiry and pedagogical reasoning process (Kavanagh et al., 2020; Kelly & Brandes, 2010). In essence, the culturally responsive school leader uses the context in which they lead to envision and create a new environment or "culture" of learning for students who have been marginalized because of class or race (Khalifa et al., 2016; Leithwood & McAdie, 2007; Leithwood & Sun, 2018).

LEAD CRITICAL PROFESSIONAL DEVELOPMENT AND TEACHER PREPARATION

Collective experimentation through capacity building sets the foundation for engagement in the profession, increased morale, shared leadership, and improved self-efficacy (Kohli et al., 2015; Matschiner, 2022). According to Leithwood and McAdie (2007), teachers' constructive efforts for required tasks strengthened when they were afforded time to plan and collaborate through high-quality professional development. Mayfield (2017) noted that the critical work in disrupting inequitable teaching practices could be mined through concerted professional development that challenges people's assumptions, examines their implicit bias, and links sociopolitical awareness with pedagogical practices.

Thus, engagement in collaborative professional development focused on changes in classroom practice and pedagogical expectations is vital for both principals and teachers. Hynds et al. (2016) examined the impact of teacher professional development in New Zealand for culturally responsive pedagogies, specifically for Indigenous Māori student academic achievement and teacher practices. As in other nations, Hynds et al. (2016) asserted that schools in New Zealand were designed to eliminate cultural differences and assimilate the Māori population, perpetuating deficit thinking as the cultural and linguistic practices of tribal groups were viewed as inferior to those of New Zealand Europeans.

Hynds et al. (2016) noted that sustainable professional development focuses on specific instructional techniques or content areas, involves collaborative rather than individual efforts, is coherent, and uses mastery experiences (Siwatu, 2011). As such, the Te Kotahitanga professional development program, the focus of this study, approached pedagogical change through self-determination and reciprocal teaching and learning while developing and strengthening relationships. Formal, structured, and rotated classroom observations with feedback to individual teachers, along with coaching sessions between teachers and facilitators, were integral to professional development.

Participants were 214 Māori students across twenty-two schools where teachers previously participated in the Te Kotahitanga professional development. To examine the impact of professional development, Hynds et al. (2016) utilized interviews with students, teachers, professional development facilitators, and principals, as well as 336 in-class observations of teaching practices. Overall, their findings revealed that seventy of the seventy-six teachers involved incorporated a relational or interactional focus into their teaching.

Within the study, students expressed that some teachers valued their identity after the professional development; however, some felt that teacher practices remained focused on remedial work, reinforcing negative stereotypes of low achievement. Teachers who made changes valued key changes, such as their own efforts around relationship-based pedagogical practices and taking instruction from traditional static approaches to more interactive and relational methods (Gay, 2010; Hammond, 2015; Ladson-Billings, 2009). However, those with low-implementation classrooms consistently revealed rote "chalk and talk" techniques with little student engagement, a lack of learning objectives or criteria, and low expectations for learning and behavior.

Hynds et al. (2016) advocated for professional development that engages principals and teachers in collaborative inquiry and coconstructive classroom coaching, repositioning teachers as learners from their minoritized students, in much the same way as advocated by Kavanagh et al. (2020). Additionally, Hynds et al. (2016) noted that this collaborative inquiry needs to be sustained systemically, raising awareness of racial justice and positive social transformation built on *asset-based approaches* sustained through education (Paris & Alim, 2014).

To foster success and promote sustainable change, the principal can ensure that the foundational conditions for professional learning, such as examining one's implicit biases, collaborative inquiry, and relationship-based pedagogical practices, are in place, giving the enactment of cultural responsiveness a greater chance within the school.

PROMOTE AN INCLUSIVE SCHOOL CLIMATE

A bevy of academic and social-emotional issues often hampers minoritized students, including low academic achievement, but they do so in a culture that unfairly disciplines them and does not accentuate their intelligence, leading to a distressing environment (Khalifa et al., 2016). As such, the increasing cultural diversity in schools, led by principals with different cultural backgrounds than their students, calls for innovative approaches to school leadership, highlighting culturally responsive practices and competences (Madhlangobe & Gordon, 2012).

In essence, the principal's focus must be to strategically plan, align goals, and build relationships that promote systemic change to create and sustain cultural inclusivity (Khalifa et al., 2016; Madhlangobe & Gordon, 2012; Tran et al., 2020). Invariably, a school's culture consists of the values and norms established by the district as well as personal attitudes, managerial actions, and experiences that leaders and teachers themselves bring to the school site (Smith, 2008). Culturally responsive school leaders help their students and teachers progress intellectually, socially, and emotionally using cultural referents as a bridge for teaching and learning (Gay, 2010; Ladson-Billings, 2009).

Madhlangobe and Gordon (2012) examined and described how a culturally responsive school leader performed her role in a culturally and linguistically diverse high school. The case study was grounded in and developed using principles of Freire's social constructivist framework, which asserts that effective learning evolves through culturally appropriate teaching practices. The case study was also grounded in Burns's transformational leadership model, where continuous inquiry into how the organization functions stimulates creativity and enables the organization to serve its stakeholders more effectively. Participants deemed culturally responsive school leaders in the preliminary study were judged by a panel of experts on equity and social justice.

Effective culturally responsive leadership from Madhlangobe and Gordon's (2012) analysis included themes such as (1) developing a *school vision* that embraces all cultures; (2) combining students' and teachers' lived experiences and school experiences; (3) understanding and using customs, sociocultural experiences, and beliefs and values of students as a basis for helping them to construct new knowledge; and (4) building a school environment that is inclusive and promotes learning.

Providing a caring relationship to teachers and placing an emphasis on encouraging teachers to demonstrate the same care for students was modeled throughout the study. In addition, Madhlangobe and Gordon (2012) found that reducing anxiety among students and teachers was a key relationship-building behavior, as it allows teachers to engage in new pedagogical practices and minority students to participate in social interactions without fear of making mistakes.

Essentially, the authors suggested using positive relationships and trust-building actions, two approaches identified by Klem and Connell (2004), Howard (2001), and Leithwood and Sun (2018) as effective at improving teacher and student performance. Effective culturally responsive leaders celebrate and acknowledge culturally responsive teaching in classroom observations and actively participate in learning activities (Madhlangobe & Gordon, 2012). Providing legitimacy to teachers' instructional behaviors builds trust and self-efficacy (Siwatu, 2011) while fostering commitment to practice new pedagogical approaches for equity.

DEVELOP POSITIVE COMMUNITY RELATIONSHIPS

A fourth tenet of culturally responsive leadership that is vital in promoting inclusivity is the ability of the principal to interact with students, families, and the school community in culturally responsive ways (Khalifa et al., 2016). Much research reveals that principal leadership strongly influences and shapes the impact of educational reform on school and community success (Stein et al., 2016). Moving beyond the schoolyard, principals must advocate for community-based initiatives aimed at creating positive life structures for marginalized students (Khalifa et al., 2016).

As such, educational leaders must have fluidity in their ability to use a variety of skills to improve school reform and community advancement. Green (2018) advocated for principals to foster school reform with direct connection to equitable community improvement—positioning the principal as a social broker in the community, linking school culture to local revitalization initiatives, and connecting curriculum to cultural realities. Drawing on the concept of bridging social capital, Green (2018) asserted that *linking social capital* allows schools to make social connections to institutions of fiscal or political "power" that move beyond one-time reform efforts to sustained social capital.

For example, the principal in Green's study focused on the needs of the community by operationalizing his vision to make the school a community-wide health care provider in partnership with local organizations, filling the need for access to health care. Additionally, the principal developed bridging social capital and strategic partnerships with local chief business officers (CBOs) to support parents comprehensively by offering a variety of adult education classes and childcare.

Finally, Green (2018) found that adopting career academies focused on preparing students to address community realities created transformational teaching and learning opportunities. For example, the school-based community garden allowed students to gain skills from local CBOs, while providing parents fresh produce that was not previously available in the community. This supported the work of DeCuir-Gunby et al. (2010), suggesting that principals create educational experiences for students of color through community service. Shifting the role of leadership to the role of supporter in community efforts is vital in student and parent engagement schoolwide.

Nonclassroom experiences in the instructional context that place value on students' cultural identity and give them a voice in their communities increase academic success (DeCuir-Gunby et al., 2010; Gay, 2010; Moll et al., 1992). By promoting overlapping school-community culturally inclusive contexts, the principal as a social broker has the power to dismantle the deficit stereotypes often faced by students and families of color (Khalifa et al., 2016).

Together, these studies illuminate the role of leadership from a social justice perspective, highlighting the principal's role fostering increased academic achievement for students of color (Griner & Stewart, 2012; Klem & Connell, 2004) while ensuring a sustained praxis with students, teachers, and stakeholders. Gay (2010) asserted that culturally responsive pedagogy is important but that it alone cannot untangle the disparities facing racially, ethnically, or linguistically diverse students.

As we'll see throughout this book, culturally responsive leadership speaks to the *macro level* of principal actions in creating a culturally responsive school. At the *micro level* are the site-based instructional leadership tactics that leaders must demonstrate to further enhance schoolwide culturally responsive pedagogical effectiveness (Gutierrez, 2021).

THE TRANSFORMATIONAL EFFECT

In examining culturally responsive leaders, two distinct themes emerged in the support they were able to provide for their teachers and the community they served (Gutierrez, 2021). Predominantly, the research site's principal and guidance instructional specialist were highly skilled in two areas of culturally responsive leadership based on tenets from Khalifa et al. (2016): (1) *promote an inclusive school climate* and (2) *engage all in positive community contexts*. Interestingly, these two culturally responsive actions intersected seamlessly with two distinct traits of transformational leadership: *idealized influence* and *inspirational motivation* (Northouse, 2019).

Although highly effective from a relational standpoint, support in this area overlooked the in-class instructional guidance necessary for deeper pedagogical refinement—the *micro level*. Therefore, the two traits are categorized within the surface level of culturally responsive leadership (see figure 7.1 in the next chapter). In addition, adherence to a character education curriculum was referenced as a schoolwide effort, taking focus away from culturally responsive pedagogical practices.

Furthermore, both teacher and administrator participants spoke to the need for shifting pedagogical collaboration to a more explicit system of feedback, centered on developing more actionable learning for culturally responsive instruction. In essence, the need for a transformational approach to culturally responsive school leadership, underpinned by instructional leadership, resonated throughout my work with the six teachers and two leaders. Culturally responsive leadership and transformational leadership emerged as tandem traits serving the *macro level* of leadership, setting the tone for the overarching philosophies leading to instructional leadership expertise guided by a lens of equity.

Promote an Inclusive School Climate through Idealized Influence

Followers (in this case, teachers) want to emulate leaders who serve as strong role models, with high moral and ethical behavior traits (Northouse, 2019). In providing a vision and a sense of collectiveness, the leader sets a foundation for new initiatives of equity. In fostering an inclusive school climate, culturally responsive school leaders help their students and teachers progress intellectually, socially, and emotionally using cultural referents as a bridge for teaching and learning (Gay, 2010; Ladson-Billings, 2009).

Throughout the school site, Sandra, the principal, referred to the intentional efforts teachers made to develop a context around building parental partnerships as well as securing a familial culture within the classroom (Gutierrez, 2021; Howard, 2001). The teachers, in mirrored fashion, often spoke of how Sandra modeled expectations in embracing the community:

> She's [the principal's] really big on our community partnerships, where supporters come out and not just give us monetary donations, but actually they give us their time. She's constantly looking for recommendations from staff to hire former students. (Marisol, kindergarten teacher)

Because of the principal's leadership tactics, teachers within my research were better equipped to mitigate the erosion of trust that had historically developed within the school community. The principal spoke of intentional efforts to reimagine community inclusion that had eroded because of prior dismissive experiences. In fact, Marisol commented on the fact that the school principal created an initiative that empowered students through community mentoring partnerships.

All teachers recognized that Sandra constantly sought assistance for the betterment of teachers, students, and parents. Angelo, like most other participants, also commented on the motivational factor in Sandra's efforts to foster an inclusive and collaborative school network:

> My principal supports community involvement by making sure we [teachers] connect with parents and make those little approaches, like, "Hey, let's get involved with our community and become one. Let's build some relationships."

In turn, Angelo recognized the possibilities that outside agencies played in supporting the long-term investment in students' education, setting the stage for ongoing collective improvement. As Northouse (2019) suggests, Sandra motivated Angelo and other participants to create an inclusive classroom environment, which spread to the entire campus, through her idealized influence.

The intersectionality of culturally responsive leadership traits and the four factors of Northouse's transformational leadership are critical in leading a culturally responsive school. Within my research, the school's leader was highly proficient in all four tandems; however, most responses from all participants highlighted the first two leadership tandems in the midrange areas (as seen in figure 6.2). Further leadership development for both novice and veteran principals, however, can inform the progression necessary for the full range of connections (Khalifa et al., 2016; Northouse, 2019).

The implication for practitioners is the importance of becoming familiar with the full gamut of leadership when honing one's skills as a culturally responsive leader. We'll look at the practicality of the last two pairs later in this chapter, as this becomes crucial when developing one's lens of equity at the district level, in the school setting, and in community school implementation. There are also implications for principal preparation programs to expand on these frameworks in order for preservice and in-service leaders to ensure academic success for culturally and linguistically diverse students.

Engage All in Positive Community Context through Inspirational Motivation

When working to engage everyone within their organization, leaders "communicate high expectations to followers, inspiring them through motivation to become committed to and a part of the shared vision" (Northouse, 2019, p. 171). Within this study, Dora (kindergarten teacher) felt inspired by the principal's open lines of communication, which created a shared purpose for the staff. Dora felt the routine messaging from the principal positively inspired both students and faculty members. She also felt the principal's morning

Figure 6.2. Midrange Culturally Responsive Transformational Leadership
Source: Adapted from Northouse (2019, p. 172). Copyright 2019 by Sage. Factors of Culturally Responsive Leadership adapted from Khalifa et al. (2016).

announcements set a positive tone daily. These efforts carried over into the school community among parents:

> She's really good at inspiring people. She inspired me a lot. Just her weekly messages that she sends out every Sunday night that tals about the week ahead, but also reflecting and inspiring at the same time.

Although Dora felt supported by the principal's efforts to engage the community, the connection to explicit classroom instruction did not appear in her responses. Instead, by affording parents opportunities to learn, Dora believed the administration supported her enactment of culturally relevant pedagogy. Through this model, motivational efforts to enact culturally responsive pedagogy suggest improvements in instructional leadership could be made in moving toward deeper instructional undercurrents (see figure 7.2).

Implications from this remind practitioners that a leader's lens of equity (an often unseen data set) can assist in attending to students' academic needs and move past the "feel-good" curriculum frameworks suggested by Ladson-Billings (1995a). Again, leadership preparation programs must assist preservice and in-service school leaders to examine both macro-level and micro-level tactics in supporting equity, social justice, and culturally responsive learning.

REVISITING THE FULL RANGE OF LEADERSHIP

The teachers and site leaders within my research readily referred to leadership traits that focused on inclusion and positive community relationships (as seen in figure 6.2). The full range of this model, however, interconnects intellectual stimulation with establishing critical self-awareness, along with merging individualized consideration and leading professional development (see figure 6.3). In doing so, leaders develop agency across the transformational culturally responsive leadership continuum.

Intellectual Stimulation Coupled with Establishing Critical Self-Awareness

One of the most critical behaviors in advancing culturally responsive pedagogy is a leader's ability to stimulate their followers'—in this case, teachers'—creativity in innovational endeavors, while challenging personal beliefs and biases (Northouse, 2019). Kezar and Eckel (2008) found that intellectual stimulation "relates to the leader's ability to engage people's minds when thinking about a new direction, stimulating creativity and innovation and challenging their own beliefs and values (in this case critical self-awareness), as well as those of the organization" (p. 381).

Simultaneously, the culturally responsive leader models the ability to critically self-reflect with a lens of racial equity, mirroring the same critical piece required of teachers in culturally responsive pedagogy (Howard, 2003; Ladson-Billings, 2009; National Equity Project, n.d.), which influences how a teacher responds to the needs of diverse learners (Hammond, 2015; Kohli, 2009). Within my study, these combined behaviors were limited to a relational component, rather than a deeper dive into innovative instructional practices (micro level) and analyzing one's biases.

Amber, the school's guidance instructional specialist, felt building and sustaining relationships with teachers was foundational to her overall support of their attempts to enact culturally responsive pedagogy. Like the school principal, Amber felt trust and open dialogue involving difficult areas of day-to-day teaching became less cumbersome because of her ability to engage with teachers. From a teaching standpoint, Victoria recognized the administration's collective efforts in relationship building as they pertained to creating

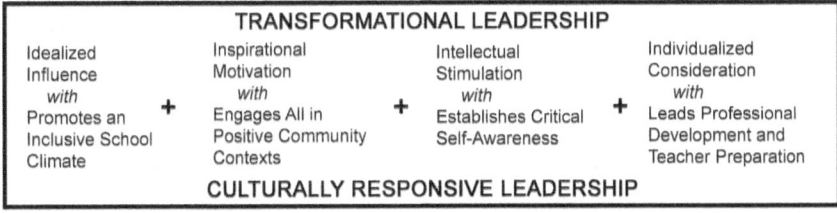

Figure 6.3. Full-Range Culturally Responsive Transformational Leadership
Source: Adapted from Northouse (2019, p. 172). Copyright 2019 by Sage. Factors of Culturally Responsive Leadership adapted from Khalifa et al. (2016).

an inclusive school community for parents. In turn, she prioritized assisting families with educational matters through positive relationships.

Although not directly related to supporting classroom instructional practices, participants acknowledged the commitment made by site administration in sustaining educational partnerships. From a leadership standpoint, the transition to specific actionable guidance in pedagogical reasoning (Kavanagh et al., 2020), innovation, and creativity must be fostered from a practical belief that all students—and all teachers—can succeed at high levels.

Individualized Consideration Centered on Leading Professional Development and Teacher Preparation

Mayfield (2017) noted that the critical work in disrupting inequitable teaching practices can be mined through concerted professional development that challenges people's assumptions, examines their implicit bias, and links sociopolitical awareness with pedagogical practices. The transformative leader acts as a coach and individualized advisor to followers (in this case, teachers), while ensuring that followers develop skills and tactics to their full potential.

Interestingly, Ladson-Billings (2009) describes coaches as those who "believe their students are capable of excellence, but they are comfortable sharing the responsibility to help them achieve it with parents, community members, and the students themselves" (p. 27). To foster success and promote sustainable change, the principal can ensure that the foundational conditions for professional learning, such as examining one's implicit biases, collaborative inquiry, and relationship-based pedagogical practices, are in place, giving the enactment of cultural responsiveness a greater chance within the school.

Within this study, teachers such as Suzanne felt that professional development in culturally responsive pedagogy shaped her realization of key areas, such as self-reflection and its relation to student outcomes. Suzanne felt she became more equipped to see her own potential stereotypes and biases as well as to find teaching techniques that fostered self-worth within her students. Lisa also recalled the ways professional development propelled her to self-reflect on her approach to culturally responsive pedagogical practices.

Based on the professional development provided by the site's leadership, participants felt that their lens of self-awareness aided in their ability to enact culturally responsive pedagogy and to see the value in the diversity of their students.

In moving forward, however, both the principal and the guidance instructional specialist alluded to the need for more personalized instructional feedback and guidance explicitly targeted to the pedagogical tactics of culturally responsive pedagogy. These findings align with more current national surveys (Woo et al., 2022), which found that many teachers do not receive professional development that adequately prepares them to address learning structures tied to cultural and racial inclusivity. If teachers should modify pedagogical practices that respond effectively to diverse learners, the principal's practices and modeling should also look to transform the school into a more culturally responsive learning environment.

Therefore, the culturally responsive school leader must support teachers in promoting a welcoming, inclusive, and accepting school climate (Khalifa et al., 2016; Kohli, 2009), while engaging in authentic critical reflection, helping teachers address issues of diversity and systemic injustices that allow students to reach the *Apex of Student Learning* (Gutierrez, 2021; Hammond, 2015; Woo et al., 2022). More importantly, as we'll explore in the next chapter, the *prepared* leader creates a culturally responsive school with their ability to foster a schoolwide academic culture, to see and combat the origins of inequities, and to learn from crisis.

Chapter 7

The Prepared Leader

A Lens of Equity

"A Just Cause is a specific vision of a future state that does not yet exist; a future state so appealing that people are willing to make sacrifices in order to help advance toward that vision."

—Simon Sinek

The *prepared* leader examines the anatomy of inequities, which often act to inhibit learning and teaching (Darling-Hammond, 2022; James & Wooten, 2022). In doing so, the *prepared* leader makes informed decisions by being critically conscious of the needs of their students and implements mechanisms to combat structural inequities. Like the two arrays of culturally responsive pedagogy, which speak to surface-level versus deep instructional undercurrents, two arrays for culturally responsive leadership emerged (Gutierrez, 2021). First, we'll look at evidence that lived in the emergent or surface level of schoolwide culturally responsive leadership.

As figure 7.1 illustrates, three distinct categories became prevalent within the school site: (1) fostering school- and community-wide inclusivity, (2) positive relationships and reinforcement, and (3) character education. The two arrays of culturally responsive pedagogy, previously discussed in chapter 4, hover parallel to the two arrays of culturally responsive leadership. As already mentioned, the two constructs are dependent on each other.

In the final section of this chapter, I'll illustrate the deep instructional undercurrents of culturally responsive pedagogy and leadership—distilled in tandem fashion. The model will serve a central role in portraying a direct facilitation to learning—the two primary foci in creating a culturally responsive school. In chapter 8, we'll include the third component to the model, in which community schools address barriers to learning and teaching. The *Apex*

126   Chapter 7

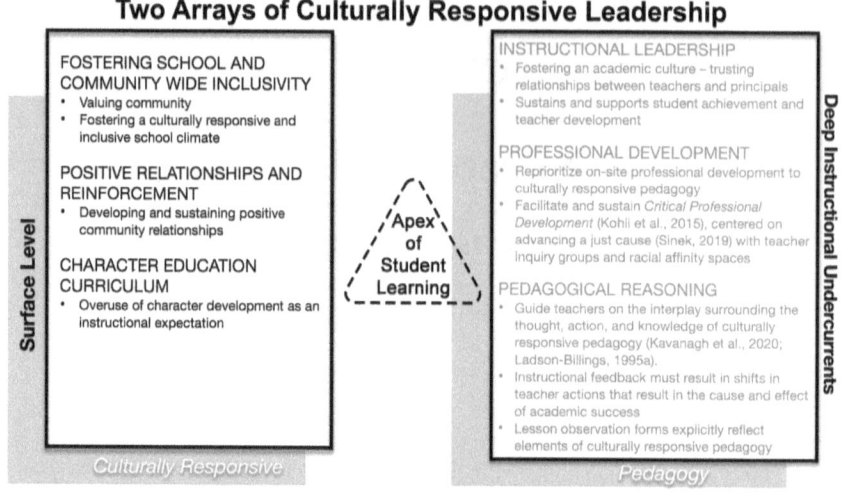

Figure 7.1. Surface-Level Culturally Responsive Leadership
Source: Adapted from Daggett (2008, p. 42). Copyright 2008 by International Center for Leadership in Education. *Apex of Student Learning* adapted from Gutierrez (2021, p. 151). Factors of Culturally Responsive Leadership adapted from Khalifa et al. (2016).

of Student Learning always remains central, which through instruction and leadership guides culturally and linguistically diverse learners to the highest levels of learning.

Fostering school- and community-wide inclusivity and positive relationships and reinforcement was discussed in the previous chapter as they pertained to the transformational effect of culturally responsive leadership. Although highly necessary, especially when implementing community school supports or laying the groundwork for school climate, the connection to in-class pedagogy (micro level) is limited. Similarly, character education, often overused, was misconceived throughout interviews with teachers as a direct component of culturally responsive pedagogy (Gutierrez, 2021).

CHARACTER EDUCATION CURRICULUM

In developing their expertise in the enactment of culturally responsive pedagogy, participants referred to using instructional time to assist students in developing positive character traits. At the beginning of the 2020–2021 school year, during the pandemic, district mandates called for the implementation of a comprehensive character education curriculum. The time commitment to the program and disproportionate suspension data for students of color aided in teachers' misconceptions of its relation to culturally responsive teaching.

Teachers began to conceive of character development as an end goal of culturally responsive pedagogical tactics. Directly correlated was a shift away from instructional feedback that focused on the true tenets of culturally responsive teaching in relation to student academic success.

Targeting Character Development

Teachers and administrators continually referred to using a character development curriculum as a component of culturally responsive pedagogy (Gutierrez, 2021). As with trauma-informed teaching, this was in direct response to how they enacted culturally responsive pedagogy on a day-to-day basis. In essence, instructional priority was placed on reinforcing positive character for diverse students, rather than on leveraging cultural knowledge for deeper levels of learning.

When asked how teachers enacted culturally responsive pedagogy, Amber, the guidance instructional specialist, spoke about teachers' ability to assist students to develop character:

> I think they [teachers] do a really, wonderful job of just character development in their kids as well and understanding that all of their kids are different, but also really promoting that message of being kind, of being a friend to others.

Although Amber's comments referenced teachers' ability to recognize student diversity, she equated culturally responsive learning outcomes with the promotion of positive character traits. For Amber, the ability to promote character development was seen as an effective pedagogical attribute of culturally responsive pedagogy. This misconception was consistent among most of the study participants.

Like most participants, Dora spoke about weekly lessons targeting character development when asked how she saw herself enacting culturally responsive pedagogy in her classroom:

> We just started our positive character curriculum, so that's just how you build strong relationships with each other in the classroom. It's basically like character training. But still, every week we're hitting a different character trait, like last week it was curiosity. That's one example, but like this week it's teamwork. So you can work as a team to help each other and it's always because we want to do our best. It always comes down to doing our best.

In building a conducive learning environment, Dora felt students' academic proficiency could be nurtured through attaining good character rather than being a result of her instructional practices. In fact, Dora relied on the canned character curriculum to facilitate relationship building, which she did not translate into constructs of her routines surrounding culturally responsive pedagogical tactics.

Like Dora, Marisol relied on the use of the positive character curriculum, which supplemented her classroom management:

> Right now, we're doing the character curriculum. I let them know, "Hey, you're on a team; when one team member is not ready, then they're not learning, so let's let them learn." So definitely I build a team kind of environment in my classroom. So we always talk about being respectful, following the rules, implementing outstanding character, acting responsibly and being respectful.

Creating a team environment and holding students accountable for others' ability to learn remained central for Marisol as she articulated her experiences in teaching from a culturally responsive mindset. For Marisol, emphasis on linking learning through character overshadowed incorporating students' cultural knowledge to promote academic success. Although creating a collaborative learning environment is critical, she did not indicate this routine developed as a result of culturally responsive planning or learning structures.

When asked how he created a safe learning environment within the realm of culturally responsive pedagogy, Angelo spoke about character development as a conduit for social capital:

> Yes, I let them know they hold the future within themselves. And that's where I went back to that statement that "I'm a character builder." Good character is what is going to make society function on a positive note. So the more you do to make yourself a positive person, the better off your foundation is for your future. So character is starting now, and if they start building their character at a young age, it starts to become a little bit easier and normal in eighth and ninth grade.

Angelo's statement demonstrated a common misconception among participants, which linked student success to character development. In Angelo's case, he felt good character would provide his students with a better chance at future success. Although he took pride in assisting students in shaping their character, he failed to mention the pedagogical skills necessary to capitalize on students' learning potential and intellectual capacities.

Like Angelo, Suzanne shared instructional decisions that showed developing students' sociopolitical consciousness was hampered by time being dedicated to character development:

> I probably could embed [sociopolitical consciousness] more within our actual curriculum, but I do spend a lot of time on our character development curriculum, so we do spend time on how we can incorporate these different characteristics.

It's just kindness and courage and all these, how can we go and incorporate that in our lives to enhance the lives of ourselves and the lives of others.

Suzanne felt that developing students' sociopolitical consciousness was hampered by the prescribed adherence to character development. Suzanne's instructional time was focused on building positive personal traits rather than allowing students to engage in sociopolitical community efforts.

Sandra, the school principal, shared similar sentiments that instructional time should be a catalyst for academic success. The principal believed academic success involved personal effort and a character trait of perseverance:

> I think while [students are at school] academic success is that they're feeling confident and they're learning, they're able to take risks and aren't afraid to fail. They'll keep at it. They put that time and effort into not just quitting, but that they keep pushing themselves through. To me, academic success is when our kids are able to persevere through personal obstacles, whether it's emotional success to when you can see a kid work through a problem that they have personally and they're able to get through that and their academic success comes with it.

Sandra saw students' self-confidence and willingness to take risks as a cyclical endeavor, which served as a key element for them to persevere toward academic success. In fact, Sandra felt students' academic success revolved around their ability to overcome a perceived emotional constraint or personal problem. For her, the cultivation of personal confidence, which allowed students to be risk takers, equated to their ultimate ability to succeed academically.

As evidenced by participant responses, the adoption of character development curriculum created confusion over pedagogical tactics that ensure cultural responsiveness. Again, stemming from the instructional focus set forth by district leaders, passed on to the principal, teachers regularly mentioned the development of positive character as a component of culturally responsive pedagogy.

Although social and emotional well-being are important, time is of the essence for our Black and underserved student populations when it comes to closing proficiency gaps. Any program that overshadows the core elements of academic success, cultural competence, and sociopolitical awareness must not be overused or perpetuate a deficit mindset based on a lack of individual character traits.

Explicit Instructional Feedback

Like many districts across the nation, lesson observation forms prescribed at the district level did not contain instructional expectations aimed at utilizing students' culture to foster academic success. As a means for instructional feedback, the competencies also lacked key elements targeting the support of cultural competence and sociopolitical consciousness as a means to reach the adaptation level of learning (as shown in figure 7.4). Amber, the school's guidance instructional specialist, alluded to the need for lesson observation forms to become more explicitly geared toward cultural responsiveness, yet she still emphasized social-emotional learning:

> It's [culturally responsive pedagogy] not embedded in there [observation form], and I think that would be a great idea because we want culturally responsive teaching to be embedded in everything that we do. Not ask, "Oh, today we're teaching about—we're learning about empathy, today is. . . ." We want it to just constantly be embedded [into teaching]. The more that you build that culture of this is something we're always looking at, just like we're checking what your objective is, just like we want to know your standard, and we want to see checking for understanding, we also want to be sure we're incorporating culturally relevant pedagogy.

Amber felt the school needed to shift to an explicit focus on culturally relevant pedagogy, with evaluation forms having embedded instructional practices around its core tenets. She felt the current form did not specifically address *teacher moves* within daily instructional practices. However, it is worth noting that when describing her ideal form, Amber did not connect teaching practices with the features of culturally responsive pedagogy but remained committed to elements of social-emotional learning.

In fact, Amber admitted that during on-site professional learning experiences, addressing student trauma had remained a priority over culturally relevant practices:

> I would say that what we do in our faculty meetings once a month is helpful with teachers—also just keeping that open line of communication when we know that a student is going through a traumatic event. Sandra [the principal] does a really great job of pulling that teacher in and supporting that family, so that's always a connection there.

As students' social-emotional well-being remained central from a site administration perspective, Amber's instructional support remained constant from a relational perspective. Her mindset was aimed at providing triage to the students and their families when encountering a traumatic event. For Amber, the realization of the school's need to shift priority to deeper levels of culturally responsive pedagogy became apparent during her participation in this study.

Like Amber, Sandra—who had been the principal for the last seven years—saw the need to shift and reprioritize instructional focus on culturally responsive tactics for the academic success of students:

> As far as my role as a principal goes, I think I could be more intentional about it [culturally relevant pedagogy] and keep it at the forefront. It is one of those things where you do professional development and you build in maybe a new concept like daily conferences, which developed from that. Our teachers still do those, but we didn't continue the conversations and continue the learning with [culturally responsive pedagogy]. We kind of presented it and now I've taken components of that and embraced them as part of our new culture [focused on trauma], so I would say that as I go into next year, I would like to be more intentional with it [culturally responsive pedagogy].

Sandra's comments referenced a need for more commitment to the areas of culturally relevant pedagogy in daily conversations with teachers, along with an intentional ongoing focus schoolwide. As an offshoot from professional learning in culturally responsive pedagogy, trauma-informed practices overshadowed the instructional focus. According to Sandra, an intentional commitment to transitioning back to professional development in cultural responsiveness would be prioritized for the following school year.

Within her enactment of culturally responsive pedagogy, Victoria felt that explicit instructional feedback tied to using students' culture would illuminate improvement efforts, yet she remained fixated on securing a socially and emotionally safe classroom:

> I think explicit feedback would help me because I would like to know where I can improve areas of culturally relevant teaching. I think my main goal, yes, aside from teaching the standards and everything, I want to make sure that my kids feel safe in the classroom, and they don't feel like "I don't want to go to school" because of trauma. So I try my best to make sure that they all understand that this is a safe place for them. So, yes, I would like to know what else I can do to make that stronger.

Although she admitted that feedback centered on cultural responsiveness would assist her, Victoria remained focused on providing a safe environment for learning. Victoria's viewpoint substantiated the importance of redefining the instructional focus toward using students' cultural knowledge for learning proficiencies. As with all participants, her mindset toward instruction remained at the relational level rather than using students' cultural competence or affirming their racial identities as a vehicle for learning.

Lisa also articulated that feedback was specifically tailored to address the needs of all students, not necessarily considering the tenets of culturally responsive pedagogy:

> In my experience, when I reflect on some feedback, it's them [the administrators] talking about how I make sure that I was not just focusing on the gifted students but pulling in those students that we know are struggling or students that are English learners, all types of students. Whether that's cultural, whether that's ethnicity, whether that's academic level, all different areas. They always touch on that, and most of the feedback has been always the question, "Did they reach all students?" So I think that's obviously focused on, just making the activity or the lesson relatable.

Lisa's recollection of instructional feedback was in relation to meeting the needs of "all students," not necessarily using students' culture as a tool for learning, nor the specific pedagogical expectations of cultural responsiveness.

Participant comments revealed that instructional practices at the school site shifted away from culturally responsive pedagogy and moved toward trauma-informed practices and social-emotional learning. In some instances, both teachers and administration referred to their trauma-informed practices as cultural responsiveness. Moreover, participants referred to using instructional time to assist students in developing positive character when discussing cultural responsiveness, which caused further misconceptions, equating character development with culturally responsive pedagogy.

Findings indicated that the school site, as a whole, was on the lower end of the continuum of enacting culturally responsive pedagogy (see chapter 4, figure 4.1), in part because of a switch in the instructional focus toward addressing student trauma and character development. As discussed in chapter 4, the site principal's view on addressing trauma necessitated a schoolwide instructional focus on social-emotional learning.

Due to the instructional focus set by site administration, teachers regularly mentioned promotion and allocation of instructional time for assessing students' social and emotional well-being. Although vital to establishing a conducive learning environment, trauma-informed practices are not built on foundations of cultural responsiveness. This misconception was further illuminated as Lisa talked about her efforts to incorporate daily conferences as an element of culturally responsive pedagogy in her classroom.

Like most of the participants in this study, Lisa commented that instructional time was used to gauge the social-emotional well-being of her students. However, instructional practices that use cultural referents to move toward the *Apex of Student Learning* within culturally responsive teaching were not mentioned (Daggett, 2008; Hammond, 2015; Ladson-Billings, 2009).

The *deep instructional undercurrents*, where themes signify higher levels of culturally responsive pedagogical effectiveness (figure 7.2), are directly supported by a school's instructional leaders. Sandra, the school principal, shared concerns similar to those noted in national studies (Woo et al., 2022), including the need for more commitment to culturally relevant pedagogy in daily conversations with teachers, along with an intentional ongoing focus schoolwide. In terms of pedagogical refinement, trauma-informed practices were a more prevalent instructional focus at the school, revealing a need for intentional and explicit feedback on culturally responsive practices.

To move further along the continuum of high-impact pedagogical practices, teachers must shift their individual and collective focus toward reprioritizing lesson design, initiating pedagogical tactics capitalizing on cultural knowledge, and designing lessons that assist students in developing a broader sociopolitical consciousness. In turn, site administrators must refocus on supporting teachers' efforts by providing explicit feedback tied to the tenets of culturally responsive pedagogy, shift lesson observation forms to reflect cultural responsiveness, and reprioritize critical professional development.

Overall, participants expressed limited exposure to explicit feedback surrounding culturally responsive pedagogy, and site administration felt it could be addressed more intentionally. This suggests a need to transform pedagogical collaboration into a more explicit system of feedback centered on developing actionable learning for culturally responsive pedagogy. Woo et al. (2022) posit that teachers must receive adequate professional learning that prepares them to address diversity and systemic injustices that exist in their classrooms.

In addition, these findings, along with actions described in the next sections, can inform principal preparation programs in developing candidates' expertise in instructional leadership, facilitating critical professional development, and becoming proficient in pedagogical reasoning—a unique cycle of instructional feedback.

CULTURALLY RESPONSIVE INSTRUCTIONAL LEADERSHIP

Wide research has been done to study the effects of both principal leadership and the tenets of culturally responsive pedagogy in isolation (Gay, 2010; Hammond, 2015; Kavanagh et al., 2020; Khalifa et al., 2016; Ladson-Billings, 2009; Leithwood & Sun, 2018). However, the effects of culturally responsive leadership (at the *micro level*) in mediating the enactment of culturally responsive pedagogy remain elusive (Khalifa et al., 2016). Knowledge, which emerges only through creation and re-creation and through invention and reinvention, can foster deeper levels of critical reflection (Freire, 1972).

Thus, little is known about the authentic "praxis," the true critical reflection between school leadership and teachers in order to guide, improve, and sustain the enactment of culturally responsive pedagogy.

Over the past half century, instructional leadership has been gradually accepted into the role set of the principal in education settings throughout the world (Hallinger et al., 2017). Paramount to this role is the principal's ability to give guidance to teachers so that they become skilled in making rapid, reasoned, and in-the-moment instructional decisions (Kavanagh et al., 2020).

Simultaneously, the instructional leader must engage teachers in mutual discussions that address social justice, race relations, and equity in relation to day-to-day instruction (Kohli, 2009). To support teachers in their development of culturally relevant pedagogy, principals must foster an academic culture in which trust becomes the catalyst for supporting teachers in all facets of their professional expertise.

Culturally Conscious Learning Partnerships

In order for teachers to enact culturally responsive pedagogy successfully within their classrooms, they need the guidance and support of culturally responsive site leaders. With equity at the forefront, both teachers and principals work in unison to interrupt a system that either implicitly or explicitly perpetuates achievement gaps for students of color (National Equity Project, n.d.). Culturally responsive leaders facilitate collaborative efforts that analyze current unjust outcomes, requiring a lens of equity at the individual, institutional, and structural levels (Khalifa, 2012; National Equity Project, n.d.).

In doing so, principals and teachers together enlighten the complexity of relationships, values, and pedagogical reasoning (Kavanagh et al., 2020) that result in decisions leading to equitable learning outcomes (National Equity Project, n.d.). At the core of culturally responsive learning partnerships is the analysis of the community relations, academic culture, and conditions that drive teacher effectiveness that equates to student learning (Hammond, 2015; Khalifa, 2012; Leithwood & Sun, 2018).

The enactment of culturally responsive pedagogy is dependent on rich critical discourse and mentorship provided by the principal within the realms of racial equity and academic achievement. As figure 7.2 illustrates, culturally responsive leadership, like culturally responsive pedagogy, carries two arrays of practices. On the right, the *micro-level* components are instructional leadership, professional development, and pedagogical reasoning provided by the school leader. Below you will read about the micro-level tactics of culturally responsive leadership.

Fostering an Academic Culture

The culture of the school, promoted by the principal as school leader, positively influences the working conditions of the teachers (Leithwood & McAdie, 2007). Leadership displayed by the principal is vital as it makes a significant difference in teachers' levels of self-efficacy, commitment, and performance (Kouzes & Posner, 2016; Siwatu, 2011). In times of change, coupled with the complex demands of meeting the needs of culturally and linguistically diverse learners, leaders must refocus improvement efforts on explicit practices that affect student learning (Leithwood & Sun, 2018). The actions and improvement efforts of the principal dictate the potential for instructional effectiveness and positive student learning outcomes.

Part of developing a strong academic culture includes developing a trusting relationship among principals and teachers. According to Dirks and Ferrin (2002), the trust that was needed for an effective academic culture required teachers to recognize two variables in their principals: (1) commitment to decisions made by or goals set by the leader, and (2) belief in the accuracy of information provided by the leader. Trust was found to be frequently associated with the perceived fairness of leadership actions. When teachers feel trusted by their administrators, they are more willing to be vulnerable and, therefore, take instructional risks to benefit diverse learners.

A relationship-based perspective, which involves the degree of respect with which the leader treats their constituents, leads to the development of this kind of trust through a perception of organizational support (Dirks & Ferrin, 2002). Trust and respect are fostered through participative decision making (PDM), as the instructional leader enacts an exchange relationship between teachers and the school in which the teachers believe that the school cares about their well-being. In turn, this belief leads to stronger teacher performance and commitment to the success of the school and its students.

Effective *prepared* leaders recognize the systemic shifts needed for culturally and linguistically diverse learners and create an academic culture that explicitly affects student learning (Leithwood & Sun, 2018). As these studies (Dirks & Ferrin, 2002; Leithwood & Sun, 2018) revealed, both instructional leadership and trust play a significant role in creating and sustaining a rich academic culture, one that supports student achievement and teacher development. More importantly, within an inclusive school culture, culturally responsive leaders play a dynamic role in developing teachers' overall capacity and self-efficacy to deliver the complexities of culturally responsive pedagogy.

Research also suggests that key strategies and practices should center around a coherent vision of accentuating the strengths of culturally and linguistically diverse learners (Darling-Hammond et al., 2021). Common

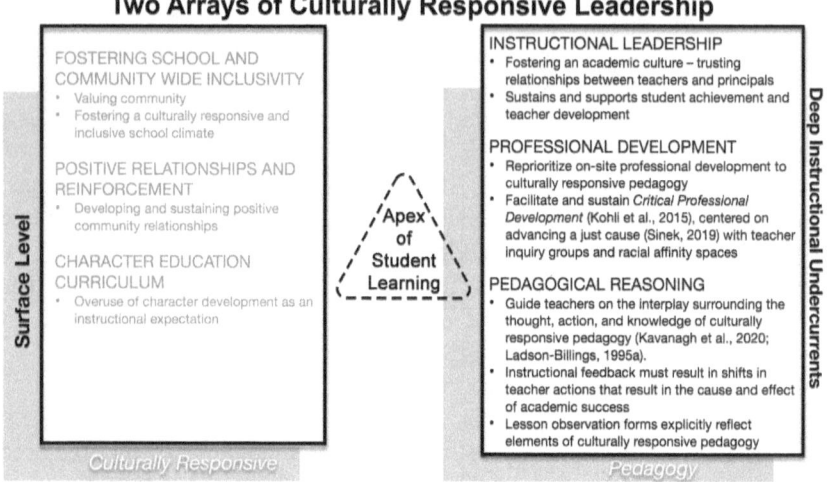

Figure 7.2. Culturally Responsive Leadership—Deep Instructional Undercurrents
Source: *Apex of Student Learning* adapted from Gutierrez (2021, p. 151). Factors of Culturally Responsive Leadership adapted from Khalifa et al. (2016). Instructional Leadership adapted from Kavanagh et al. (2020) and Ladson-Billings (1995a).

high-impact practices are drawn from professional development that provides a framework for

- the unique ways culturally and linguistically diverse students learn and develop within social contexts, intentionally focused on how cultural, social, emotional, and physiological lived experiences shape learning;
- how grade-level content and curriculum goals can intentionally align with real-time instructional tactics that leverage students' cultural strengths; and
- aligning content with pedagogy, then intentionally designing lessons toward higher levels of cognition, as informed by formative and summative assessments and supported by an inclusive learning environment.

To foster success and promote sustainable change, the principal can ensure that the foundational conditions for professional learning, such as examining one's implicit biases, collaborative inquiry, and relationship-based pedagogical practices, are in place. Brown (2004) examined the current state of preparation and professional development models for school leaders, arguing that substantial changes are needed to foster equitable learning practices, such as culturally responsive teaching.

Brown (2004) advocated for educational leadership frameworks that specifically promote and deliver social justice frameworks (Gooden & Dantley, 2012; Kelly & Brandes, 2010), while engaging in problem-based learning, moving beyond knowledge acquisition to mastery experiences in adaptation (Daggett, 2008; Kavanagh et al., 2020; Siwatu, 2011). Brown (2004) noted that effective transformational leaders take responsibility for their learning, share a vision of possibilities for social change, and promote awareness through critical self-reflection, extending the claims made by Gay and Kirkland (2003).

In order to support this understanding, principal preparation programs must promote and incorporate community-based learning and civic responsibility opportunities. Through social action, adult learners become better equipped to make decisions on important sociopolitical issues and to take actions to solve them (Brown, 2004). Given that transformational leadership has a tremendous impact on school culture, teacher self-efficacy, and student engagement (Leithwood & Sun, 2018; Siwatu, 2011), this form of preparation is vital for school inclusivity and cultural responsiveness.

If implementation of culturally responsive teaching is to be sustained, leadership must play a central role in modeling the necessary practical, philosophical, and pedagogical conditions at the site. It's widely accepted that student achievement is impacted by the principal who participates as a learner with staff, one who mentors leadership in others (Fullan & Quinn, 2016; Kavanagh et al., 2020; Khalifa et al., 2016) to foster equitable learning environments. In taking theory to practice, the principal must embody the expected outcomes of professional learning communities or run the risk of creating a disjointed or short-lived set of academic goals.

Sound professional development practices also illuminate the influential efforts of school leadership in building congruent targets for schoolwide goals tied to student achievement. More importantly, building teachers' self-efficacy in developing lessons for deeper learning and enacting complex pedagogical practices are vital in securing a shared language among teachers.

REPRIORITIZE ON-SITE PROFESSIONAL DEVELOPMENT

In building on one of the core tenets of culturally responsive leadership (Khalifa et al., 2016), which calls for leading professional development and teacher preparation, principals must facilitate and build a foundation for critical engagement, increased teacher capacity, and improved teacher self-efficacy (Kohli et al., 2015; Matschiner, 2022). Vital to any initiative focused on instructional practices is time to plan and collaborate through high-quality professional development (Leithwood and McAdie, 2007).

Thus, engagement in collaborative efforts focused on changes toward deep instructional undercurrents in classroom practice and pedagogical expectations must be prioritized over surface-level features. In addition, research suggests that professional development with the greatest impact on student achievement allows teachers to embrace key changes, such as their own efforts around relationship-based pedagogical practices and taking instruction from traditional static approaches to more interactive and relational methods (Gay, 2010; Hammond, 2015; Hynds et al., 2016; Ladson-Billings, 2009). These experiences shape pedagogical change through self-determination, reciprocal teaching and learning, and developing and strengthening relationships.

Professional development that engages principals and teachers in collaborative inquiry and coconstructive classroom coaching, repositioning teachers as learners from their minoritized students (Hynds et al., 2016; Kavanagh et al., 2020), is vital in sustaining actions that translate to deeper learning (Darling-Hammond & Darling-Hammond, 2022).

FACILITATE CRITICAL PROFESSIONAL DEVELOPMENT

Professional development directly addressing race and racism with preservice and in-service teachers remains elusive and relatively unexplored on a wide scale (Matschiner, 2022). In successful culturally responsive schools, the principal drives the implementation and sustainability of this effort. It is widely known that teacher development and self-efficacy require ongoing reflection and mentorship.

Critical to principal preparation programs are the foundational tenets of racial-equity professional development, which equip preservice and in-service leaders to better serve their schools. From a lens-of-equity perspective, racial-equity professional development holds that (1) racism remains evident in school experiences; (2) like all members of society, teachers' racial identities influence their performance through the beliefs they hold and enact; and (3) focused attention is needed to mitigate educational barriers based on race and racism in schools (Kohli, 2009; Matschiner, 2022).

Through critical professional development, collaborative inquiry can be sustained systemically while raising awareness for racial justice and positive social transformation built on *asset-based approaches* (Kohli et al., 2015; Matschiner, 2022; Paris & Alim, 2014). The most compelling question facing educators today is this: How does racial-equity professional development translate to actions in the classroom?

As mentioned, this is certainly a contentious undertaking, as both teachers and leaders report walking a fine line with race-related topics in the confines of school. Woo et al. (2022) reported that educators expressed the need for more support in addressing politicized issues, such as racism, in their schools, including coherent messaging from principals and support from preparatory programs and in-service professional development. As we've seen in America today, these opinions are often split along political and racial lines.

For example, nearly all Black principals (92 percent) reported that they believed systemic racism existed in schools, compared to 61 percent of White principals surveyed (Woo et al., 2022). Because these topics are so essential to the core tenets of culturally responsive teaching, it is imperative that leaders are intentional in preparing teachers to navigate these topics in a safe environment.

Racial Affinity Spaces

An often unexplored and underused aspect of professional development is the relational-strengthening power of racial affinity spaces. Although early practices began outside of schools as racialized groups of teachers sought communal support in dealing with institutional racism (Mosely, 2018), current efforts include White teachers in order to build racial inclusivity (Matschiner, 2022). Racial affinity spaces can drive critical conversations in developing teachers' lenses of equity and commitment to social justice.

As teachers enter this healing-centered and relationally safe space, sharing testimonials of oppression illuminates paths to eradicate both implicit and explicit biases in school. Kohli (2009) posits that in sharing their lived experiences, teachers of color can enlighten their White counterparts on the trauma that racism can cause students. Racial affinity spaces, when properly incorporated into on-site professional development, can support teachers' efforts in supporting the learning of students of color.

One example is shedding light on "discrimination based on factors affiliated with race or ethnicity such as language, religion and culture" (Kohli, 2009, p. 237). Much needed discourse can then take place in using students' culture and funds of knowledge as assets rather than deficits to learning. Along with building racial sensitivity and empathy, these spaces can secure collective expectations surrounding intolerance for racial slurs, dismantling cultural invisibility in the curriculum, and examining the existence of racial hierarchies that work to oppress students of color (Kohli, 2009).

Due to a void in teacher preparation programs using this practice, it's imperative that culturally responsive leaders facilitate these opportunities for in-service teachers. Emerging research, however, indicates that Black teacher residency models are seeing the value of this form of professional development (National Center for Teacher Residencies, n.d.).

Teacher Inquiry Groups

Building on the foundational aspects of racial affinity spaces, teacher inquiry groups provide both White teachers and teachers of color a platform to engage in cooperative dialogue, build unity, and secure a shared sense of curricular leadership (Kohli et al., 2015). The significance of inquiry groups is that they allow teachers to reflect on pedagogical practices in a safe dialogical format. More importantly, in addition to the instructional mentoring provided in pedagogical reasoning, tactics that sustain oppression can be illuminated and dismantled in real time.

Culturally responsive leaders intentionally allot time and immerse themselves within these smaller learning communities. In doing so, site leaders set the tone and foster an inclusive school culture not just for students but for teachers as well. Mason et al. (2021) posit that "leadership impacts school outcomes in a variety of ways including building a productive school climate and facilitating collaboration and professional learning communities among teachers" (p. 8). Current and future Black teachers deserve spaces where racialized experiences and personal identity are valued, and where their voices are included in schoolwide decision making (Mason et al., 2021; Matschiner, 2022).

At the heart of teacher inquiry groups are the collective learnings around cultural competence and sociopolitical awareness that remain elusive in pedagogical outcomes (Gutierrez, 2021). Site leaders and instructional coaches can initiate conversations based on information from student data, classroom observations, and parent panels. Through race-conscious reflection and conversation, effective teacher inquiry groups lead to pedagogical practices that build awareness and affirmation for students of color (Kohli, 2009; Matschiner, 2022).

For teachers and classified employees alike, the learning (sometimes through grieving) is just as important as the curriculum itself. Critical professional development allows educators to engage emotionally and cognitively—lending cohesion for a collective lens of equity. Relational life therapist Terrence Real (2022) argues that when we learn to live relationally and ecologically, all members begin to take responsibility for their thinking. Within these experiences, the individual accepts emotions that spawn from relationally inclusive group settings.

Teachers of color and in particular Black teachers need a safe space to share their realities, and White teachers (80 percent of the teaching force) can learn from the power of race-conscious reflections. Relationally, these spaces can heal experiences from our past, where emotional security allows the implicit to be made explicit (perhaps critical conversations around racial biases). In the process of healing comes a commitment to evolve.

Real (2022) explains that our brains are built to coregulate, allowing for new information to become habitual and, from a racial relationship standpoint, undergo a social restructuring. This ability to evolve, in essence, lends power for both personal and collective transformation. These practices are critical as the racial and cultural enlightenments gained can be transferred into the classroom, where vulnerability surrounding one's performance and ability to accept feedback often drives student success.

PEDAGOGICAL REASONING

At the core of culturally responsive learning partnerships—either between teacher and student or between principal and teacher—is the mediation and analysis of instructional practices that transform teacher effectiveness (Hammond, 2015; Hynds et al., 2016; Leithwood & McAdie, 2007; Leithwood & Sun, 2018). Practice in a complex domain like classroom teaching involves the integration of understanding, skill, relationships, and identity to provide equitable learning structures for students (Grossman et al., 2009).

Looking at the development of novice teachers, Kavanagh et al. (2020) examined to what extent and in what ways teacher educators (TEs) mediated novice teachers' opportunities to engage in pedagogical reasoning. In investigating activities for teacher learning such as rehearsals, learning labs, and mediated fieldwork, the authors asserted that pedagogical reasoning illuminates the interplay between thought, action, identity, and knowledge (invisible behaviors), as opposed to the prioritization of rote and step-by-step approaches to teaching (visible behaviors) such as scanning the room or using nonverbal cues.

To examine the work of the TEs, Kavanagh et al. (2020) drew on the framework of Grossman et al. (2009) for studying teacher education pedagogy, which includes the constructs of representations, decompositions, and approximations of practice. *Representations of practice* refers to how TEs support novice teachers to envision professional practice and may include observing recordings of teaching, modeling, or analyzing lesson plans. *Decomposition of practice* involves breaking down or categorizing the practice of teaching into named parts. With this, novices cultivate refined professional language, allowing them to describe and interpret the art of teaching. Lastly, *approximation of practice* gives novices an opportunity to try out their craft in a safe environment. For example, in low-risk experiments in acting out the practice of teaching, novice teachers receive instructive feedback, experience trial and error, and strengthen their thinking and depth of knowledge (Kavanagh et al., 2020). In culturally responsive schools, the principal takes on the role of TE, essentially becoming the primary source for mentoring teachers' learning in practice.

Because learning is continuously re-created and shared by teachers and students (Ladson-Billings, 2009), pedagogical reasoning has the potential to support decision making informed by historical and ongoing structures of oppression, racial affirmation, or students' cultural funds of knowledge within the teaching context (Kavanagh et al., 2020; Kohli, 2009; Moll et al., 1992; Paris & Alim, 2014). In this case, the *invisible* aspects are teachers' recognition of how racism operates in classroom resources, in environments, and, most importantly, within oneself.

In contrast, the *visible* work is building on this inner knowledge and securing culturally responsive pedagogical practices that humanize students' racial identities and leverage students' intellectual strengths (Kohli, 2009; Ladson-Billings, 2009; Thomas, 2023). Figure 7.3 demonstrates the continuous flow of instructional feedback followed by action—keeping the *Apex of Student Learning* at the center of the pedagogical reasoning universe.

The implications for student learning are twofold, as these actions suggest that (1) developing current teachers' capacity to teach for cultural responsiveness could involve the same approximation of practices used to support novice teachers, and (2) designing and implementing professional development

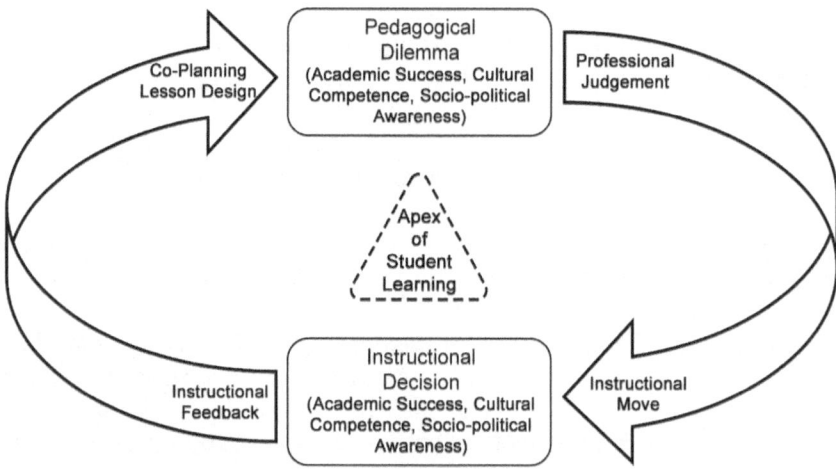

Figure 7.3. Culturally Responsive Pedagogical Reasoning

Source: Adapted from Daggett (2008, p. 42). Copyright 2008 by International Center for Leadership in Education. *Apex of Student Learning* adapted from Gutierrez (2021, p. 151). Pedagogical Reasoning adapted from Kavanagh et al. (2020).

for culturally responsive teaching could focus on pedagogical reasoning through a lens of equity.

With this framework in mind, principals would observe (and record) a culturally responsive lesson and progress through each step with teachers. How a teacher handles a pedagogical dilemma (whom to call on, when to scaffold, when to hold back) is noted in relation to the professional judgments they make. For example, are judgments based on affirming Black students' cultural knowledge in real time, or do powerful student dialogue (teachable moment) and cognitive interactions dictate a shift in utilizing an engagement strategy?

These observable instructional moves ultimately remain focused on fluid decisions based on academic success, cultural competence, and sociopolitical awareness (Kavanagh et al., 2020; Ladson-Billings, 2009). Most importantly, both the teacher and the leader develop automaticity in making invisible moves—the *adaptive* ability to identify dilemmas and then make informed, rapid, and reasoned instructional decisions—while instructional feedback then leads to culturally responsive coteaching efforts.

Lesson observation forms should be explicit in terms of the culturally responsive "look fors" and the expected observable outcomes. Embedding key factors within the lesson observation rubric assists both teachers and instructional leaders in developing common language for subsequent dialogue, feedback, coteaching, and professional development. As illustrated in figure 7.4, a condensed version of ideologies described in this book serves as a concise yet robust template for observable teaching and learning.

All observation forms may look different depending on the district, but some essential elements cannot be overlooked. For example, instructional leaders must be able to note how and when teachers make judgments that stem from a pedagogical dilemma. Then, based on observation, leaders must have space to reflect on and coach the teacher on the instructional moves that led to academic success or perhaps highlight their ability to adapt in real time. In essence, the form must note the visible moves and invisible tactics used as the lesson progresses toward deeper levels of learning.

In addition, site leads and principals may observe the teacher recognizing students' need to refocus and employ a short stint of mindfulness. It is also extremely important for principals to provide feedback on teachers' use of interpersonal efforts, in the manner of leveraging students' power languages. As mentioned, power languages are conduits of attunement, positive interrelation constructs, and cultural affirmation between the teacher and student. In side-by-side fashion, lesson design progression and rubric "look fors" in content, instruction, culture, and interpersonal dynamics (Gutierrez, 2021; Massachusetts Department of Elementary and Secondary Education

Culturally Responsive Lesson Observation

Lesson Design	Lesson "Look Fors"
• Introduction / Opening • Direct Teaching (Acquisition) • Guided Practice One (Application) • Guided Practice Two (Assimilation) • Independent Practice (Adaptation) • Closure	• **Content:** The subject matter that students are engaging with, and the substance of the materials that students are analyzing and discussing. • **Instruction:** Teacher employs deep instructional undercurrents with observable strategies that facilitate learning towards the Apex of Student Learning in a gradual release manner (dependent to independent). • **Culture:** The classroom's culture and learning ecosystem include observable rituals, routines, and structures that promote racial affirmation and inclusion. • **Interpersonal:** The observable authentic relationships and socially safe dynamics between teacher-to-student, as well as positive social and racially affirming relationships between students.

Pedagogical Reasoning:

    Visible Moves (scanning room, non-verbal cues, giving praise) "Routine"

    Invisible Moves (decisions that affirm cultural knowledge) "Adaptive"

Mindfulness Practice:

Use of Power Languages:

Higher Level Thinking Progression Notes:
(Acquisition, Application, Assimilation, Adaptation)

Rubric can be used in each section or individual action (i.e.: Interpersonal – 5)
(5) Always (4) Often (3) Sometimes (2) Occasionally (1) Rarely (0) No Evidence

Figure 7.4. Culturally Responsive Lesson Observation Template
Source: Commissioned by author.

[MDESE], 2021) center teachers' focus on ensuring students reach the *Apex of Student Learning* (adaptation level).

The following are descriptions of the four categorical "look fors" in more detail (MDESE, 2021):

Content: The subject matter that students are engaging with and the substance of the materials that students are analyzing and discussing.

Teacher Actions:

- Encourages students to examine and discuss examples and occurrences of stereotypes and biases—leading to students' ability to examine sociopolitical issues.
- Aligns lessons to common core state standards while delivering content clearly, accurately, and with coherence to objective(s).
- Affirms students' identities while creating materials that showcase sensitive or difficult content in socially just ways and invites students to engage in civic discourse.

Instruction: Teacher employs deep instructional undercurrents with observable strategies that facilitate learning toward the *Apex of Student Learning* in a gradual release manner (dependent to independent).

Teacher Actions:

- Demonstrates depth and breadth of the lesson and contextualizes it in students' racial identities, cultural experiences, and funds of knowledge.
- Instruction ensures *information processing* through fostering personal connections to learning scaffolding, checking for understanding, and adjusting instruction (reteach) when needed.
- Uses *pedagogical tactics* to progress to the adaptive level of learning while leveraging cooperative learning structures throughout (see "Culturally Responsive Lesson Design" in chapter 5).

Culture: The classroom's culture and learning ecosystem include observable rituals, routines, and structures that promote racial affirmation and inclusion.

Teacher Actions:

- Arranges classroom in a manner that promotes collaboration and socially affirms students' identities while celebrating diversity.
- Uses language that is racially affirming and purposeful while connecting content to both communal and independent learning.
- Models positive and reinforcing language to promote students' cultural identity as an asset to learning.

Interpersonal: The observable authentic relationships and socially safe dynamics between teacher and student, as well as positive social and racially affirming relationships between students.

Teacher Actions:

- Uses students' primary and secondary power languages, exhibiting relational presence in creating authentic relationships with individual students (and whole class).
- Seizes the opportunity to leverage students' attention system by incorporating mindfulness into daily routines (four minutes) and is cautious not to overemphasize the practice.
- Shows intolerance for harmful racial comments and sets boundaries that protect all students of color.

As mentioned, all lesson observation templates may differ; however, it's vital that consistent and coherent language is built among the entire team. In addition, rubric markers must be clear and used for the purpose of building positive discourse and necessary adjustments for learning goals. The metrics seen in figure 7.4 are merely a sample for guiding discussions after formal or informal lesson observations. More important, obviously, are the rich conversations based on thorough notes, student engagement, and the teacher's own outlook on their performance.

As the principal offers instructional feedback, a main topic of discussion is the teacher's ability to tailor learning toward the *Apex of Student Learning*. Then, subsequent instructional mediation and dialogue (in a safe environment) drive the coplanning of culturally responsive lessons based on teacher expertise (see "Culturally Responsive Lesson Design" in chapter 5). This in turn facilitates higher levels of learning at more efficient rates. How? When principals help teachers develop automaticity in textural practices, helping them make rapid and reasoned in-the-moment instructional decisions, shifts in awareness for cultural contexts are built in real time.

Most crucial is that teachers are encapsulated with direct support during those *mastery experiences* of culturally responsive teaching, which are the most influential in developing self-efficacy (Siwatu, 2011). The game changer for teachers is that this form of support can also inform "knowledge about historical and ongoing structures of oppression, or students' cultural funds of knowledge and linguistic resources" (Kavanagh et al., 2020, p. 9) within day-to-day instructional practices.

When embedded within the role of the principal, this instructional mentorship secures teacher vulnerability, courage, and personal responsibility to perfect their enactment of culturally responsive teaching. Dialogue surrounding using students' cultural knowledge as assets, affirming racial identities, and promoting learning progressions are interchangeable in the feedback process.

TEACHER SELF-EFFICACY

As teachers become more proficient in their ability to enact culturally responsive strategies through safe conversations with their leaders, instruction becomes more effective and efficient. However, simply assisting teachers in developing the knowledge and skills associated with cultural responsiveness may not accurately predict ongoing classroom practice. Instructional leaders must sustain the impact of self-efficacy and commitment of teachers (Freeman et al., 2022; Hallinger et al., 2017; Hattie, 2012) by providing experiential practice and pedagogical reasoning (Kavanagh et al., 2020).

Therefore, the culturally responsive school leader must first nurture teachers' vulnerability, which revolves around building courage and self-efficacy beliefs (Brown, 2018; Hattie, 2012; Siwatu, 2011) through guided practice and sound feedback. Siwatu (2011) concluded that mastery experiences (executing the practice of culturally responsive teaching) were the most influential aspect to help an individual develop self-efficacy. The most effective items listed included "use the interests of students to make learning meaningful for them" and "develop a personal relationship with students" (Siwatu, 2011, p. 363).

Vicarious experience was found to be valuable as well, as it afforded teachers the opportunity to watch other teachers carry out successful approaches to culturally responsive pedagogy, although firsthand opportunities were still the most effective. The study also illuminated tensions leading to the development of less self-efficacy, such as merely engaging in classroom discussion without procedural and conditional knowledge.

This study illuminates the need for school principals to (1) incorporate activities that build self-efficacy, such as lesson demonstrations with pedagogical reasoning for both preservice and in-service teachers; (b) model development and writing of culturally responsive lessons; and (3) build sustaining efforts to infuse critical professional development that fosters dialogue and reflection concerning racial equity in authentic, firsthand experiences. These findings also suggests that sustained quality instruction that empowers students intellectually, social-emotionally, and politically (Ladson-Billings, 2009) requires that teachers feel efficacious when employing teaching strategies that are culturally responsive (Siwatu, 2011).

Implications for building self-efficacy also pertain to preservice candidates' commitment to pursue the completion of their credentials and ultimately enter the workforce (Freeman et al., 2022). Practice in complex domains like classroom teaching involves the integration of understanding, skill, equitable relationships, and contextual cultural knowledge to accomplish learning structures with students (Grossman et al., 2009; Hammond, 2015; Kavanagh et al., 2020). From a social justice perspective, creating a culturally responsive school requires the leader to foster increased engagement and academic achievement for all students, no matter their racial, cultural, ethnic, or linguistic background.

Rather than creating contention, culturally responsive leaders also build unity and provide shared decision making in the analysis of inequitable outcomes. In creating a culturally responsive school, figure 7.5 serves as a model to merge the *micro-level* tactics of culturally responsive pedagogy (left side) and culturally responsive leadership (right side) along the continuum of deep instructional undercurrents. Both simultaneously enhance the capacity of the other, as actions serve as the *direct facilitators* to learning in guiding culturally diverse students toward the *Apex of Student Learning*.

As we'll see in chapter 9, these direct facilitator actions are critical for building comprehensive Black teacher pipelines and residency models within districts.

In chapter 8, the *secondary* focus, community schools, will cement the framework for overall shifts—a *package framework* for a high-impact culturally responsive school. The analogy used to portray an environment necessary for racially and linguistically diverse students to achieve high levels of learning may surprise you.

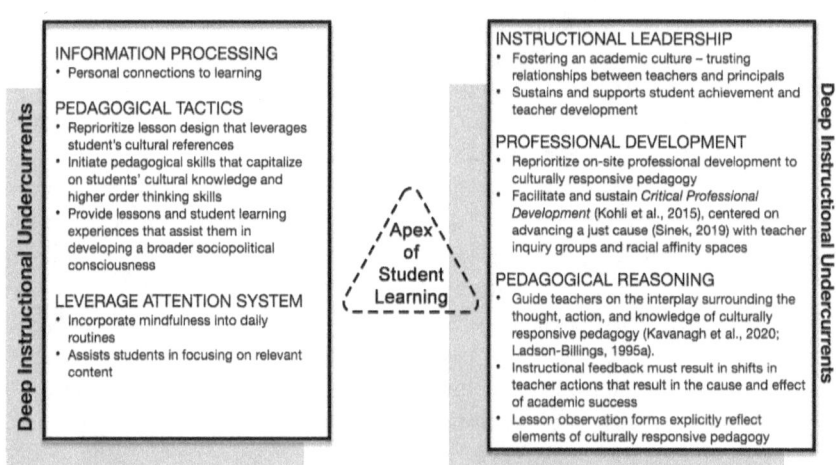

Figure 7.5. Primary Focus: Direct Facilitators to Learning
Source: Commissioned by author.

Chapter 8

The Culturally Responsive School

"A mind that remains in the present atmosphere never undergoes sufficient development to experience what is commonly known as thinking."

—Carter G. Woodson

In 2020, at the height of the pandemic, Adam Silver, the commissioner of the National Basketball Association, stunned the sports world by enacting an isolation zone, creating a *bubble effect* for the league. In essence, the bubble protected the league's players and staff from the threat of the coronavirus, allowing them to thrive without infection, recouping $1.5 billion in estimated lost revenue for the league (James & Wooten, 2022). At its highest level, health experts and business executives around the world witnessed what educators refer to as data-informed decision making.

The data pointed to uncertainty, so the leagues' top executive placed a safe community inside an unsafe environment. The data, in this case individual health and threat of infection, forced the action. During that pivotal moment in league history, Silver was forced to define his *just cause*, based on what he committed to build for the immediate and unpredictable future (James & Wooten, 2022; Sinek, 2019). Silver was the *prepared* leader.

THE BUBBLE EFFECT

Imagine, for a moment, if we created a *bubble effect* for Black and historically marginalized students—this protective encapsulation *is* the culturally responsive school. And the culturally responsive leader, guided with transformational traits, also becomes the *prepared* leader in facilitating this environment.

Through a lens of equity, the *just cause* becomes the school's commitment to protect students from violence. It would protect students from racism and from further trauma by affirming their cultural experiences. It would ensure that Black students' culture, identity, and genius are *visible*, while shattering the institutionalized racial hierarchies so many minority teachers and students have experienced (Kohli, 2009). In this environment, teachers would move past the perceived "race work" and develop Black intellectual thought frameworks within a pro-Black culturally responsive lens (Thomas, 2023). Teachers would not come to teach in this community; the teachers *are* the community (Ladson-Billings, 2009). The *bubble effect* would ensure that Black students' dreams are not betrayed—their dreams would become a reality.

Along with the overarching features mentioned in chapter 2, the high-impact culturally responsive school possesses five keys to students' academic and emotional success: (1) inclusive and culturally responsive leadership, (2) authentic connections to parents and the community, (3) critical professional development for teachers, (4) culturally responsive pedagogical practices that move toward higher levels of learning, and (5) effective instructional guidance and mentoring through pedagogical reasoning (Adelman & Taylor, 2018; David & Cuban, 2010; Gutierrez, 2021; Kavanagh et al., 2020; Kohli, 2009; Ladson-Billings, 2009; Partnership for the Future of Learning, 2019).

In essence, the bubble would be a unified encapsulated educational environment in which students' culture, school, and community *overlap* with commonalities of languages, values, and experiences (Brown, 2022). The culturally responsive school continually improves by using multiple, coherent methods specifically tailored for the students and community it serves. More importantly, in simulating the most effective *turnaround* schools, the coordinated strategies require a unified, comprehensive approach, one that strives for continuous improvement in student achievement (Adelman & Taylor, 2018; David & Cuban, 2010).

When fully implemented, the culturally responsive school *becomes* the culturally responsive community school (CRCS), cementing equitable academic outcomes for Black and historically marginalized students. As shown in figure 8.1, when the primary and secondary components of the culturally responsive framework are fully interconnected, providing the foundation for developing the *whole child*, student success is unlocked through intentional and equitable practices (Adelman & Taylor, 2018; Gutierrez, 2021).

Within this *bubble effect* for building a CRCS, culturally responsive pedagogical practices and culturally responsive leadership serve as the primary focus (or direct facilitators to learning), complemented by a secondary focus—community schools, which address barriers to learning and teaching. When secured through collective efforts of systemic equity, the CRCS is *inviolable* (Emdin, 2023, 5:45)—meaning its safety will never be penetrated by racism, microaggressions, nor racial stereotypes, and Black students' academic performance will thrive beyond expectations.

PRIMARY FOCUS
Direct Facilitation of Learning

- Culturally Responsive Pedagogy: Information Processing, Pedagogical Tactics, Leverage Attention System
- Culturally Responsive Leadership: Instructional Leadership, Professional Development, Pedagogical Reasoning

Deep Instructional Undercurrents

SECONDARY FOCUS: COMMUNITY SCHOOLS
Addressing Barriers to Learning and Teaching
(Combating Childhood Poverty)

Short-Term Solutions

- Supplemental and expansion to the Supplemental Nutrition Assistance Program (SNAP) in the form of food-pantries and community gardens (NASEM, 2019).
- Workforce development and job placement for 18 to 25-year-old community residents (NASEM, 2019).

Long-Term Solutions

Integrated Student Supports
- Medical and Dental Care
- Behavioral and Mental Health Therapy
- College Completion - Adult Education
- Personalized Reading Intervention
- Trauma-Informed Care

Expanded Learning Time
- Linking Learning to Career Exploration (Live or Virtual)
- Real-World Problem Solving Tied to Sociopolitical Issues
- Mentoring and Learning Enrichments (i.e. Music Production)

Active Family and Community Engagement
- Parent Teacher Home Visits
- University Visits / Academic Advising
- Parent Leadership Development

Collaborative Leadership and Practices
- Culturally Responsive Education Lab
- Black Educator Residency
- Comprehensive and Coherent Professional Development

Figure 8.1. Primary and Secondary Culturally Responsive Framework
Source: Commissioned by author.

As we've established throughout this book, the primary focus is to cultivate the deep instructional undercurrents of cultural responsiveness (leadership and teaching), which act as direct facilitators of learning. Through a lens of equity, the *prepared* leader is critically conscious to the needs of their students and builds partnerships to combat structural inequities. In the United States, the anatomy of inequity begins with childhood poverty, with school-aged children experiencing growing rates of homelessness and food insecurity (Darling-Hammond, 2022).

Ample research also points to significant correlations between child poverty and school achievement, lack of career options leading to well-paying employment, and criminal behavior (National Academies of Sciences, Engineering, and Medicine [NASEM], 2019). The implementation of CRCSs shows promise in bridging the gap to higher levels of learning and the coordination of equitable social services. As shown in figure 8.1, CRCS structures must aim to combat childhood poverty with short-term initiatives such as food assistance programs and workforce development and job placement.

Then, in adhering to areas such as integrated student supports and community engagement, grant dollars can positively impact long-term educational outcomes. In fact, recent cost-benefit research suggests every dollar spent on community school efforts and wraparound services equates to a fifteen-dollar return on social and economic benefits for communities (Maier et al., 2017). If culturally responsive schools (with an embedded community school) are in fact *turnaround* schools, then policies for implementation must include factors addressing childhood poverty. Put simply, if placed in a community stricken by poverty, the only goal of the CRCS is to eradicate poverty within that community.

SHORT-TERM SOLUTIONS: COMBATING CHILDHOOD POVERTY

Although many children are resilient in the face of the negative impacts of poverty, the association between poverty and poor outcomes, such as adverse childhood experiences, material hardship, low birth weight, or mental health problems, remains prevalent in our public schools. By some accounts, nearly 9.6 million U.S. children live in families below the poverty line (13 percent), while 7 percent live in deep poverty—a family of four living on fourteen thousand dollars a year (Darling-Hammond, 2022; NASEM, 2019).

Nationally, the child poverty rate for Black children (18 percent) is more than double that of White children (8 percent) and for children living with a single parent (22 percent) than for those living with two parent families (9 percent) (NASEM, 2019). In Fresno County, in California's Central Valley, a staggering 45.3 percent of Black children live below the poverty line, while 13.6 percent White children do (American Community Survey, 2022).

According to NASEM, several factors positively impact childhood poverty in terms of annual government spending, such as the Medicaid program (estimated cost ninety billion dollars) directed at children, the Children's Health Insurance Program (CHIP), and the Child Tax Credit (CTC) (NASEM, 2019). Interestingly, a recent factor in the decline of child poverty is associated with increases in maternal employment. In addition, the Earned Income Tax Credit (EITC) has been successful in supplementing household incomes and thereby encouraging single parents to work. That said, community schools can play a significant role in two distinct areas for families living in poverty—addressing food insecurities and providing workforce development opportunities.

Supplemental Food Assistance

National studies show a growing trend in school-aged children experiencing poor health and educational outcomes stemming from food insufficiencies within the household (Bovell-Ammon et al., 2022). Community schools and the funding embedded can emulate a growing trend within community colleges and state universities in providing food assistance services to the students and families they serve. The correlation between healthy nutrient (food) intake and the critical growth and brain development of school-aged children is one of the most foundational aspects of educational well-being.

Although many families living in poverty may already qualify for the Supplemental Nutrition Assistance Program (SNAP), the community school can provide additional food assistance in partnership with national and local food banks. According to the NASEM (2019), SNAP is "by far the single most important federal program for reducing deep poverty; it is estimated that eliminating SNAP would nearly double the fraction of children in families with incomes below the deep poverty threshold" (p. S-5).

The U.S. Congress introduced the advance CTC payments in response to the pandemic, with research indicating its association with overall reductions in childhood poverty and with improved nutritional intake for children (Bovell-Ammon et al., 2022). However, the expiration of the CTC is associated with an estimated 25 percent increase in food insufficiency (Bovell-Ammon et al., 2022), along with a decrease in spending on items such as shelter, medical care, and educational expenses (Ouellette et al., 2004).

These findings are critical, as they inform the culturally responsive leader of the correlations of food insecurity with immediate and long-term effects on physical health, mental health, and educational achievement. At the local level, community schools can offset the ill effects of food insecurity by leveraging community partnerships. The culturally responsive leader can accomplish this by doing the following:

- Ensuring families without SNAP are connected to a social worker for eligibility applications and assistance
- Working with local nonprofits or national food banks to open a food pantry on-site
- Partnering with university or industry agriculture departments to build on-site greenhouses and gardens for sustainable fruits and vegetables

School districts looking to implement a supplemental food pantry program within their community school can look to national organizations such as the Wonderful Company, Feeding America, and the Salvation Army. At the local level, initiatives such as Food Bank for the Homeland in Omaha, Nebraska; Fresno Metro Ministries in Central California; or Capital Area Food Bank in Washington, DC, are prime examples of potential partnerships.

Workforce Development Packages

Community school grant dollars can be leveraged to build partnerships with local or federal agencies providing basic skills through education and specified training programs. Well-implemented community schools essentially act as a supportive social network that connects young adults to sustainable employment opportunities. Through trusted community partnerships, young adults or young single parents are given direct access to career apprenticeships and workforce development. In overseeing these initiatives, the culturally responsive leader ensures that Black young adults are cared for and that employment is nondiscriminatory.

The significance of work programs is twofold: academic achievement of children living in poverty is often hampered by unstable and unpredictable income, causing further stress and everyday challenges for families (NASEM, 2019), and increases in family income that afford the use of formal childcare (or prekindergarten) are linked to positive school achievement (Duncan et al., 2009).

On a national level, community schools could implement three key components, like organizations such as WorkAdvance, which connects young adults in Tulsa, Oklahoma, to successful career pathways (WorkAdvance, n.d.). The community school's work development division could provide similar options, such as the following:

- Career Launching Strategies: Resume building, interview skills, and soft skills

- Resources and Mentoring: Transportation, clothing for interviews and daily shifts, and tools for specific jobs
- Job Placement: Connections with employment based on skills and talents

In Central California, community schools could partner with local organizations such as Career Nexus, which provides internships and job skills training and looks to prepare a more diverse workforce within the Fresno County region (Career Nexus, n.d.). This agency works collaboratively with prospective employers to create meaningful work-based learning experiences and identifies the shifting skills young adults need to be well prepared for industry. The focus of organizations such as Career Nexus is promising in terms of assisting in the work to build a Black teacher pipeline.

Within the expanded and enrichment learning time framework, community schools can leverage funds to build on existing career technical education (CTE) classes and provide job skill development. Effective culturally responsive schools embed CTE opportunities for Black students to ensure technical skills, knowledge, and professional development are afforded for them to succeed in future careers, such as teaching and leadership. Students who complete a blended academic-career curriculum are more likely to pursue postsecondary education, have a higher GPA in college, and are more likely to complete college (California Department of Education, 2022).

Because the NASEM committee's evidence showed promise in programs like WorkAdvance, it's important for community schools to simulate the positive effects of implementing career and job development initiatives. Implications for both food assistance and workforce development can bridge the gap to combat childhood poverty with the community ecosystem in the short term. Effective implementation of community schools attacks structural inequities, helps close achievement gaps for low-income students, and prepares students for college and career (Partnership for the Future of Learning, 2019).

The two short-term factors (food assistance and workforce development) are virtually untapped in the planning and implementation of current community schools; however, they serve as a unique foundation, complementing the supports of each of the four pillars.

LONG-TERM SOLUTIONS: SERVING THE WHOLE CHILD

The culturally responsive community school is a "place-based strategy where schools partner with students, families, educators, community organizations and agencies and local government to support the whole child and family and to improve teaching and learning" (Maier, 2022, p. 20). As seen in figure 8.1, CRCSs are built on a foundation of culturally responsive teaching and leadership that includes information processing, pedagogical tactics, leveraging the attention system, pedagogical reasoning, and professional development (Gutierrez, 2021).

In addition, the CRCS reflects students' academic needs, cultural assets, and local contexts. On top of the equity that culturally responsive teaching and leadership already provide, the CRCS ensures "access to resources, opportunities, and supports to advance learning and healthy development" (Partnership for the Future of Learning, 2019, p. 4). More importantly, comprehensive studies indicate that well-implemented programs lead to positive results for low-performing students in high-poverty schools (Maier, 2022), bridging the growing achievement gaps faced by students of color (Maier et al., 2017).

Bridging Leadership to Community

High-impact CRCSs are led by effective culturally responsive leaders—the *prepared* leader who works through a lens of equity. As shown in figure 8.2, the four tenets of culturally responsive leadership (Khalifa et al., 2016) lead to powerful advocacy for each community school pillar (Partnership for the Future of Learning, 2019). For example, pillar four, Collaborative Leadership and Supports, is highly dependent on the leader's ability to cultivate *trust*

Figure 8.2. Culturally Responsive Leadership for Community Schools
Source: Commissioned by author.

through promoting an inclusive school and organizational environment (Madhlangobe & Gordon, 2012).

In fact, the arrows indicating *trust, respect, access,* and *impact* in figure 8.2 represent the essential building blocks in forming partnerships with communities and families to support the success of Black students.

Integrated Student Supports

As mentioned earlier, the looming economic inequality students face has long created out-of-school opportunity gaps that CRCSs must look to close. The culturally responsive principal (school leader) models the ability to critically self-reflect through a lens of racial equity, which influences how they respond to and ultimately *impact* positive student outcomes. The hallmark of integrated student support structures are the partnerships with multiagency providers that address barriers to learning.

Along these lines, a prominent feature growing across the nation are school-based health centers. Community agencies that know and understand local contexts provide seamless care to students and families, specifically in addressing students' social-emotional learning, providing trauma-informed counseling, and affording mental health care (Maier et al., 2017).

The significance of these services is twofold: the obvious positive impact reaches the child's social and emotional well-being, while equally important is the time saved from lost instruction stemming from teachers' added responsibilities to mitigate students' needs *during* class time (Partnership for the Future of Learning, 2019). Academic interventions such as personalized literacy instruction during the extended learning time are also essential.

Black students working on their teacher apprenticeships while in high school can serve as mentors in providing this service. Reading and literacy experts from local universities can assist in training high school mentors in reading strategies, such as phonemic awareness, fluency, vocabulary, and comprehension. In addition, university partnerships would also provide college completion classes for parents and young adults enrolled in workforce development programs.

In Alameda County, California, the community school provides a framework for several collaborative structures that are poised to enhance the work surrounding culturally responsive practices. As shown in figure 8.2, community school plans built by the culturally responsive leader can leverage collaborative elements such as "transformative leadership, capacity-building, dynamic partnerships, a shared vision and goals, and the importance of schools' connections to the surrounding community" (Partnership for the

Future of Learning, 2019, p. 36). In taking the whole-child approach in pillar one, the following are elements of a high-quality CRCS (Maier et al., 2017):

- Attention to all aspects of students' academic, social, emotional, physical, psychological, and moral development
- Securing a CRCS climate that is safe and provides all students and families with a trusting relationship

The alignment and development for integrated student supports must be congruent with student achievement data, social and emotional needs, and the coherence of professional development. In essence, both observable and measurable indicators must be aligned with and target the expected outcomes for the school's most vulnerable students.

Expanded and Enrichment Learning Time and Opportunities

In building on pillar one, the effective CRCS leader extends and allows *access* to professional development for expanded learning staff, creating coherence for schoolwide culturally responsive pedagogy that results in positive outcomes for culturally and linguistically diverse students. Mentoring and learning enrichments for students might involve the arts or sciences, depending on student surveys and availability of local agencies specializing in those areas. For example, experiences in music production, ballet, or dissecting organs in a lab could be coupled with mentorship by experts in the field.

In addition, effective CRCSs offer teachers collaborative supports from partnering organizations during the school day by supplementing learning through STEAM (science, technology, engineering, arts, and math) and other teaching internships (Partnership for the Future of Learning, 2019). Mentors are highly significant in that these individuals provide increased access to rich cultural and social expertise while fostering trusting relationships with families and supporting students' academic and social-emotional needs.

In Meriden, Connecticut, for example, community school funding was leveraged to partner with the YMCA and the Boys and Girls Club to offer one hundred minutes of extended learning engagement. Professional development between teachers and community partners centered on the review of curriculum, alignment of the school's instructional goals with enrichment supports, and allowing community partners to engage in professional learning communities (Partnership for the Future of Learning, 2019).

Culturally responsive professional learning in this manner brings community voice into the fold in terms of learning goals, as Ladson-Billings (1995a) suggests students must be guided to develop a critical lens to see the inequities around them and be empowered to present solutions to sociopolitical issues. According to the Partnership for the Future of Learning (2019) and Maier et al. (2017), high-impact implementation for pillar two must involve professional development that integrates regular-day and extended-day programming, thereby allowing teachers and community school staff to develop coherent practices and shared language.

The CRCS leader ensures that these collaborative relationships revolve around a lens of equity tied to culturally responsive practices. Within this pillar, other notable characteristics of high-quality CRCSs are (Maier et al., 2017) these:

- High expectations and strong culturally responsive instruction equating to learning
- Providing ample resources and access to meaningful learning—tailored to the needs of the whole child

Active Family and Community Engagement

High-impact school leaders advocate and continually garner partnerships with community-based initiatives that have positive impacts on Black students' educational success, building on current models, along with reform efforts (Green, 2018; Khalifa et al., 2016; Stein et al., 2016). In showing *respect* for the students and community they serve, the collective capacity of all partnerships allows for powerful decision making. This is a critical component in building learning experiences based on academic success, cultural competence, and sociopolitical awareness (Ladson-Billings, 2009), the through line in fostering cultural responsiveness in the extended learning sphere.

In the planning and subsequent implementation of the CRCS, partnering with families and community agencies becomes even more important in *respecting* the current challenges of the community. Initial stakeholder meetings must be welcoming and centered on illuminating the assets and strengths of the community while simultaneously learning about the root causes of issues and barriers to learning (Partnership for the Future of Learning, 2019). In this phase, school leaders are also cognizant of community members' work schedules, transportation methods, and home languages—accommodating every type of need.

School leaders also understand that home visits may be necessary to build trust with parents, and in many rural communities a home–school liaison or migrant coordinator is leaned on to build on existing relationships. According to the Partnerships for the Future of Learning (2019), parent-teacher home visits played a significant role in Sacramento School District's ability to engage parents and build trusting and respectful school relationships. In fact, the efforts showed a decrease in absenteeism by 24 percent, while parents and students also reported an increase in trust and overall communication with the school (Partnership for the Future of Learning, 2019).

Many districts across the nation are building strong frameworks for effective family engagement into strategic plans for continuous improvement. In cities like Cleveland, Ohio, and Austin, Texas, parents and community members are engaged in building district aims for student success, as well as being afforded professional development opportunities for leadership (Partnership for the Future of Learning, 2019). In counties such as Fresno, California, where there are high rates of poverty for Black children, parents' cultural knowledge and academic aspirations could inform dual-enrollment offerings in partnership with local universities.

The next section will highlight the possibilities that college dual enrollment plays in building culturally responsive education labs for both parents and students. In shaping the framework for high-quality CRCSs, these characteristics are also foundational within pillar three (Maier et al., 2017):

- Creating a cohesive and aligned partnership with families and community, allowing informed decision making to emerge from cultural assets and strengths
- Students and parents experiencing a school climate that is welcoming, trusting, and safe

Collaborative Leadership and Supports

When establishing collaborative leadership and support practices, the principal's focus must be to strategically plan, align goals, and build relationships that promote systemic change for cultural inclusivity (Center for Black Educator Development [CBED], n.d.; Khalifa et al., 2016; Madhlangobe & Gordon, 2012; Tran et al., 2020). In doing so, this fourth pillar essentially completes the relational *trust* surrounding cultural responsiveness schoolwide. The coherence, in turn, comes when all stakeholders are immersed and equally invested in professional learning communities, committees focused on culturally responsive instruction and assessments, and leadership development strategies (Partnership for the Future of Learning, 2019).

Leveraging local university partnerships is a critical factor within the implementation structures surrounding collaborative leadership and supports. In using data to assess the school's context or the region-by-region performance within a district, higher education collaborations must expand in planning for continuous improvement.

An often untapped piece is creating a culturally responsive education laboratory (CREL) within the extended hours of the school day. The CREL would offer a robust adult literacy program in which university researchers and professors facilitate parent-student evidenced-based reading instruction while adhering to a culturally responsive and racially inclusive setting (Hammond, 2015; Kohli, 2009; Ladson-Billings, 2009). Through this partnership, middle school and high school students act as literacy coaches to younger students—garnering leadership and mentorship experiences. More importantly, these Black students would see their racial and cultural identity as an asset and come to see the teaching profession as a possibility.

The CREL also serves as an affinity space for Black students enrolled in the education pathway at the local university. Kohli (2009) and CBED (n.d.) call for teacher preparation programs that validate students' racial identity, push back on cultural invisibility in the curriculum, and dismantle racial hierarchies in teacher education. While finalizing their coursework, teacher residents, both Black and White, begin to build community surrounding their lived experiences and strategize (preservice) how to prevent racism in their classrooms (Kohli, 2009).

Learning to create classroom structures as suggested by Hammond (2015) and designing lessons anchored by academic success, cultural competence, and sociopolitical awareness (Ladson-Billings, 2009) would be a primary basis of the CREL. As suggested by Kavanagh et al. (2020), CREL students could be given opportunities for *approximation of practice* in low-risk experiments in acting out teaching, receive instructive feedback, experience trial and error, and strengthen their thinking and depth of knowledge.

This is a snapshot in braiding community school grant dollars in launching the beginning stages of the Black teacher pipeline. As we'll see in chapter 9, culturally responsive pedagogical practices can be the focus of both apprenticeships and mentorships for Black youth, in a setting where younger underperforming students need academic interventions. Then, within this practice, the affinity spaces would begin to mirror those of the existing professional development and professional learning communities within the school. Future teachers would begin to understand the cohesion surrounding racial justice and internalize the goals and vision of the CRCS.

The above description of creating a culturally responsive education lab fits close descriptions of key policy principles within the framework of pillar four. A major component of turnaround schools is the creation of "mechanisms for systems-level collaborations between the district, city offices, community-based organizations, and other community partners (colleges and universities) to align and integrate the work" (Partnership for the Future of Learning, 2019, p. 65) for the betterment of Black and historically marginalized students.

At the discretion of local control, community school grant dollars call for creativity and must be built on the philosophy of mitigating barriers to learning. The high-impact CRCS must leverage space that equates to providing extended learning opportunities for those who underperform—whether that means focusing on foster youth, English emergent learners, or Black students.

In New York City, for example, the community school strategic plan is formulated around silo-breaking ways of reimaging educational partnerships and aligning policies with local agencies (Partnership for the Future of Learning, 2019). In doing so, successful community schools take a cradle-to-career approach, constantly integrating the local context and filling gaps based on student needs. Across the nation, in nearly all school districts, the need to rebuild the Black teacher pipeline is critical. Resource allocations based on providing Black students extended learning, reading intervention, and exposure to the arts can be fused with the culturally responsive education lab.

In fact, high-quality implementation is dependent on school personnel and community partners (colleges and universities) being organized into professional learning communities focused on specific issues identified in local data and strategies that emphasize shared ownership for the CRCS in planned improvements in policies, practices, and procedures (Partnership for the Future of Learning, 2019). According to Maier et al. (2017), other features can bolster the success of a CRCS within pillar four:

- Creating a coherent culture of teacher collaboration and critical professional learning
- Using data and the assessment of local contexts as tools for continuous improvement and shared accountability

BRIDGING THE GAP

The implications for braiding culturally responsive leadership traits within the CRCS framework are paramount, as schools of education at the university level look to support future site- and district-level leadership. These act as the *invisible and visible* lenses of equity. School- and district-level leaders either intentionally forge success mechanisms for Black students or they don't. Professional development is either built to address learning outcomes for Black students or it is not. The encapsulated educational environment must be sealed with cultural responsiveness and initiatives that promote a positive racial identity for Black and historically marginalized students.

How will CRCS leaders measure success?

Currently, there are no metrics of accountability at the national or state levels tying student performance to community school grant funds. At present, districts are allowed local control to plan and implement specific programmatic features associated with the specific needs of the community served. A 2020 RAND study found that New York City's graduation rates were higher, along with elementary and middle school math scores, in community schools when compared to noncommunity schools (Maier et al., 2017).

In effect, every dollar spent must be directly funneled toward the academic and social-emotional needs of our most vulnerable student populations. At the transforming stage (highest level of positive impact), Campo (2023) suggests benchmarks show increases in graduation rates, postsecondary enrollment, workforce development, economic development, and micro-credential attainment for young adults.

For Black and historically marginalized students, we must ask ourselves: Are academic outcomes equitable? Are graduation rates, along with college and career readiness markers, equitable? Are suspensions and expulsions decreasing? Are student perceptions around safety, racism, and cultural inclusivity indicating positive and impactful trends? It is not inconceivable that in the next five years accountability for community school dollars (as well as federal funds) will include those equitable markers, along with overall health metrics, food distribution data, and family engagement.

The very core of this book is illustrated in figure 8.3, the model for success within the culturally responsive school system—*the work* in securing equitable academic outcomes for Black and historically marginalized students. The structure of the culturally responsive school has one end goal, and that is for students to perform beyond expectations. As mentioned, the infrastructure

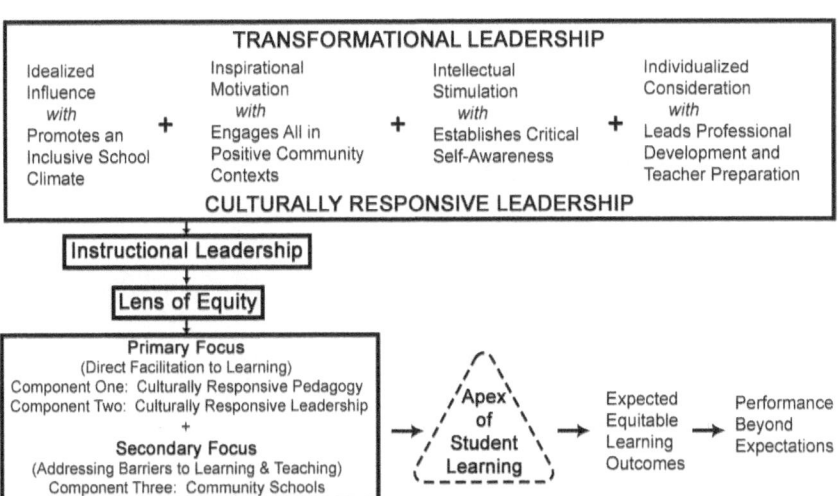

Figure 8.3. Components of a Culturally Responsive School
Source: Commissioned by author.

must be built around the ideology of a *bubble effect*, one that continually protects Black students from all aspects of inequity.

For long-term sustainability, this system only develops with an overarching culturally responsive and transformational leader—the *prepared* leader (James & Wooten, 2022; Khalifa et al., 2016; Northouse, 2019). Is this work happening in your district?

As we'll explore in chapter 9, the CRCS is, in fact, the epicenter for the resurgence of the Black teacher pipeline across America. Along with breaking the barriers of systemic inequities and mindsets, the CRCS must be unified within a comprehensive prekindergarten through twelfth-grade experience—with intentional partnerships at the university level. This entire educational continuum shapes the *whole child*, foundationally and fundamentally building on Black students' cultural strengths and lived experiences.

The sustainable effects are unlikely to hold unless alliances are formed with community agencies and local universities that also possess a lens of equity in confronting unjust educational outcomes. Finally, as discussed, the CRCS is led by the culturally responsive leader, the *prepared* leader, one who orchestrates a *just cause*—a vision not of current realities but of an untold future where all Black students thrive academically, socially, and emotionally. Creating the CRCS is not a *here-and-now* endeavor; rather, it's part of a liberated future that educators must continually cultivate.

Chapter 9

Building the Black Teacher Pipeline

"We have to talk about liberating minds as well as liberating society."

—Angela Davis, American political activist

To preface this chapter, it is essential to state that rebuilding the Black teacher pipeline in America and creating culturally responsive community schools are not isolated endeavors. Black teachers, both preservice and in-service, can have positive lasting effects on educational attainment when their own and their students' racial and cultural identities are affirmed. So, as the national narrative surrounding the need for more Black teachers continues to grow, equal importance must be placed on the development of culturally responsive schools (see figure 8.3).

Why? Because the recruitment of future Black teachers starts the moment the child walks into their kindergarten classroom. It's cyclical in nature if one truly sees the pipeline. And we must ask ourselves, "Are we protecting them within a *bubble effect*—a high-impact culturally responsive school?"

This book illuminates and closes gaps not only in student achievement but also those that inhibit the development of Black teacher pipelines. Recent research proves how powerful it is, academically and social-emotionally, for Black students to be taught by Black teachers. Yet despite these positive impacts, we must ask, Why are school districts not doing more to invest in and create their own Black teacher pipelines? Answering that question is the goal of this chapter.

Two of the nation's leading organizations strengthening pathways and advancing policies for young future Black educators, the Center for Black Educator Development and the National Center for Teacher Residencies' Black Educators Initiative, will be highlighted. In addition, key elements and starting points will be shared from the Teachers of Color Alliance for Educational Empowerment, a grassroots Black teacher pipeline in California's Central Valley.

LIBERATION OVER INCARCERATION

Today, there are nearly seven times more Black males incarcerated in our American prison system (nearly 365,000) than teaching (approximately 53,000) in our public school classrooms (Bureau of Justice Statistics, 2021; National Teacher and Principal Survey, 2021). Figure 9.1 paints a stark picture of this reality. For most of these inmates, if not all of them, having at least one Black teacher may have inspired them to stay in school (Mason et al., 2021) and perhaps altered their path into the criminal justice system.

A step further: having a Black male teacher could have provided a positive role model, resulting in "cultural synchronicity," and perhaps inspired these individuals to pursue college and serve in the field of education (Freeman et al., 2022; Ingersoll et al., 2022). More eye-opening, research shows that having one Black male teacher has three times larger an impact on Black male students' college-going aspirations than having a Black female teacher—specifically for the socioeconomically disadvantaged (Gershenson et al., 2021). If you ever wondered if your school is part of the solution—it is.

Much of the work to rebuild and sustain a more just educational system starts with examining district-level and schoolwide culture, along with

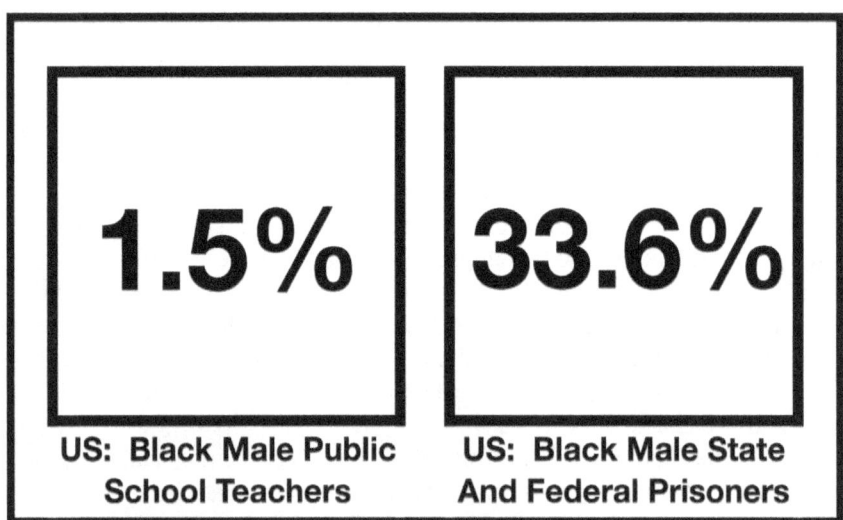

Figure 9.1. U.S. Black Male Teacher versus Prisoner Percentages
Source: Adapted from National Teacher and Principal Survey (2021) and Bureau of Justice Statistics (2021). Commissioned by author.

classroom pedagogical tactics that affirm students' racial identities, using them as assets. In essence, it's as much a *liberation* of reimagined systemic practices as it is an *enlightenment* for the betterment of the students we serve.

Educational dollars earmarked for racially diverse subgroups to meet performance standards must be equally dispersed to university teacher and leader preparation programs. When legislators fight for dollars to *reach* our Black and other historically marginalized students of color, they are really asking if those dollars are *reaching teachers' and leaders' pedagogical tactics and mindsets*. Fundamentally, and in real time, this sentiment is also embedded within an ideological framework that will inherently produce future Black educators.

State governors and state superintendents of education must begin to have critical conversations with college presidents about allocating funds that directly support culturally responsive and racially affirming educational pathways. In turn, the trickle-down effect ultimately meets the needs of high school students' postsecondary teaching aspirations—for example, (1) securing dual-enrollment education pathways for students to earn an associate of arts degree while simultaneously earning a high school diploma (community college faculty funding), (2) Black teacher apprenticeships that focus on providing mentorship and real-time pedagogical experiences (university faculty funding), and (3) Black teacher residencies in partnership with local school districts (university professor in residence funding). In addition to this, Gershenson et al. (2021) posit that policies must also be explored in providing professional development for the largely non-Black teacher workforce to better serve Black students through culturally relevant pedagogical practices.

PIPELINE WITHIN A PIPELINE

As mentioned in chapter 2, following the *Brown* decision in 1954, nearly sixty thousand Black educators were essentially erased from the teaching profession. As Black students began to attend all-White schools (Thomas, 2023; Wright, 2022), Black teachers did not abandon their students; they were dismissed from their jobs. In the United States today, Black, Indigenous, and people of color (BIPOC) make up nearly 37 percent of the adult population (age eighteen and older), while BIPOC children (birth to age eighteen) account for roughly 50 percent of the total population (Gist & Bristol, 2022). Within the next five to seven years, it is not inconceivable that students of color will make up nearly 65 percent of the nation's student population, calling for more answers and accountability for culturally responsive teaching and curricular shifts that affirm students' racial identities.. Because of this, leaders today must prioritize the recruitment, pedagogical support, and retention of Black teachers. All students' educational advancement depends on it.

According to the 2022 Nation's Report Card, Black students' reading scores (pre- and postpandemic) in both fourth and eighth grades continue to lag nearly thirty points below their White peers (U.S. Department of Education, 2022). In fact, White students, according to the National Assessment of Educational Progress, scored below proficiency in reading as well.

You're probably thinking: "My universal design for learning is, well, not so universal." That is the beauty of culturally responsive pedagogy—teachers own the curriculum; the curriculum doesn't own them.

In efforts to rebuild the Black teacher pipeline for student achievement (Gist & Bristol, 2022), lawmakers must equally advocate for the development of culturally responsive community schools. As described in chapter 8, these schools are all-inclusive and become the natural fit for future Black teachers' successful emergence into the profession (as seen in figure 9.2). Too often, however, widespread support for teacher diversity is oversimplified as a call for racial parity, without explaining the magnitude of positive outcomes that Black teachers provide for all students—even as they help Black students in particular (Young & Easton-Brooks, 2022).

Among these drivers are culturally relevant practices, which allow Black teachers to read student behavior through an appropriate lens, leverage their existing community relations, build connections that create a sense of belonging, and embrace the hidden curriculum by cultivating self-esteem and pride by celebrating Black students' racial identity (El-Mekki, 2023; Freeman et al.,

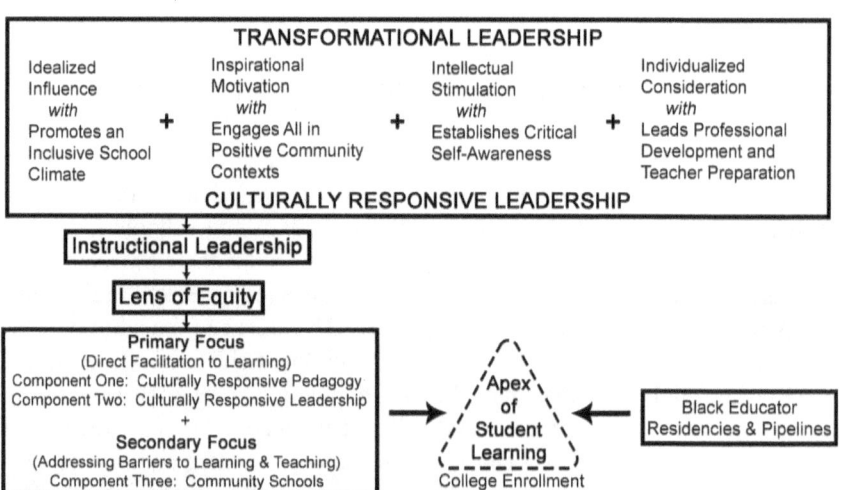

Figure 9.2. The Black Teacher Residency Pipeline
Source: Commissioned by author.

2022; Gershenson et al., 2021; Young & Easton-Brooks, 2022). The "added value" for all students when assigned to Black teachers (Freeman et at., 2022) is *so clear* it goes unseen in many *in-practice* educational spheres and educator preparation programs.

Research abounds that distills the immediate and long-term impacts of same-race teachers of color in closing stubbornly persistent educational attainment gaps:

- Black students (especially disadvantaged males) who have at least one Black teacher by third grade are 13 percent more likely to graduate high school and 19 percent more likely to enroll in college than students not taught by a Black teacher (Gershenson et al., 2021).
- Black students who have at least one Black teacher in kindergarten to fifth grade scored significantly higher in reading and mathematics compared to students of color who did not have a Black teacher (Easton-Brooks, 2021).
- Black students who have at least one Black teacher are provided highly educated role models, a crucial "counterexample" to the mindset that higher education is unattainable (Gershenson et al., 2021).
- Black and Latinx students are less likely to lose instructional time due to disciplinary referrals when they have a teacher of the same race (Lindsay & Hart, 2017).
- Students of color and White students report having positive perceptions of their teachers of color and report experiencing rigorous coursework with positive relationships (Carver-Thomas, 2018).
- Black students experience fewer out-of-school suspensions and special education referrals, coupled with a more positive social-emotional educational experience, when assigned to Black teachers (Bristol & Martinez-Fernandez, 2019).

If Black teachers are more impactful for Black students' educational attainment, then national focus should naturally center on replicating these practices and behaviors for all non-Black teachers (Gershenson et al., 2021). And therein lies the cyclical context of this book: we know that non-Black teachers can, as Ladson-Billings (2009) demonstrated, provide a culturally responsive learning environment for Black students.

Because nearly eight in ten public school teachers or roughly 79 percent in the United States are White (Schaeffer, 2021), the need for cultural congruency and culturally responsive expertise among them is paramount. Figure 9.2 illustrates the cyclical nature of the culturally responsive school system, which propels Black students to enroll in college, therefore securing the potential to guide them into educational careers.

Yet today, nearly sixty-five years post-*Brown*, we must ask ourselves, Why are we still experiencing racial disproportionalities within the teaching profession? And what are the barriers leading to these outcomes? The essence of this book is that we will not see long-term improvements in teacher diversity (especially Black teachers) unless we see long-term sustainability in creating culturally responsive schools.

As we'll discuss later, there are obvious clues in regard to college readiness, but even deeper than that are those answers that inspire Black students to turn to the teaching profession in general. Moving forward, it's imperative that non-Black teachers nationwide gain high levels of expertise in both culturally responsive practices and antidiscriminatory mindsets. These constructs work hand in hand for the educational success of students of color. So finding answers within this cross-race relational learning structure has implications for Black teacher pipelines and residencies.

As illustrated in figure 9.2, the culturally responsive model school can better serve culturally and linguistically diverse students, but the workload is heavy. Simultaneously, this school plays a significant role in both the short- and long-term recruitment and retention of Black educators. In fact, according to the Black Educator Initiative (BEI), one of the most alluring factors in recruiting prospective Black teacher residents are antiracist and social justice frameworks embedded in school culture (Madhani et al., 2022).

Mason et al. (2021) explain that "school leaders have the opportunity to elevate the voices of Black educators and ensure that their perspective is included in school-wide decision-making" (p. 9). In addition, Black teacher residents, like school-aged students, expressed that the school leader provided a sense of belonging and that they thrived when mentorship was built into the program (Gershenson et al., 2021; Khalifa et al., 2016; Madhani et al., 2022; Young & Easton-Brooks, 2022).

Cradle to Career

Addressing college readiness upon earning a high school diploma remains the crux for millions of students of color across America. As mentioned throughout this book, instruction that engages diverse students in realizing their own racial and cultural genius allows for greater chances to excel within standardized levels of proficiency and twenty-first-century learning, in turn allowing for greater preparation in meeting the requirements to enter college.

In order to paint a picture of the current situation, we need to look at the number of Black students that our educational system prepares to enter university. Then we must examine if we truly have culturally responsive schools in place. I'll focus on California, arguably the most ethnically diverse state in the nation, as it pertains to Black students. Then, dear reader, you are welcome to examine other states' graduation rates and college eligibility for Black students as you wish. At that point, you may realize that cradle to career is not such a cliché after all—illuminating and dismantling barriers becomes real work.

In California, the 2021–2022 Black student high school graduation rate was a mere 78 percent, compared to White students who graduate at 91 percent (California Department of Education, n.d.-c). Of the nearly twenty-one thousand Black students who graduated, only 8,704 (41.3 percent) met the A–G requirements to apply for the California State University (CSU) or University of California systems (California Department of Education, n.d.-c). Even more concerning are the actual enrollment numbers in relation to college applications.

In the fall of 2022, one CSU campus enrolled only 10 percent of the Black students who applied, although it admitted nearly 90 percent of them (personal communication), which amounted to 140 Black students. Meanwhile, during the previous 2022 spring semester, only 2 Black students out of 441 total candidates (0.5 percent) completed a teaching credential (personal communication). Other CSUs in California hover between four and seven total Black students completing their credentials annually (personal communication).

To put this into a better perspective, consider the following hypothetical calculation. If the roughly 155 colleges and universities in California (University Review, n.d.) produced five Black credential earners per year, that would equal nearly 775 Black teachers annually. Considering that 5.1 percent of California's K–12 students are Black (California Department of Education, n.d.-b), it would take eight years based on the above scenario to see the additional six thousand Black teachers needed to align the racial make-up of the workforce with the students being taught (Gershenson et al., 2021).

Put another way, *every single* Black student (8,704) in California who met the A–G requirement in spring 2022 would have had to enroll in college and major in education and complete their credential to meet the goal. By this calculation, California would see alignment in racial comparison by the spring of 2027, assuming each student completed their degree and credential within the five-year time frame.

These nonscientific scenarios are not meant to be pessimistic. Rather, these hypothetical calculations serve as reminders in examining the day-to-day pedagogical practices, support structures, academic counseling, and college-going experiences set forth throughout the kindergarten-to-twelfth-grade system for Black students (see figure 9.2). The educational outcomes of our Black youth that are produced in *our systems* quite literally equate to their ability or inability to pursue their dreams.

PATHWAYS INTO TEACHING FOR BLACK YOUTH

Nearly 50 percent of Black teachers in the nation are graduates of historically Black colleges and universities (HBCUs), despite those colleges being only 3 percent of the nation's educational institutions (Freeman et al., 2022). The obvious question: *What pathways or strategies are present within the HBCU system that K–12 and college programs can learn from to support Black students to pursue the teaching profession?* Knowing these answers has implications for policy and practice that may enhance and expedite the influx of Black educators needed in all sectors of our educational system.

These answers also have implications for the ongoing work of organizations such as the Center for Black Educator Development and the BEI residency network in conjunction with the National Center for Teacher Residencies (NCTR). Most importantly, our nation's K–12 school systems could work to simulate the Afrocentric benefits from HBCUs as part of their locally controlled funding schemes, strategic plans tied to grant proposals, and overall targeted pedagogical expectations in meeting accountability measures.

So what do we know?

Personal Motives

According to Freeman et al. (2022), the HBCU students' pathways into teaching hinged on three significant factors: development of competences or self-efficacy, culturally responsive pedagogical practices, and the demand for teachers in their fields of study (mathematics and science). Mirroring the teacher-student relationships described throughout this book, the HBCU students spoke of their own K–12 experiences—feeling that teachers had high expectations for their academic success—as well as holding a childhood identity of becoming a professional within the area of expertise.

For example, a love of science compelled students to dream of becoming a physician or health care professional (Freeman et al., 2022). In addition, self-efficacy was tied to love and passion for teaching, suggesting the importance of leaders' modeling, engaging in reflective dialogue related to affirming students' racial identities, and allowing for approximations of practice in safe spaces (Kavanagh et al., 2020; Kohli, 2009; Siwatu, 2011).

Culturally Responsive Pedagogy

Student-teacher candidates within the HBCU study readily centered their positive experiences with faculty who taught from a culturally responsive lens. Of significance were students' stories of teachers having high expectations of them, along with mentoring them in a familial atmosphere (Freeman et al., 2022). These findings support concepts centered on students' success being driven by feeling cared for while having a foundation of critically conscious teaching that leverages their cultural strengths and knowledge (Goodwin et al., 2022; Hattie, 2012; Howard, 2001; Milner, 2011).

Content focused on equitable opportunities for students to develop personalized deep learning while affirming their racial identities and cultural strengths (Adelman & Taylor, 2018; Darling-Hammond & Darling-Hammond, 2022; Kohli, 2009; Ladson-Billings, 2009) cemented their pursuit of teacher preparation coursework. HBCU students take these learnings and carry them into their own pedagogical practices once granted a position of their own (Freeman et al., 2022).

Being exposed to high expectations stemming from culturally responsive teaching was a common theme within the college coursework. Teaching candidates spoke of being led with a strengths-based epistemology, which allowed for self-trust in their teaching skills (Freeman et al., 2022; Ladson-Billings, 2009), again carrying this mindset into their own teaching careers. These findings have major implications for building teacher preparation programs that lead to teacher residency initiatives. For example, the use of culturally responsive pedagogy would strengthen Black students' enjoyment and self-efficacy in education pathway dual-enrollment classes, allowing them to earn an associate of arts degree and high school diploma simultaneously.

To reach such goals, community colleges must ensure that professors' epistemological frameworks rest on (1) conceptions of self and others, (2) enriching social relations, and (3) conceptions of investigative knowledge (Hammond, 2015; Howard, 2001, Ladson-Billings, 2009; Milner, 2011). In California, for example, dual-enrollment courses can be taught by high school teachers holding a subject-specific master's degree, further illuminating the proven power of recruiting Black single-subject teachers (Gershenson, 2021; Young & Easton-Brooks, 2022).

Demand for Black Teachers

Although specific to Freeman et al. (2022), where the focus was on a demand for Black science and mathematics teachers, the nation needs a critical mass of teachers of color in general (Gist & Bristol, 2022). In fact, Gershenson et al. (2021) explain that to align the national racial composition of Black teachers to Black students, our college preparation programs and teacher residency initiatives would need to produce a total of 256,000 more Black teachers. Put simply, well-prepared Black teaching candidates are in such high demand that teaching positions are virtually guaranteed.

However, aside from realizing their high demand (along with the assumed ease for employment), teachers' affinity for the profession remained centered on their school experiences as children (Freeman et al., 2022). Childhood experiences within their educational environment that cultivated their self-efficacy, usually based on an enjoyment of learning, mirrored the experiences in preservice training. In addition, supportive instructors, mentors, and structures were prevalent in mitigating barriers.

Fortunately, there are national organizations gaining momentum and garnering millions in philanthropic funding for the support, recruitment, and retention of Black teachers. A "North Star" within this endeavor is the Center for Black Educator Development (CBED), based in Philadelphia, Pennsylvania. The organization is led by Sharif El-Mekki, a former nationally recognized school principal, who founded the CBED with one goal—increase the pipeline of Black teachers (CBED, n.d.). El-Mekki's mission is simple: *to ensure equity in the recruiting, training, hiring, and retention of quality educators who reflect the cultural backgrounds and sociopolitical interests of the students they serve.*

School districts across the nation searching for methods to better serve Black students would be wise to emulate the educational offerings built into the CBED. A hallmark of the organization's focus is the Freedom Schools Literacy Academy model, which offers teaching apprenticeships and access to in-classroom pedagogical experiences, mentorship, and professional development to high school students, college students, and classified employees (CBED, n.d.).

More importantly, students in kindergarten through second grade are immersed in literacy enrichment and phonemic awareness, built within a culturally responsive and racial affirming epistemology. In 2022, the Freedom Schools Literacy Academy report card results indicated the following:

- Students showed significant increase in interest in entering the teaching profession and working with Black children.
- College students reported an increase in interest in entering the teaching profession, which was directly tied to their coaches' serving as excellent mentors.
- Nearly 85 percent of the students in kindergarten through second grade improved one or more reading levels.
- Positive racial identity among all student participants increased.

Programmatically, this model can be replicated in community schools across the nation. Community school grant dollars and ESSA Title I funds can serve as building blocks to initiate a Black teacher pipeline in school districts.

In California specifically, school districts charged with addressing significant and persistent disparities in academic performance for student subgroups could embed the Literacy Academy model directly into pillar four of the community school, *collaborative leadership and supports*.

Similar to the work of the CBED, the NCTR is a nonprofit organization dedicated to developing, starting, supporting, and expediting the impact of teacher residency initiatives (NCTR, n.d.). The NCTR's mission is to *dismantle the historical inequities within the teaching profession by supporting teacher residencies in preparing diverse and culturally responsive educators.* The NCTR began its BEI in 2019 with grant funds explicitly focused on the recruitment, support, and retention of future Black teachers.

In just three years, the BEI has expanded from its initial eight residency partners, to twenty within the overall NCTR network (Madhani et al., 2022), due in part to the five-year twenty-million-dollar expansion grant provided by the Ballmer Group. Successful recruitment efforts within the BEI framework are the following:

- Program recruitment materials describe in detail a commitment to diversity, equity, and inclusion while uplifting the voice and perspectives of the partnering communities.
- The recruitment process explicitly and deliberately extends personalized outreach to Black students while offering teaching supports and mitigating barriers to entry.
- Financial support is provided in the form of stipends and scholarships.

Once the recruits entered their residencies, many shared specific recommendations for future programmatic efforts. Like the factors touched on from HBCUs, these can inform professional development opportunities at the K–12 level, leadership development at the college level, and forming Black teacher pipelines within school districts. Teacher residents' recommendations included the following (Kohli, 2009; Madhani et al., 2022):

- Hire Black recruiters, organize Black alumni panels, and find Black mentors to be part of the recruitment process.
- Support career pathways for Black high school graduates—work with school leadership to intentionally build education pathway dual-enrollment courses.
- Create and support racial affinity groups that allow Black resident voices to be heard and to discuss ways to change the system.
- Develop closer relationships with school leaders to partner on equity initiatives.

Although more rich longitudinal data will surface with time in retention efforts, the BEI has had a significant impact on the recruitment and job preparedness for young Black preservice educators. In fact, BEI programs on average had 16 percent more Black residents than other residencies in the NCTR network (Madhani et al., 2022).

Why do national organizations such as the CBED and the NCTR's BEI matter? The obvious reasons are to build capacity in the recruitment of Black teachers. However, lack of awareness can lead to a lack of resources and policy attention. As already mentioned, state superintendents and state governors can look at the educator pipeline and residency models described above when making investments in supporting, recruiting, and retaining Black teachers.

TEACHERS OF COLOR ALLIANCE FOR EDUCATIONAL EMPOWERMENT

In 2021, based on philosophies and research inherent to culturally responsive schools, the office of the Fresno County Superintendent of Schools began planning a partnership with Central Unified School District and local universities aimed to increase the number of Black students entering the teaching profession. In writing the initial grant, the initiative was dubbed the Teachers of Color Alliance for Educational Empowerment (TCAEE).

The entire blueprint uses the ideology of a comprehensive kindergarten through credential completion continuum (see figure 9.2), founded on two distinct philosophies: *empowering Black students* and *transforming educators through a culturally responsive lens*. In 2023, renewal funding in the amount of nearly half a million dollars was secured from the California Regional K–16 Education Collaboratives Grant in support of TCAEE and other residency models. Currently still building capacity in a "pilot program" structure, the initiative has immersed both teachers and principals from one elementary school, one middle school, and two feeder high schools in professional development focused on culturally responsive pedagogical practices.

One of the main concepts built into the programmatical framework at each of the four school sites is building an academic college-going culture within the curriculum and overall mission of the schools (Gooden & Dantley, 2012; Kelly & Brandes, 2010; Leithwood & Sun, 2018). This begins with rigorous and engaging content that is directly related to students' racial identities and cultural assets. Teachers at each of the four sites have embraced the ideology of becoming "champion teachers" who lead from a lens of equity and have taken the initiative to support colleagues in learning about culturally responsive pedagogical tactics (as described in chapters 3 through 8). In fact, two champion teachers commented:

Our students of color need the support, examples of hope—many times at a young age, seeing is believing.
This is going to help Black students feel more comfortable and accepted.

Potential Long-Term Impacts

Commitment to social justice

- Transforming the education of racially marginalized youth requires the development of a racially diverse and conscious teaching force (Kohli, 2009).

Valuing experiential knowledge

- The TCAEE can create a culture that centers on the experiences and narratives of students of color, equipping educators to better understand and address racial inequities within their school of employment (Kohli, 2009).
- Pedagogical practices will continually create and re-create expertise in deeper learning, based on instructional leadership focused on culturally responsive teaching, explicit instructional feedback, and pedagogical reasoning (Kavanagh et al., 2020; Ladson-Billings, 2009; Leithwood & Sun, 2018).
- Racial affinity spaces and teacher inquiry groups will remain a consistent practice for both in-service and preservice residents in order to build synergy and collegiality focused on high-impact instruction and using students' racial identity as assets (Kohli et al., 2015).

Interdisciplinary empowerment

- The dual-enrollment instructors will draw on the fields of psychology, sociology, Black intellectual thought, Black history, and the educational advances made by Black scholars, as these interdisciplinary pedagogical practices empower students to strive for a multitude of educational pathways (El-Mekki, 2023; Kohli, 2009; Thomas, 2023).
- The local CSU and its school of education will develop a culturally responsive certification pathway for preservice students that leads directly into Central Unified School District's TCAEE teacher residency program.

- Mentorship programs will be developed for Black male high school students enrolled in the education pathway and for middle school Black male students enrolled in the junior teacher's academy.

Goals of the Teachers of Color Alliance

1. Increase the percentage of highly qualified Black teachers in Fresno County, as well as building a pipeline of culturally responsive educational leaders in underserved communities.
2. Increase the percentage of Black students and students of color in Central Unified School District earning an associate of arts degree from the local community college (simultaneously earning a high school diploma).
3. Increase the percentage of Black students and students of color graduating from Central Unified School District who are CSU/UC eligible.
4. Create a direct teacher pipeline between Central Unified School District and the local CSU, increasing the percentage of Black students earning a bachelor's degree and obtaining a California teaching credential.

By 2030, the goal is to support and recruit seventy Black teachers within Fresno County, specifically to become employed in the Central Unified School District.

Program Supports

- High school dual-enrollment cohort model
- Coteaching with CTE education pathway teacher
- Embedded professional development—culturally responsive pedagogical practice
- Chrome laptop device for each student
- Elementary school partnership for work experience—California Teaching Fellows Foundation funding
- Employment within community school structure or after-school program—grant funded
- Mentoring for elementary students provided by the local CSU

Highlights

- Simultaneous high school diploma and associate of arts degree completion
- CBEST certification embedded within dual-enrollment classes (African American history emphasized within general education coursework)

- University guidance to admission beginning in ninth grade
- Immediate enrollment in teacher induction classes
- Potential for "one-year" credential program
- Bachelor's degree and a teaching credential from the local CSU
- Priority placement within Central Unified School District's employment needs

Sample Professional Development for Culturally Responsive Pedagogy

The Culturally Relevant Teaching: Transforming Educators strand of Advancement Via Individual Determination (AVID) professional development is designed for administrators, site coordinators, teachers, and site team members who are ready to conduct self-examination and address issues of race, class, gender, and accountability through a growth mindset. Over the course of three days in a summer institute setting, participants work in collaborative groups to explore strategies and lessons that empower students through examination, validation, and celebration of their own and others' culture.

The professional development strands provide frameworks of effective methodologies that validate the cultures of students in the classroom and on the campus. The goal of professional learning is to enhance each site's curriculum and empower students to make culturally relevant learning connections to content in order to increase subject-matter comprehension. Teachers will gain expertise in creating culturally responsive lessons (see chapter 5) that are targeted to the *Apex of Student Learning*, mirror students' cultural contexts, and enlighten sociopolitical consciousness, while incorporating rigor for various learning styles.

The local community college and CSU would pave the road for upskilling nearly twenty-five Black students annually through the "direct pipeline" approach in receiving a bachelor's degree along with a California teaching credential. Although beyond the scope of this book, high school academic counselors play a critical role in recruiting students (as far down as fifth grade) into the TCAEE initiative.

Although in its infancy, initial markers are encouraging when considering TCAEE schools compared to non-TCAEE schools within Central Unified School District. For example, the middle school currently has thirty-seven Black students actively involved in the Black Student Union, compared to the non-TCAEE middle schools that do not currently have a Black student union. For the 2023–2024 school year, there is nearly a 300 percent increase in Black student enrollment within the TCAEE middle school junior teacher cohort.

The TCAEE elementary school doubled the number of educators receiving professional development in culturally responsive practices, now poised to collaborate in grades one through three. The high school TCAEE cohort is showing a nearly 300 percent increase in Black students enrolled in the education pathway, which will put them on track to earn an associate of arts degree while graduating from high school. The other high school within the TCAEE has now secured an education pathway within the dual-enrollment offerings, and initial enrollment is targeting ten Black students for year one. Lastly, there were twelve champion teachers in year one, compared to sixteen champion teachers in year two.

The beauty of national and grassroots efforts in building effective Black educator pipelines is in the modeling of cohesive and collective efforts that can be replicated in any district. All these efforts work to eradicate barriers such as lack of experimental preparation, collegial isolation, and racially insensitive spaces (Carver-Thomas, 2018). Examples of creative work in braiding funds, such as federal dollars earmarked for socioeconomically disadvantaged students, community school grant dollars, educator effectiveness block grants, and local initiatives, allow district leaders to build programs of their own.

A VISION FOR THE FUTURE

In his seminal book *Ratchetdemic: Reimagining Academic Success*, Chris Emdin posits, "The roadmap to freedom has been drawn by our ancestors and hidden in the hearts and minds of our youth" (2021, p. 173). Culturally responsive schools resurrect students' ancestors and allow freedom to no longer be cast in the shadows. Culturally responsive schools embody the human capital theory, in which education and schooling are explicitly catered to Black youth in preparing them to contribute to the labor force and to catapult their genius for the betterment of the community (Nafukho et al., 2004).

Culturally responsive schools use educators' imaginations as a resource, and students' cultural and lived experiences ignite critical learning collusions (Howard, 2001; Milner, 2011). In this space, students' community is thrust into the classroom, rather than the curriculum being blind to their cultural strengths and historical power.

As educators, our purest purpose is to become the conduits of the hopes and dreams of our students. Lesson plans must be written not only as blueprints to student engagement, higher levels of thinking, and content mastery but as *tickets to liberation*. Our schools (your classroom) and the belief systems we employ must be transformed into a coherent culturally responsive climate every day. As the intensity mounts and the impatience ensues, it is our task *and* obligation to ensure that every action, every policy, and every commitment is equitable for Black and historically underserved students.

Despite the swinging pendulum of our educational history, there is hope for unification in the name of our students, and there is hope in the growing coalitions of culturally responsive schools. It is my hope that this book has crystallized what those schools look like and how they can be brought to scale.

And remember, I'm not a holiday celebration. I'm not a multicultural dress-up day. I'm not a social-emotional framework. I am not trauma.

I am deep rooted in demanding that our educational system is free of racism, and I unapologetically ensure that Black and historically marginalized students' genius is affirmed for academic success, cultural competence, and sociopolitical consciousness. My lens of equity looks to a prioritization of the recruitment and empowerment of Black teachers.

Our *affirmative action* is affirmative action.

Our students' lives depend on this notion—but do you see us?

References

Adelman, H. S., & Taylor, L. (2018). *Improving school improvement.* Los Angeles Center for Mental Health in Schools and Student/Learning Supports at UCLA. http://smhp.psych.ucla.edu/pdfdocs/improve.pdf

Ahmad, F. Z., & Boser, U. (2014). *America's leaky pipeline for teachers of color: Getting more teachers of color into the classroom.* Center for American Progress. http://files.eric.ed.gov/fulltext/ED561065.pdf

American Community Survey. (2022). *Children living below poverty level 2016–2020.* Healthy Fresno County Community Dashboard. https://www.healthyfresnocountydata.org/indicators/index/view?indicatorId=189&localeId=247&localeChartIdxs=1|2|3|4

Becerra, X. (2019). *Juvenile justice in California.* California Justice Information Services Division, California Department of Justice. https://openjustice.doj.ca.gov/resources/publications

Bernal, D. D. (2016). Critical race theory, Latino critical theory, and critical raced-gendered epistemologies: Recognizing students of color as holders and creators of knowledge. *Qualitative Inquiry, 8*(1), 105–26.

Bourdieu, P. (2003). *Firing back: Against the tyranny of the market.* Verso Books.

Bovell-Ammon, A., McCann, N. C., Mulugeta, M., Ettinger de Cuba, S., Raifman, J., & Shafer, P. (2022). Association of the expiration of Child Tax Credit advance payments with food insufficiency in US households. *JAMA Network Open, 5*(10). doi:10.1001/jamanetworkopen.2022.34438

Boyko, T., Briggs, P., Cobb, M., Dragoo, H., Ferreira, L., O'Connor, J., & Sanders, J. (2016). *AVID culturally relevant teaching: A schoolwide approach.* AVID Press.

Bristol, T. J., & Martinez-Fernandez, J. (2019). The added value of Latinx and Black teachers for Latinx and Black students: Implications for policy. *Policy Insights from the Behavioral and Brain Sciences, 6*(2), 147–53.

Brown, B. (2018). *Dare to lead: Brave work, tough conversations, whole heart.* Random House.

Brown, B. A. (2022). *Lifting our voices: Field guide #4: Planning forward with cultural relevance in the classroom.* California Association of African-American Superintendents and Administrators. https://ccee-ca.org/wp-content/uploads/2022/07/CAAASA-Field-Guide-4.pdf

Brown, K. (2004). Leadership for social justice and equity: Weaving a transformative framework and pedagogy. *Educational Administration Quarterly, 40*(1), 77–108.

Bureau of Justice Statistics. (2021). *National prisoner statistics, 2021*. U.S. Department of Justice, Office of Justice Programs. https://bjs.ojp.gov/sites/g/files/xyckuh236/files/media/document/p21st.pdf

California Assessment of Student Performance and Progress. (2022). *English language arts/literacy and mathematics: Smarter balanced summative assessments*. California Department of Education. https://www.cde.ca.gov/ta/tg/sa/sbacsummative.asp

California Department of Education. (n.d.-a). *2018–19 suspension rate—State report disaggregated by ethnicity*. https://dq.cde.ca.gov/dataquest/dqCensus/DisSuspRate.aspx?year=2018-19&agglevel=State&cds=00

California Department of Education. (n.d.-b). *2019–20 enrollment by ethnicity and grade*. https://dq.cde.ca.gov/dataquest/dqcensus/EnrEthGrd.aspx?cds=00&agglevel=state&year=2019-20

California Department of Education. (n.d.-c). *2021–22 four-year adjusted cohort graduation rate: Statewide report*. https://dq.cde.ca.gov/dataquest/dqcensus/CohRate.aspx?cds=00&agglevel=state&year=2021-22

California Department of Education. (n.d.-d). *California school dashboard: Academic performance*. https://www.caschooldashboard.org/reports/ca/2019/academic-performance

California Department of Education. (n.d.-e). *Dropouts by ethnic designation by grade*. https://dq.cde.ca.gov/dataquest/DropoutReporting/DrpGradeEth.aspx?cDistrictName=State&CDSCode=00000000000000000&Level=State&TheReport=GradeEth&ProgramName=All&cYear=2016-17&cAggSum=StTotGrade&cGender=B

California Department of Education. (2021). *Foster youth in California schools: Data and outcomes*. https://www.cde.ca.gov/ds/sg/fosteryouth.asp

California Department of Education. (2022). *CTE general public fact sheet*. https://www.cde.ca.gov/ci/ct/gi/ctegeneralfacts.asp

California Department of Education. (2023). *Certificated staff by ethnicity for 2017–18: Teachers*. https://dq.cde.ca.gov/dataquest/Staff/StaffByEth.aspx?cYear=2017-18&cChoice=StateNum&cType=T&cGender=&Submit=1

Campo, S. (2023, January). *Stages of development*. National Center for Community Schools, Children's Aid. https://www.nccs.org/wp-content/uploads/2023/01/CSF_Stages-of-Development-Jan-2023.pdf

Career Nexus. (n.d.). *A workplace ecosystem serving people, business, & community*. Retrieved January 30, 2023, from https://careernexus.org

Carle, A., Smith, A., & Thomas, A. (2013). *Adverse experiences*. https://www.childtrends.org/indicators/adverse-experiences

Carver-Thomas, D. (2018). *Diversifying the teaching profession: How to recruit and retain teachers of color*. Learning Policy Institute. https://doi.org/10.54300/559.310

Center for Black Educator Development (CBED). (n.d.). *Center for Black Educator Development*. Retrieved March 11, 2023, from https://www.thecenterblacked.org

Centers for Disease Control and Prevention (CDC). (2016, April 1). *Adverse childhood experiences.* https://www.cdc.gov/violenceprevention/acestudy/

Chan, E. (2007). Student experiences of a culturally sensitive curriculum: Ethnic identity development amid conflicting stories to live by. *Journal of Curriculum Studies, 39,* 177–94.

Chapman, D. (2015). *The 5 love languages: The secret to love that lasts.* Northfield.

Cholewa, B., Goodman, R., West-Olatunji, D., & Amatea, C. (2014). A qualitative examination of the impact of culturally responsive educational practices on the psychological well-being of students of color. *Urban Review, 46*(4), 574–96.

Cohen, D., Moffitt, S., & Smith, K. (2018). The influence of practice on policy. In D. E. Mitchell, R. Crowson, & D. Shipps (Eds.), *Shaping education policy: Power and process* (2nd ed., pp. 162–86). Routledge.

Daggett, W. (2008). *Rigor and relevance from concept to reality.* International Center for Leadership in Education.

Darling-Hammond, L. (2022, May 2). *Possible futures: The policy changes we need to get there.* Kappan. https://kappanonline.org/possible-futures-policy-changes-darling-hammond/

Darling-Hammond, L., Bae, S., Cook-Harvey, C. M., Lam, L., Mercer, C., Podolsky, A., & Stosich, E. L. (2016). *Pathways to new accountability through every student succeeds act.* Learning Policy Institute.

Darling-Hammond, L., & Bransford, J. (Eds.). (2005). *Preparing teachers for a changing world: What teachers should learn and be able to do.* Jossey-Bass.

Darling-Hammond, K., & Darling-Hammond, L. (2022). *The civil rights road to deeper learning: Five essentials for equity.* Teachers College Press.

Darling-Hammond, L., Flook, L., Schachner, A., & Wojcikiewicz, S. (with Cantor, P., & Osher, D.). (2021). *Educator learning to enact the science of learning and development.* Learning Policy Institute. https://doi.org/10.54300/859.776

David, J. L., & Cuban, L. (2010). *Cutting through the hype.* Harvard Education Press.

DeCuir-Gunby, J., Devance Taliaferro, J., & Greenfield, D. (2010). Educators' perspectives on culturally relevant programs for academic success: The American Excellence Association. *Education and Urban Society, 42*(2), 182–204.

Dirks, K. T., & Ferrin, D. L. (2002). Trust in leadership: Meta-analytic findings and implications for research and practice. *Journal of Applied Psychology, 87*(4), 611–28.

Doucet, F. (2017). What does a culturally sustaining learning climate look like? *Theory into Practice, 56*(3), 195–204.

Duncan, G., Gennetian, L., & Morris, P. (2009). Parental pathways to self-sufficiency and the well-being of younger children. In C. J. Heinrich and J. K. Scholz (Eds.), *Making the work-based safety net work better: Forward-looking policies to help low-income families.* Russell Sage Foundation.

DuVernay, A., Averick, S., Barish, H. (Producers), & DuVernay, A. (Director). (2016). *13th* [Film]. Netflix. Retrieved from http://www.netflix.com

Easton-Brooks, D. (2021). Ethnic-matching in urban schools. In H. R. Milner IV (Ed.), *Handbook of urban education* (pp. 234–52). Routledge.

Edwards, S., & Edick, N. (2012). Culturally responsive teaching for significant relationships. *Journal of Praxis in Multicultural Education, 7*(1), 1–18.

El-Mekki, S. (2019). *Who is preparing teachers for our students? Who is teaching the teachers?* Philly's 7th Ward. https://phillys7thward.org/2019/09/who-is-preparing-phillys-teachers-for-phillys-classrooms/

El-Mekki, S. (2023, March). *Reviving the legacy of the Black teaching tradition* [Video]. TED Conferences. https://www.ted.com/talks/sharif_el_mekki_reviving_the_legacy_of_the_black_teaching_tradition

Emdin, C. (2016). *For White folks who teach in the hood . . . and the rest of y'all too: Reality pedagogy and urban education.* Beacon Press.

Emdin, C. (2021). *Ratchetdemic: Reimagining academic success.* Beacon Press.

Emdin, C. (Host). (2023, January 31). What Now? #HipHopEd on navigating the traumas of our era #TyreNichols [Audio podcast episode]. In *Hip Hop Ed.* https://twitter.com/i/spaces/1ypKddAoEOyKW

Faulkner-Bond, A. (2022, April 21). *Culturally and linguistically responsive assessment: Myths and opportunities.* WestEd. https://www.wested.org/wested-bulletin/equity-in-focus/culturally-linguistically-responsive-assessment-myths-opportunities/

Fenwick, L. T. (2022). *Jim Crow's pink slip: The untold story of Black principal and teacher leadership.* Harvard Education Press.

Fisher, D., & Frey, N. (2015). *Unstoppable learning: Seven essential elements to unleash student potential.* Solution Tree Press.

Franquiz, M. E., & Ortiz, A. A. (2016). Every Student Succeeds Act—A policy shift. *Bilingual Research Journal, 39*(1), 1–3.

Freeman, K. E., Winston-Proctor, C., & Grant, O. B. (2022). Pathways into the teaching profession for African American science and mathematics graduates from historically Black colleges and universities. In C. Gist & T. Bristol (Eds.), *Handbook of Research on Teachers of Color and Indigenous Teachers* (pp. 255–62). American Educational Research Association.

Freire, P. (1972). *Pedagogy of the oppressed.* Herder and Herder.

Freire, P. (1985). *The politics of education: Culture, power and liberation.* Teachers College Press.

Fullan, M., & Quinn, J. (2016). *Coherence: The right drivers in action for schools, districts, and systems.* Corwin.

Fuller, P., Murphy, M., Chow, A., & Franklin Covey (Firm). (2020). *The leader's guide to unconscious bias: How to reframe bias, cultivate connection, and create high-performing teams.* Simon & Schuster.

Gay, G. (2002). Preparing for culturally responsive teaching. *Journal of Teacher Education, 53*(1), 20–32.

Gay, G. (2010). *Culturally responsive teaching: Theory, research, and practice* (2nd ed.). Teachers College Press.

Gay, G. (2013). Teaching to and through cultural diversity. *Curriculum Inquiry, 43*(1), 48–70.

Gay, G., & Kirkland, K. (2003). Developing cultural critical consciousness and self-reflection in preservice teacher education. *Theory into practice: Teacher reflection and race in cultural contexts, 42*(3), 181–87.

Gershenson, S., Hart, C. M. D., Hyman, J., Lindsay, C., & Papageorge, N. (2021). The long-run impacts of same race teachers (Working Paper 25254). National Bureau of Economic Research. https://www.nber.org/system/files/working_papers/w25254/w25254.pdf

Gist, C. D., & Bristol, T. J. (Eds.). (2022). *Handbook of research on teachers of color and indigenous teachers*. American Educational Research Association.

Gist, C. D., Bristol, T. J., Carver-Thomas, D., Hyler, M. E., & Darling-Hammond, L. (2021). Motivating teachers of color and indigenous teachers to stay in the field. In *Building a More Ethnoracially Diverse Teaching Force: New Directions in Research, Policy, and Practice* (pp. 61–65). Kappan Special Report.

Gonzalez, J. (2017, September 10). *Culturally responsive teaching: 4 misconceptions.* https://www.cultofpedagogy.com/culturally-responsive-misconceptions/

Gooden, M., & Dantley, M. (2012). Centering race in a framework for leadership preparation. *Journal of Research on Leadership Education, 7*(2), 237–53.

Goodwin, B., Rouleau, K., Abla, C., Baptista, K., Gibson, T., & Kimball, M. (2022). *The new classroom instruction that works: The best research-based strategies for increasing student achievement*. ASCD.

Green, T. L. (2018). School as community, community as school: Examining principal leadership for urban school reform and community development. *Education and Urban Society, 50*(2), 111–35.

Griner, C. G., & Stewart, M. L. (2012). Addressing the achievement gap and disproportionality through the use of culturally responsive teaching practices. *Urban Education, 48*(4), 585–621.

Grissom, J. A., Egalite, A. J., & Lindsay, C. A. (2021). *How principals affect students and schools: A systematic synthesis of two decades of research.* Wallace Foundation. http://www.wallacefoundation.org/principalsynthesis

Grossman, P., Compton, C., Igra, D., Ronfeldt, M., Shahan, E., & Williamson, P. (2009). Teaching practice: A cross-professional perspective. *Teachers College Record, 111*(9), 2055–2100.

Gutierrez, H. (2021). *The enactment of culturally responsive pedagogy: A case study of one elementary school* (Order No. 28411816) [Doctoral dissertation, Fresno State]. ProQuest. https://www.proquest.com/dissertations-these/enactment-culturally-responsive-pedagogy-case/docview/2510349293/se-2

Gutierrez, R. (2002). Beyond essentialism: The complexity of language in teaching mathematics to Latina/o students. *American Educational Research Journal, 39*, 1047–88.

Hallinger, P., Hosseingholizadeh, R., Hashemi, N., & Kouhsari, M. (2017). Do beliefs make a difference? Exploring how principal self-efficacy and instructional leadership impact teacher efficacy and commitment in Iran. *Educational Management Administration & Leadership, 46*(5), 800–819.

Hammond, Z. (2015). *Culturally responsive teaching and the brain: Promoting authentic engagement and rigor among culturally and linguistically diverse students*. Corwin.

Hattie, J. A. (2012). *Visible learning for teachers: Maximizing impact on learning*. Routledge.

Hollingsworth, J., & Ybarra, S. (2009). *Explicit direct instruction: The power of the well-crafted, well-taught lesson*. Corwin.

Howard, T. C. (2001). Telling their side of the story: African-American students' perceptions of culturally relevant teaching. *Urban Review, 33*(2), 131–49.

Howard, T. C. (2003). Culturally relevant pedagogy: Ingredients for critical teacher reflection. *Theory into Practice, 42*(3), 195–202.

Hyland, N. (2009). One White teacher's struggle for culturally relevant pedagogy: The problem of the community. *New Educator, 5*(2), 95–112.

Hynds, A., Hindle, R., Savage, C., Meyer, L., Penetito, W., & Sleeter, C. (2016). The impact of teacher professional development to reposition pedagogy for indigenous students in mainstream schools. *Teacher Educator, 51*(3), 230–49.

Ingersoll, R., May, H., Collins, G., & Fletcher, T. (2022). Trends in the recruitment, employment and retention of teachers from under-represented racial-ethnic groups. In C. Gist & T. Bristol (Eds.), *Handbook of Research on Teachers of Color and Indigenous Teachers* (pp. 823–39). American Educational Research Association.

Intercultural Development Research Association (IDRA). (2022). Culturally responsive practices in four critical levels. https://www.idra.org/wp-content/uploads/2022/11/Culturally-Responsive-Practices-in-Four-Critical-Levels-%E2%80%93-Set-IDRA-EAC-South-2020.pdf

James, E. H., & Wooten, L. P. (2022). *The prepared leader: Emerge from any crisis more resilient than before*. Wharton School Press.

Jha, A. P. (2021). *Peak mind: Find your focus, own your attention, invest 12 minutes a day*. HarperOne.

Kagan, S., & Kagan, M. (2009). *Kagan cooperative learning*. Kagan Publishing.

Kavanagh, S., Conrad, J., & Dagogo-Jack, S. (2020). From rote to reasoned: Examining the role of pedagogical reasoning in practice-based teacher education. *Teaching and Teacher Education, 89*, 1–11.

Kelly, D. M., & Brandes, G. M. (2010). "Social justice needs to be everywhere": Imagining the future of anti-oppression education in teacher preparation. *Alberta Journal of Educational Research, 56*(4), 388–402.

Kezar, A., & Eckel, P. (2008). Advancing diversity agendas on campus: Examining transactional and transformational presidential leadership styles. *International Journal of Leadership in Education, 11*(4), 379–405.

Khalifa, M. (2012). A re-new-ed paradigm in successful urban school leadership. *Educational Administration Quarterly, 48*(3), 424–67.

Khalifa, M. A., Gooden, M. A., & Davis, J. E. (2016). Culturally responsive school leadership: A synthesis of the literature. *Review of Educational Research, 86*(4), 1272–1311.

Kinney, A. (2015). Compelling counternarratives to deficit discourses: An investigation into the funds of knowledge of culturally and linguistically diverse U.S. elementary students' households. *Qualitative Research in Education, 4*(1), 1–25.

Klem, A. M., & Connell, J. P. (2004). Relationships matter: Linking teacher support to student engagement and achievement. *Journal of School Health, 74*(7), 262–73.

Knight, J. (2013). *High-impact instruction: A framework for great teaching.* Corwin.

Kohli, R. (2009). Critical race reflections: Valuing the experiences of teachers of color in teacher education. *Race Ethnicity and Education, 12*(2), 235–51.

Kohli, R., Picower, B., Martinez, A. N., & Ortiz, N. (2015). Critical professional development: Centering the social justice needs of teachers. *International Journal of Critical Pedagogy, 6*(2), 6–24. https://libjournal.uncg.edu/ijcp/article/view/1057

Kouzes, J., & Posner, B. (2016). *Learning leadership.* John Wiley & Sons.

Ladson-Billings, G. (1992). Reading between the lines and beyond the pages: A culturally relevant approach to literacy teaching. *Theory into Practice, 31*(4), 312–20.

Ladson-Billings, G. (1995a). But that's just good teaching! The case for culturally relevant pedagogy. *Theory into Practice, 34*(3), 159–65.

Ladson-Billings, G. (1995b). Toward a theory of culturally relevant pedagogy. *American Educational Research Journal, 32*(3), 465–91.

Ladson-Billings, G. (2009). *The dreamkeepers: Successful teachers of African American children* (2nd ed.). Jossey-Bass.

Ladson-Billings, G. (2022). *The dreamkeepers: Successful teachers of African American children* (3rd ed.). Jossey Bass.

Leithwood, K., & McAdie, P. (2007). Teacher working conditions that matter. *Education Canada, 47*(2), 42–45.

Leithwood, K., & Sun, J. (2018). Academic culture: A promising mediator of school leaders' influence on student learning. *Journal of Educational Administration, 56*(3), 350–63.

Lindsay, C. A., & Hart, C. M. (2017). Exposure to same-race teachers and student disciplinary outcomes for Black students in North Carolina. *Educational Evaluation and Policy Analysis, 39*(3), 485–510.

Lopez, I. H. (2014). *Dog whistle politics: How coded racial appeals have reinvented racism and wrecked the middle class.* Oxford University Press.

Loveless, T. (2017). How well are American students learning? *2017 Brown Center Report on American Education, 3*(6), 23–33.

MacGregor, K. (2015, September 26). Social capital and "grit" help poor students succeed. *University World News.* https://www.universityworldnews.com/article.php?story=20150925161144888

Madhani, N., Shand, R., & Austin, K. (2022). *Recruitment and retention of Black educators: Promising strategies at eight U.S. teacher residencies.* National Center for Teacher Residencies. https://nctresidences.org/wp-content/uploads/2022/07/Recruitment-and-Retention-of-Black-Educators-Full-Report-FINAL-July-2022.pdf

Madhlangobe, L., & Gordon, S. (2012). Culturally responsive leadership in a diverse school: A case study of a high school leader. *NASSP Bulletin, 96*(3), 177–202.

Maier, A. (2022, December). The case for community school districts. *School Administrator, 11*(79), 18–24.

Maier, A., Daniel, J., & Oakes, J. (2017, December). *Community schools as an effective school improvement strategy: A review of evidence.* Learning Policy Institute. https://learningpolicyinstitute.org/media/136/download?inline&file=Community_Schools_Effective_BRIEF.pdf

Many, T. W., & Sparks-Many, S. K. (2015). *Leverage: Using PLCs to promote lasting improvement in schools.* Corwin.

Marzano, R. J., Pickering, D. J., & Pollock, J. E. (2001). *Classroom instruction that works: Researched-based strategies for increasing student achievement.* McREL.

Mason, S., Cole-Malott, D., Teoh, M., Ravenell, A., El-Mekki, S., & Seaton, K. (2021, September 28). *To be who we are: Black teachers on creating affirming school cultures.* Teach Plus and the Center for Black Educator Development. https://teachplus.org/teachplus-cbed-tobewhoweare/

Massachusetts Department of Elementary and Secondary Education (MDESE). (2021). *Educator evaluation: Classroom instruction videos and sample observation & feedback calibration activities.* Retrieved January 26, 2023, from https://www.doe.mass.edu/edeval/resources/calibration/videos.html

Matschiner, A. (2022). A systematic review of the literature on inservice professional development explicitly addressing race and racism. *Review of Educational Research, 0*(0), 1–37.

Mayfield, V. (2017). The burden of inequity—And what schools can do about it. *Phi Delta Kappan, 98*(5), 8–11.

Milner, H. R. (2011). Culturally relevant pedagogy in a diverse urban classroom. *Urban Review, 43*(1), 66–89.

Moll, L. C., Amanti, C., Neff, D., & Gonzalez, N. (1992). Funds of knowledge for teaching: Using a qualitative approach to connect home and classrooms. *Theory into Practice, 31*(2), 132–41.

Morrison, K. A., Robbins, H. H., & Rose, D. G. (2008). Operationalizing culturally relevant pedagogy: A synthesis of classroom-based research. *Equity and Excellence in Education, 41*(4), 433–52.

Mosely, M. (2018). The Black teacher project: How racial affinity professional development sustains Black teachers. *Urban Review, 50*(2), 267–83. https:doi.org/10.1007/s11256-018-0450-4

Nafukho, F. M., Hairston, N. R., & Brooks, K. (2004). Human capital theory: Implications for human resource development. *Human Resources Development International, 7*(4), 545–51.

National Academies of Sciences, Engineering, and Medicine (NASEM). (2019). *A roadmap to reducing child poverty.* National Academies Press. https://doi.org/10.17226/25256

National Center for Education Statistics. (n.d.-a). *Public high school 4-year adjusted cohort graduation rate (ACGR), by selected student characteristics and state: 2010–11 through 2017–18.* U.S. Department of Education, Office of Elementary and Secondary Education. https://nces.ed.gov/programs/digest/d19/tables/dt19_219.46.asp

National Center for Education Statistics. (n.d.-b). *Percentage distribution of enrollment in public elementary and secondary schools, by race/ethnicity and state or jurisdiction: Fall 2003 and fall 2013*. U.S. Department of Education. https://nces.ed.gov/programs/digest/d22/tables/dt22_203.70.asp

National Center for Education Statistics. (2018). *Number, percentage distribution, and SAT mean scores of high school seniors taking the SAT, by sex, race/ethnicity, first language learned, and highest level of parental education: 2017 and 2018*. U.S. Department of Education, Digest of Education Statistics. https://nces.ed.gov/programs/digest/d18/tables/dt18_226.10.asp

National Center for Education Statistics. (2019a). *Number of 2015–16 public school principals and percentage distribution of public school principals, by 2016–17 status and selected principal or school characteristics: 2016–17*. U.S. Department of Education. https://nces.ed.gov/surveys/ntps/tables/pfs1617_fl02_p1n.asp

National Center for Education Statistics. (2019b). *Spotlight A: Characteristics of public school teachers by race/ethnicity*. School and Staffing Survey (SASS), U.S. Department of Education. https://nces.ed.gov/programs/raceindicators/spotlight_a.asp#info

National Center for Teacher Residencies. (n.d.). *Black educators initiative: Empower, transform, inspire*. https://nctresidencies.org/programs-services/black-educators-initiative/

National Commission on Excellence in Education. (1983). *A nation at risk: The imperative for education reform*. U.S. Government Printing Office.

National Equity Project. (n.d.). *The lens of systemic oppression* https://www.nationalequityproject.org/frameworks/lens-of-systemic-oppression

National Teacher and Principal Survey. (2021). *Public school teacher data file, 2017–18*. U.S. Department of Education, National Center for Education Statistics. https://nces.ed.gov/surveys/ntps/tables/ntps1718_21011202_t1n.asp

Northouse, P. G. (2019). *Leadership: Theory and practice* (8th ed.). Sage.

Ouellette, T., Burstein, N., Long, D., & Beecroft, E. (2004). *Measures of material hardship: Final report*. U.S. Department of Health and Human Services, Office of the Assistant Secretary for Planning and Evaluation.

Paris, D. (2012). Culturally sustaining pedagogy: A needed change in stance, terminology, and practice. *Educational Researcher, 41*(3), 93–97.

Paris, D., & Alim, H. S. (2014). What are we seeking to sustain through culturally sustaining pedagogy? A loving critique forward. *Harvard Educational Review, 84*(1), 85–100.

Partnership for the Future of Learning. (2019). *Community schools playbook*. Retrieved from https://futureforlearning.org

Pinar, F. W. (2013). *Curriculum studies in the United States: Present circumstances, intellectual histories*. Palgrave Macmillan.

Powell, R., & Chambers Cantrell, S. (2021). *A framework for culturally responsive practices: Implementing the culturally responsive instruction observation protocol (CRIOP) in K–8 classrooms*. Myers Education Press.

Real, T. (2022). *Us: Getting past you and me to build a more loving relationship*. Rodale.

Rebora, A. (2022, November 1). Shifting the "cognitive load" in classrooms. *ASCD, 80*(3). Retrieved from https://www.ascd.org/el/articles/shifting-the-cognitive-load-in-classrooms?_hsmi=232413309&_hsenc=p2ANqtz-_EGnZw4w56WI2SdTPLTrlaqahDM1Q_OoulqhKZNmj-QVTjpz&1WiqgPXd_HRYKDn_5qPO2IGNVMB2H1Ly_IdiKf7hnnQ

Reeves, D., Frey, N., & Fisher, D. (2023). *Confronting the crisis of engagement: Creating focus and resilience for students, staff, and communities.* Corwin.

Rogers, J., Kahne, J., Ishimoto, M., Kwako, A., Stern, S. C., Bingener, C., Raphael, L., Alkam, S., & Conde, Y. (2022). *Educating for a diverse democracy: The chilling role of political conflict in blue, purple, and red communities.* UCLA's Institute for Democracy, Education, and Access.

Schaeffer, K. (2021, December 10). *America's public-school teachers are far less racially and ethnically diverse than their students.* Pew Research Center. https://www.pewresearch.org/fact-tank/2021/12/10/americas-public-school-teachers-are-far-less-racially-and-ethnically-diverse-than-their-students/

Schmeichel, M. (2012). Good teaching? An examination of culturally relevant pedagogy as an equity practice. *Journal of Curriculum Studies, 44*(2), 211–31.

Sinek, S. (2019). *The infinite game.* Penguin Business.

Siwatu, K. O. (2007). Preservice teachers' culturally responsive teaching self-efficacy and outcome expectancy beliefs. *Teaching and Teacher Education, 23*, 1086–1101.

Siwatu, K. O. (2011). Preservice teachers' culturally responsive teaching self-efficacy-forming experiences: A mixed methods study. *Journal of Educational Research, 104*(5), 360–69.

Sleeter, C. (2012). Confronting the marginalization of culturally responsive pedagogy. *Urban Education, 47*(3), 562–84.

Smith, P. M. (2008). Culturally conscious organizations: A conceptual framework. *Libraries and the Academy, 8*(2), 141–55.

Stein, K. C., Macaluso, M., & Stanulis, R. N. (2016). The interplay between principal leadership and teacher leader efficacy. *Journal of School Leadership, 26*(6), 1002–32.

Substance Abuse and Mental Health Services Administration (SAMHSA). (2018). Retrieved from https://www.samhsa.gov/capt/practicing-effective-prevention/prevention-behavioral-health/adverse-childhood-experiences

Thomas, D. J., III. (2023). Gatekeepers and guardians of Black intellectual thought: Black male teacher-coaches combating an anti-Black epistemic order. *Teacher College Record, 125*, 3.

Tran, H., Buckman, D. G., & Johnson, A. (2020). Using the hiring process to improve the cultural responsiveness of schools. *Journal of Cases in Educational Leadership, 23*(2), 70–84.

U.S. Department of Education. (n.d.-a). *Every Student Succeeds Act (ESSA).* https://www.ed.gov/essa?src=rn

U.S. Department of Education. (n.d.-b). *No Child Left Behind (NCLB).* https://www2.ed.gov/nclb/landing.jhtml

U.S. Department of Education. (2022). *Reading assessment.* Institute of Education Sciences, National Center for Education Statistics, National Assessment of

Educational Progress (NAEP). Retrieved January 3, 2023, from https://www.nationsreportcard.gov/dashboards/achievement_gaps.aspx

University Review. (n.d.). *California colleges list.* Retrieved March 9, 2023, from https://www.universityreview.org/california-colleges/

Villavicencio, A., Conlin, D., & Pagan, O. (2022). Research-practice partnerships in pursuit of racial justice in schools: Navigating a hostile sociopolitical climate. *Educational Policy, 37*(1), 250–75. https://doi.org/10.1177/08959048221130353

Wald, J., & Losen, D. J. (2003). Defining and redirecting a school-to-prison pipeline. *New Directions for Youth Development, 2003*(99), 9–15.

Williams, A. (2011). A call for change: Narrowing the achievement gap between White and minority students. *Clearing House: A Journal of Educational Strategies, Issues and Ideas, 84*(2), 65–71.

Woo, A., Wolfe, R. L., Steiner, E. D., Doan, S., Lawrence, R. A., Berdie, L., Greer, L., Gittens, A. D., & Schwartz, H. L. (2022). *Walking a fine line—Educators' views on politicized topics in schooling: Findings from the State of the American Teacher and State of the American Principal surveys* (RR-A1108-5). RAND Corporation. https://www.rand.org/pubs/research_reports/RRA1108-5html

WorkAdvance. (n.d.). *Build a brighter future.* Retrieved January 30, 2023, from https://www.workadvance.org

Wright, Z. (2022). *Dismantling a broken system: Actions to bridge the opportunity, equity, and justice gap in American Education.* Solution Tree Press.

Young, E. (2010). Challenges to conceptualizing and actualizing culturally relevant pedagogy: How viable is the theory in classroom practice? *Journal of Teacher Education, 61*(3), 248–60.

Young, J. L., & Easton-Brooks, D. (2022). The impact of teachers of color on school belonging: A conceptual framework. In C. Gist & T. Bristol (Eds.), *Handbook of Research on Teachers of Color and Indigenous Teachers* (pp. 637–44). American Educational Research Association.

Zenner, C., Herrnleben-Kurz, S., & Walach, H. (2014). Mindfulness-based interventions in schools—A systematic review and meta-analysis. *Frontiers in Psychology, 5*(603), 1–20.

Zoch, M. (2017). "It's important for them to know who they are": Teachers' efforts to sustain students' cultural competence in an age of high-stakes testing. *Urban Education, 52*(5), 610–36.

About the Author

Dr. Hank Gutierrez is president and founder of Culturally Responsive Educators and a longtime K–12 educator and motivational speaker for both students and K–16 educational leaders. With over twenty-five years of experience in culturally responsive teaching and leadership, he continues to create new possibilities within district partnerships, programmatic change, community school development, and instructional expertise. He works daily with teachers as well as district and university leaders to shape the imagination for teacher pipelines and residency models, safe schools, leadership capacity, and culturally responsive educational spaces in order to bolster the academic achievement of Black and other racially minoritized students.

Dr. Gutierrez wants the book to be known as the "Michael Jordan" of cultural responsiveness, as it pertains to teachers' ability to achieve greatness. He loves Air Jordan sneakers, listening to hip-hop, and coffee. He's free to discuss this book over a cup of coffee anytime!

www.ingramcontent.com/pod-product-compliance
Lightning Source LLC
Chambersburg PA
CBHW032042300426
44117CB00009B/1159